THE
PRINCE
OF PEACE

Big shout out to the author of this movement, Kiyan Josiah Prince.

You don't know it Kiyan, but you've positively impacted thousands of people.

I liken Kiyan to Jesus. One person's life sacrificed for many people's lives to be saved – but only if they choose.

I'd like to dedicate this book to the kids who are hurting and need that opportunity to see that they do have greatness in them and can change.

Mark Prince

Mark Prince collaborated with Paul Zanon on this book. Paul has written five other books, including Jimmy Tibbs' colourful life story. Three of his first five publications reached the number one bestseller spot in their respective categories on Amazon. He often co-hosts a boxing show on Talksport and is a regular contributor to Boxing Monthly magazine.

THE PRINCE OF PEACE

Trinity Mirror Sport Media

THE PRINCE OF PEACE

Trinity Mirror Sport Media ☯

First published in Great Britain and Ireland in 2018 by
Trinity Mirror Sport Media, PO Box 48, Old Hall Street, Liverpool, L69 3EB.

www.tmsportmedia.com
@SportMediaTM

Trinity Mirror Sport Media is a part of Trinity Mirror plc.
One Canada Square, Canary Wharf, London, E15 5AP.

1

Trade paperback ISBN: 9781910335895.
eBook ISBN: 9781911613114.

Design and typesetting by Trinity Mirror Sport Media
Editing and production: Simon Monk, Chris Brereton.
Design: Lee Ashun.

Photographic acknowledgements:
Trinity Mirror, PA Images, the Mark Prince personal collection.
Every effort has been made to trace copyright.
Any oversight will be rectified in future editions.

Printed and bound by CPI Group (UK) Ltd, Croydon, CR0 4YY.

Contents

Acknowledgements

Love and Thanks

Special thanks to, my mother (Marva). I thought I was only like Dad for much of my life, but as I grew older and wiser I realised I may have looked just like him, but I was your protege. Your tidy nature, your dedication to God, your heart for people, your resilience, your forgiving attitude, your fighting spirit through challenges, even at death's door. You're a true champion and warrior in the game of life. Thank you for your constant love and belief in me, your prayers for when my life's been a mess and your joy at seeing me rise.

Words can't express my gratitude for all your sacrifices you have made for your children mum. Tears flow as I write this because you're such an amazing woman. And finally, year in, year out, you always encouraged me to write this book and never ever gave up on that. Mum I salute you!

Big shout out to my dad. Thanks for doing the best you could with what you had. I know you loved us all! You have passed on some strong genes and you taught me how to fight to the last bell or get knocked out trying. I also need to say, I have no bitterness in me towards you. I love you, Dad.

My brothers Colin and Clarence (Junior), my sister Natalie (Chris), I have nothing but love for you.

I want to thank my children, Tannisa, Kiyan, Jodeci, Kishon, Malik and Micaiah. I want to thank you for being my greatest teachers. You've taught me responsibility, patience, love and given me the motivation to continually be a better man. I'd also like to offer my sincere thanks to the mothers of my children Tracy, Kim and Laurel.

Acknowledgements

I'd like to express my gratitude to my wife who has brought me much joy, fulfilment, and peace. I have grown so much since I met you walking out of Highams Park station with your sons in 2012. You didn't think much of me then but boy has that changed. Our friendship slowly grew and became strong as time passed. Your belief in me has never waned, your prayers for me have been a powerful blessing and your love for me makes me work harder to achieve my goals. You feel it when I'm hurting and your appetite for laughter is unquenched. I love the fact that you take that saying 'The way to a man's heart is through his stomach,' literally. I have never lacked good tasty food served on a tray with love! Thank you for your commitment and service of love in all its forms. I love you Dazsine.

I'd also like to say a warm thanks to everyone who took the time to get their shovels out and dish the dirt on me, including Darren Cumberbatch, Kevin Bachin-Singh, Andy Evans, Joe Gallen, Andy Sinton, Laban Roomes, Carly Carew, Les Quinn, Cham Joof, Paul Furlong, Chris Rogers, Mark Grant (Slider), Luca Rosi, Spencer Fearon, Rio [Gianluca Di Caro] for his excellent photos, and a big thank you to everyone who has supported me through the good times or the bad times. Just because your name is not mentioned here, you know exactly who you are.

A special thanks to Queens Park Rangers Football Club family for all their love and support they have given to Kiyan whilst he was at QPR and most importantly after he was murdered.

Finally, a few words about my ghostwriter. First time I met Paul Zanon was in 2013. I was at a WBC event where they presented Riddick Bowe with a WBC belt for his accomplishments as a former heavyweight champion. Paul was cool but

I had no idea our initial meeting would grow into a working relationship then into a genuine friendship a few years later.

Then in 2017, thanks to Jordan Carss, our KPF website designer who said 'Do you know a guy named Paul Zanon? He wrote Jimmy Tibbs' book, the famous boxing trainer. You should work with him to get your book done. Shall I make the introductions?' 'Go on then,' I said.

I remembered meeting Paul. Our initial meeting was a positive one. Not long after we met, he said he would love to work with me. I found Paul easy to get on with, he understood me and I swiftly got the feeling after speaking with him that this was destined to be. He was the chosen one. I couldn't have met a more compatible person to work with.

Writing a book is really personal. You let someone into the good, the bad and the ugly parts of your life. That person meets friends, family and sees all your dirty laundry, past and present.

What was wonderful is not only did I love Paul but so did my wife, my children, my mum, my brothers and sister. They all really enjoyed being with him and all my friends he interviewed commented on how blessed he is. But I already knew that and would smile in agreement when they would update me on their meetings with him.

I see Paul as family now, especially now that we have had working disagreements. You never really know someone until you don't see eye to eye on something. We happily worked things out together. Nothing changed. We still had a good friendship. I've got nothing but love for this awesome writer. He has written some brilliant books and I pray that my story will add to his ever building quality collection.

I got so used to meeting with Paul at 10am every Friday,

Acknowledgements

that I still wake up Fridays thinking, 'Is Paul coming today?' A friendship is born when you realise that someone really gets you. May God bless you and your family, Paul Zanon.

Mark Prince, January 2018

You often hear people saying, 'If I was to win the lottery, I'd work for a good cause for nothing.' Well, Mark hasn't won the lottery and campaigns tirelessly against reducing knife crime, with often little or no financial return. He has told me his story in an evocative, yet intimate manner and left no stone unturned. It's been a sincere pleasure working with him. I can honestly say he's become a close friend and somebody I confide in.

I also need to say a very big thank you to Mark's family Clarence Jr, Natalie, Colin, Marva, for always responding to any of my dialogue requests with enthusiasm and energy. Many thanks too to Mark's lovely wife, Daz, for making me feel like your house was a home from home and for also increasing my waistline by four inches with your delicious Jamaican cuisine.

To my parents, Alex and Rita, and my brother Lorence – I may have failed everything at school, but you always said I would come good! Thanks for the unconditional support.

Last but not least, a big thank you to the Trinity Mirror Sport Media team; to Steve Hanrahan for giving me a chance to work with the crew again; Paul Dove, Simon Monk, Rick Cooke, Lee Ashun, Chris Brereton, Claire Brown and all who helped along the way.

Paul Zanon, January 2018

Prologue

Goodbye Kiyan

"More than 750 mourners gathered for the funeral of a promising young footballer who was stabbed outside his school" **BBC website – 22 June 2006**

22 June 2006. The date when Tracy and I had to bury our 15-year-old son Kiyan.

Normally when people get buried, they dress them in nice clothes, but our daughter Tannisa said to Tracy: "Don't get them to dress him up. Just put pyjamas on him. He's going to sleep now, so have them put his best pyjamas on him."

That's what they did.

I don't remember much about the drive to the church. I was in a daze. When we got there, the coffin was carried by me, Kiyan's cousin Mathew, and his four uncles – Junior, Colin, Dean and Darren. Not a dry eye between us.

The turnout at the Seventh Day Adventist Church in Holloway was immense. It was full inside, and outside hundreds of people spilled out onto the stairs. I wish I could have appreciated the occasion more and thanked everyone who came.

As well as family and hundreds of friends, there were loads of kids there from Kiyan's school. His team-mates at QPR were all lined up in their kit, which was beautiful. Most of the people in attendance wore pink, Kiyan's favourite colour.

Even the police officers and family liaison officers involved in the case asked if they could come. Tracy said: "Of course."

They asked: "How do you want us to dress? Full uniform?"

"Come however you want to come."

None of them wore their uniforms – they all wore something with pink, like a shirt or a tie. That was such a lovely gesture.

Also, my friend Slider and his nephew had loads of t-shirts printed up with Kiyan's face on and some nice words on them. They weren't the sort of shirts that made you feel sad, they were uplifting and celebrated his life.

You can mentally prepare yourself for any occasion, but it's only when you're put into that scenario that your natural reaction overrides everything.

When the service started, I was hugging and kissing Tracy, making sure she was OK, when suddenly, this primal, wailing noise came out of me.

This guy from the church came over and said in an aggressive tone: "Hold yourself together man." Kind of like, 'How dare you release these emotions in this way. Firm up.'

I'd known this man for years and he's a good guy, but he went about this the wrong way. When he said that, all my built-up emotions over the last few weeks were about ready to explode.

I could have easily laid into him in the church. Instead, I looked at him. My eyes basically said, 'Are you insane? I will kill you in here brother. Move.' He instantly understood and walked away with a look of intense fear. I was that close to punching him.

The service was very sad, but some lovely tributes were read out from a number of people, including my brother Junior and Phil Hearne, Kiyan's headmaster, who said: "He was a beautiful young man, the kind of which in 22 years in schools I have never seen before."

Joe Gallen from QPR stood up and did a lovely speech. We'd only asked him on the day. It was that much more special because he didn't have time to prepare for it, so it came from the heart.

When he went up, he looked around and could see everyone was crying. Hundreds of people outside and inside, and as far as I could see everyone had tears in their eyes. It was so sad.

Joe picked up on this and decided he was going to try and make them laugh by being really honest about Kiyan, his character and personality. He wanted his speech to be joyous and uplifting. Fair play to him, because it was a risk and might have backfired.

Joe started by saying that he'd only ever remembered Kiyan joking and smiling. He told the story of the first time he saw Kiyan at the training ground and when he said: "Look at the size of this guy. He's huge!" everyone burst out laughing.

A few years later, Joe said: "Selfishly, I thought if everyone's crying, then I'll start bloody crying as well and I didn't want to do that."

I did the eulogy, which was tough. I basically explained how my son was a role model and that he was the true definition of how a Prince should behave, by name and by nature.

The whole experience was so surreal. I went from feeling like I was going to collapse, to feeling like I was talking about someone else's son. As if Kiyan was still alive.

When we left the church and headed to the burial service at New Southgate Cemetery, I looked out of the window of the car and could hear people shouting: "There's that boy."

The hearse had KIYAN in flowers and people soon realised who was passing them, with many of them clapping. I was amazed by the number of people who were stopping, paying their respects along the way.

The burial itself was obviously very sad. Up to now, Tannisa hadn't cried properly, but as Kiyan's coffin was going into the ground, the emotions got to her for the first time. I held her and said: "Let it all out, let it all out."

I felt at this point that I needed to say a few words about Tracy and Kiyan, to make sure he hadn't died in vain.

I told everyone what a fantastic job Tracy had done to bring up Kiyan, how she'd given him every opportunity to grow up into a good, upstanding man.

Then I told all the men present that we had to step up. To be good role models to our kids. To feed them love and discipline.

I finished by saying: "Start opening up your feelings to your kids. Let them know about your life's struggles, what it's like to be a man. And if you don't know what it's like, start asking God. 'Help me to be a man. Help me be a dad for my son.' Lead by example. My son followed what I done. I could have told him all kind of stuff, but if I never lived it, I would never have been able to show him.

"He told me before he left, 'I'm proud of you Dad.' My son had some deep insight.

'Why son?' 'Because you never give up. You keep smiling, you keep dealing with people and I love that about you Dad.'

"And that's rested here [as I tapped my heart]. And no doubt, us as parents, we all want our children to say wonderful things, that we were an example to them.

"So let's make some changes in our life from now. Go home and focus. Change things. Don't let this go and you just shed tears and it's all over. Nah. Let's make Kiyan count if we love him. Let's show him. God bless all of you, man."

Looking back, it was an awesome funeral. I don't understand how those two words can go together, but it was. Kiyan brought awesome with him and handed out a piece of it to everyone he crossed paths with.

I love you Kiyan. Rest in peace, son. X

1

Born Fighter

"Mark was always a happy-go-lucky kind of person at school, who always had a smile on his face. Unless you upset him that is. Then you could see the red mist descend." Paul Furlong, 2017, former professional footballer

"If you don't get an abortion, I'll leave you. We can't afford no more children."

"I don't care if I have to live off cornmeal porridge. I'm having dis Pickney. You go. God will look after me," Mum screamed back.

'Pickney' is Jamaican for child and she stuck to her guns, because this Pickney was born on 10 March 1969. I weighed in at 6lbs 14oz. Hardly a light heavyweight boxer in the making, but I was heavier than my two brothers and sister, who were barely 6lbs.

I might have been small as a baby, but my appetite for destruction started at a young age. Mum said that I was walking after 11 months and was on a mission to explore every inch of our one-bedroom loft flat in Finsbury Park. One morning, I got up off the bunk bed I was on, walked over to the paraffin heater and started shaking it. The television was in the bedroom and my older brother Clarence Jr [known as Junior] and sister Natalie [known as Chris], were watching some programme and I was annoying them.

"Stop it Mark. I want to watch the rest of *Catweazle*," Chris shouted. But I wouldn't stop. When they turned around again, I'd banged it over and these flames had lit up the bed.

Chris jumped up and ran into the kitchen to tell Mum. When she came out and saw what was going on, she started screaming, "Fiiiiirre! Prince come!"

Remember back in the early 1970s fire resistant stuff wasn't a big thing. Everything caught fire; quickly.

Junior and Chris ran behind the settee, while Dad came up and tried to pick up the mattress, which was proper lit up by now. As he tried to bung it out the window of our third-floor flat, the curtains caught fire and everything started getting out of control. He ran down to the landlord on the ground floor and then straight afterwards called the fire brigade.

They tried to throw the heater out of the window, but it wouldn't open wide enough, so they tried putting everything out as best they could. Thankfully the fire brigade arrived quickly and stopped the fire from spreading any further. Close call.

We didn't stay in that flat much longer. Nothing to do with the fire – it was getting very cramped. A year after I was born, my younger brother Colin followed and by now, all four of us kids were growing up quickly. That's when we moved to a house in Wood Green, which is where Mum still lives to this very day.

As you can imagine, it didn't take me long to start getting up to mischief again. One morning, Mum needed to take Junior and Chris to school and knowing she'd only be five minutes tops, she left little baby me on my own. She took a risk, but as she knew she'd be quick, she thought it would be OK. Me on the other hand, I decided to go looking for her.

Our neighbour at the end of the road saw this little kid walking the street on his own and picked me up. He put a note through Mum's door to let her know that he'd taken me back to his house safely. I can only imagine the panic when she walked through the door and realised I'd gone.

From an early age I was always a good runner, which came in handy for my boxing training and for running away from certain other people. More about that later.

Moving from Finsbury Park to Wood Green was something my parents took in their stride. Perhaps that had something to do with the fact that they'd both had major moves earlier in their lives and this was just a small stepping stone.

Mum and Dad met in London. Believe it or not, it was boxing that brought them together. My Dad, Clarence, came over from British Guyana in 1962, as a 20-year-old professional boxer, with a record of two wins, both knockouts. His brother, my uncle Buddy, was living in Finsbury Park at the time and sent for him. Why? I'm not really sure. Maybe he saw an opportunity on the boxing front. All I know is that Uncle Buddy wasn't a boxer, more of a hustler, who at a later stage did a bit of bird for his ingenious ways of creating revenue.

I loved my Uncle Buddy as he was such a laid-back, cool guy and I used to love hearing him talking fast in his thick Guyanese accent. Our summer holidays spent with him and his girlfriend in Leeds were the absolute best, although I never liked his dogs.

He had these Alsatians and they were straight out vicious. These dogs lived outside on chains in these kennels he'd built for them and he trained them to guard the house.

I'll never forget one holiday when Uncle Buddy had forgotten to lock them up in their kennels and in the middle of the night they managed to get inside the house. He had said to us about the back door latch sometimes coming off and that the dogs could come inside, but we just thought he was trying to scare us.

So there we were sleeping downstairs on the settee when all of sudden one of them comes strolling in, starts growling and sniffing right next to me. I closed my eyes, stopped breathing and starting praying, 'Oh God. Please help me!' The dog hung around for a couple of minutes before going back out, but it seemed like hours.

RIP Unc and thanks for the memories.

Mum was working in the tourist industry in Jamaica at the time, but after only a few months of the job, she was laid off. She got her two weeks' wages and decided to go to the labour office every day to try and find a job as quickly as possible.

Just as she was about to give up hope, an opportunity came her way. There was a boxer called Joe Bygraves, who was fighting an American called Wayne Bethea, on 22 September 1962 at the national stadium in Kingston.

Bygraves was born in Jamaica, but had moved to the UK and ended up marrying an English woman. He was now back in Jamaica training for this fight.

Someone told my mum that Bygraves's wife needed some help around the house they were renting, so my Mum went over and had a chat with her. They needed a maid from nine in the morning until one in the afternoon. The pay was two Jamaican dollars a day. Mum almost fell over when she heard the wages. Back then, a maid would get 25 cents from seven in the morning until seven at night, so she obviously accepted.

A few weeks into the job, Mum was in the kitchen having a conversation with Bygraves's wife. "How do you cope with all these black people piling into Britain?" my mum asked.

Mrs Bygraves laughed and replied: "It's fine!"

Why Mum asked that question, she's not even sure to this day. It can't have done much harm, because a couple of weeks later she was asked whether she'd like to come to England and work. Her first reaction was that she didn't want to leave Jamaica, but she ended up saying: "If the opportunity comes, I'll take it."

Bygraves's wife said she'd see what she could do.

As promised, she sorted all the paperwork and within no time, Mum was with the family as a live-in maid in Stanmore. This is where she met Dad. Funnily enough, she wasn't keen at first, although he really liked her. But Dad was persistent, very charming, and after a few weeks, Mum fell for him.

Apparently Dad was staying with Joe Bygraves because he was guaranteed a place to train, eat well, and would have a roof over his head. Unfortunately, he decided to bite the hand that fed him. At the time, Dad was being managed by Al Philipps and he told Al that Joe wasn't training him right.

This got back to Joe and he and Dad had a blazing argument, which ended with my dad getting kicked out. That's when my parents decided to get a home of their own.

Dad carried on with the boxing until 1966, by which time he'd clocked up a record of 10 wins – all stoppages – and 11 losses. Mind you, those losses were debatable and as kids, we remember him telling us about those decisions. One fight, he knocked his opponent down a few times, clearly beat him, but somehow this guy finished on his feet. When the judges announced the winner and put the opponent's hand up, Dad was so hurt that he cried back to his changing room.

A natural middleweight, just under six feet, he fought on some big bills at Wembley Empire, on the undercard for Billy Walker, Brian London, Terry Downes and Jack Bodell. As the late great matchmaker Ernie Fossey told me many years later: "Your dad had a vicious left hook on him. He'd knock out a lot of good boxers in sparring. Very well known fighters."

It was lovely for me to hear that from Ernie, because I've never seen Dad boxing and never found any footage. I'd just like to be able to see him move and throwing his punches, just so I could say: "Ah yeah that's my dad!" I've also never been to Guyana. I need to go and see what the deal is. I hear the Princes are big over there.

From 1966 to 1971, Mum and Dad had got married, and started a family. After Colin was born, Dad came back for one last fight. However, it wasn't having four kids that made him hang up the gloves.

He was on the way to a party and was so excited that when he crossed the road, he didn't look. His friend shouted "PRINCE," and he jumped up at the last second and ended on top of the bonnet of the car. When the car chucked the brakes on, he rolled off and got badly hurt. He ended up with a fractured eye socket and a deep cut on his forehead that scarred him for life.

Dad's boxing career being cut short due to an injury is something I'd be able to relate to about 25 years later.

With professional boxing off the table, Dad started working

at the Gestetner factory down Broad Lane in Tottenham. They made duplicating machines, or photocopiers as they're now known. That ended up being his job for life.

★★★★★★★★★★★★★★★★★

Racism was just a part of everyday life growing up and it came in different forms. First, there was the kind of racism where people would think in a misinformed way and ask ignorant questions when we went out.

For example, when we were little kids, white people would touch us like we were from the zoo. "Aaahhh. Look at your hair! You probably don't even need to comb your hair, do you?"

It wasn't in a horrible way, but it was weird trying to understand why they were acting like that. Then you had the more blatant kind. I can remember people regularly walking past us, or driving in a car and leaning out shouting "nigger" or "wog". "Get the fuck out of our country. Go back home."

I *was* home! Idiots.

And then there was the police. My first experience with the Old Bill was when I was eight, although it soon became a regular thing. On this occasion, they pulled me over as I was on my way back from the shops and said: "Where do you get that stuff from? You nicked it, didn't you?"

"No. I've just been to get some stuff for my mum," I replied. Then they started going through my bags and said: "You better behave yourself. If you nick anything, you're in big trouble."

That was scary. I kept thinking, 'They're the police. They can take you away and lock you up.' I was shitting my pants.

I also started to realise a lot of white people would pre-judge black youths. When I walked past a white woman on the bus, they would visibly clutch their bag and move it close to them, as if you were trying to steal it. They couldn't be more wrong.

I knew that it was a part of growing up as a black person, but it was hard to get to grips with the inequality.

Now I'm not trying to make out that all my experiences with white people were negative. I had white friends at school and the local policeman, PC Manely, was also a really decent guy. He lived just down the road, had two nice daughters and we got on with him and his family really well.

These days Wood Green is a multicultural area, whereas back then we were the only black people on our road. The nearby areas like Finchley, Hornsey, Muswell Hill and Crouch End were mostly white people.

There were loads of kids at my school from Muswell Hill and they'd have all new bikes and all the latest gear. They weren't broke like we were.

Money was tight growing up in the Prince household. Very tight. We used to take it in turns to get stuff. Mum would get one of us a pair of trousers one week, then someone else the week after, fourth or fifth week you might get something again like a pair of shoes.

But there were also a lot of hand-me-downs. We were wearing flares when flares were done. People would take the piss out of us when we were in church. One time I needed some shoes for school and my mum bought me a strong-looking pair of shoes, hoping they'd last longer and be tougher. Some of the kids at school took the piss and said: "Prince, what you wearing there bro? Falkland boots?!" because the war was on at the time. They thought it was funny but I hated it.

Despite money being tight, the quality of the food my parents put on the table was always good, which was not great for them as I was a seriously big eater. When Mum used to put the food down, she used to tell us to wait, because it was too hot. But by the time she came back, I'd already chowed it down.

But it wasn't the sort of food our neighbours were eating. It was all soul food. Dad loved his Guyanese cuisine. Stuff like turn cornmeal. We'd have it with loads of gravy and fish. Oats in some form was a regular thing – breakfast, lunch and dinner. Tapioca and porridge. Cornmeal porridge. You didn't leave the house without having your oats.

Mum cooked some great Jamaican dishes like jerk chicken and Mannish water, a goat soup which was really spicy. Although Dad was also really good in the kitchen and cooked some tasty Guyanese dishes like pepper pot and also his legendary fried dumplings, he also used to make us eat some mad stuff.

Mum used to tease him for some dishes he ate back in Guyana, like iguana lizard, but he'd also make stuff like octopus, which even though it looked horrible, it would taste surprisingly nice because of the way he'd prepare and cook it.

However, no matter how he made okra I couldn't swallow that slimy stuff and nearly threw up. I'd be heaving so much and Dad would say: "If you vomit that, I'm gonna beat you."

I never let it come out my mouth and ended up being at the table for what seemed like hours, before chewing and swallowing it. Even now I'm not a fan.

It wouldn't have been so bad if slimy okra was where Dad drew the line, but it got a lot worse. He was always into health foods and would come up with these stories about men who lived in some little village up a mountain in Guyana and how they'd lived to 100 years old, because they were eating stuff like pure honey and goat's milk.

One time when I was about eight, Dad had read somewhere that drinking your own piss was good for you. Dad drank it and then made us do it. Mum was shouting: "No, Prince. Don't let them do that."

"It's good for them," he replied.

We pissed in a plastic Tupperware bowl and then had to down it. There was no questioning Dad. You just did as you were told. Even my sister Chris had to do it. It was like drinking warm sea water. You'd think I'd down it, but no. I was sipping it like lemonade because I couldn't take it all in one gulp. I don't know what I was thinking.

Dad was a great cook and even better bread-maker. He was known for making the best wholemeal bread. I liked the way he would plait it and put it in the oven, a bit like when girls plait hair when they're braiding it. The stuff he made was heavy and when he sliced it, you knew you were getting a piece of bread.

Believe it or not, I never ate shop-sliced bread until I was about 13, when I had a paper round. My parents said: "Now you've got your own money, start buying things that you want."

Because we'd never had sliced bread, we decided to buy a few loafs, but compared to what Dad made, that floppy, wafer sliced bread was like a cracker for us. We'd eat 15 slices! I remember me and my brothers telling our mates and they'd laugh. "Shut up! You don't eat no 15 slices of bread," they'd say. We'd look back seriously and say: "Yeah we do. Sometimes we eat 20."

The other thing we bought was cereal, as we'd never been used to eating that either. Instead of a normal sized breakfast bowl, we'd eat out of these massive Pyrex dishes that you'd make macaroni cheese in. We'd fill that up with Bran Flakes, Shreddies, or any cereal that had some body to it. Rice Krispies were dead to us. That was airy stuff.

We used to add tinned Carnation condensed milk, which we'd water down first. With six people in the house, there was no point in us buying normal milk, because it wasn't going to last that long.

The Carnation milk was thick back then, kind of like the original Ribena was, so you'd get good usage from it. Now the current generation get the watered-down version.

Despite the amount we ate, we never got fat. Mind you, that might have had something to do with Dad's influence and discipline. From as young as I can remember, everyone in our neighbourhood knew Dad was a boxer.

It wasn't because he told anybody, it was more to do with his training. Doing his sprints and shadow boxing in the middle of our road was probably the giveaway. Everyone on our road and even the people from the flats opposite used to watch Dad when he trained. He'd get a right old audience.

And if he wasn't in the street, he'd be in the garden in his tracksuit, bouncing around like Jersey Joe Walcott as we tried to punch him in the stomach. Then he'd lie down and have us walking over his belly to strengthen his abs.

Our training started around the age of eight. We'd come home from school and whether Dad was there or not, you better be training. That included my sister. She wasn't put through all the boxing training, but she had to skip and run every day.

The dining room is where we would skip after school. If Dad came home and I wasn't sweating enough, then I had to skip outside, looking through the window watching everyone eating dinner. Sometimes I'd splash water on my face to make out I was sweating, but he always knew and made me skip more.

On the days Dad was home, we'd skip for about half an hour straight, do our groundwork and some other bits. That would last just over an hour. Then we'd spar with Dad in the garden with either these big black Everlast gloves, or you'd have the old pair which were filled with horse hair. When you squeezed them, they'd crunch.

There was also this old brown leather punch bag and we'd watch Dad pound it for about eight rounds. They must have made them bags good back then, because it's still knocking around somewhere at Mum's house.

At that stage, I hated the training and sparring, probably because I was forced to, but most of the time I gave it my all. However, one time I asked Junior to hit me. I fell back and hit my head on the cupboard so Dad would let us stop. It didn't work though. Mind you, the training was to come in handy.

One day, me and Colin were walking home from primary school to have some lunch and some kid from secondary school walked past and kept looking at me. Mum always used to say "be careful of 'dem boys."

I had a rubber which you'd put on top of your pencil and it was shaped with two fingers, which basically meant 'up yours.' I was 10 years old and this kid was three years older.

I got the pencil out with the rubber and held it up to this kid. He started running for us and I turned and grabbed Colin, yelling: "Run!" We were scared but managed to outrun him.

Looking at Colin nowadays, he's a very daunting figure. He got into weightlifting, built himself up and became world kickboxing champion. But back then, he'd get teased the most at home, but we'd let nobody pick on him outside.

We didn't think we'd see this guy again. We didn't realise he'd followed us home. A few days later he waited for us down the road, hid behind a wall and as we passed he caught us by surprise.

There I was walking and talking with Colin when he suddenly disappeared. When I looked around the corner, this guy had him in a neck lock and was saying: "Yeah. I've got you now." Colin was pooping himself and crying. All of a sudden, my whole concept of fear changed, because he had Colin.

It didn't matter that this kid was three years older than me.

"Let him go man. Let him go," I said. The guy laughed and said: "Why? What you going to do?"

He threw Colin to the side. I let loose with some combination punching and didn't give him a chance to land a single shot. Colin was like "Bruv! I'm so proud of you." I was pretty amazed too, because only five minutes before I was shitting myself.

When I got home, I told my brother Junior and he figured out who this guy was. A few days later, this kid got a beating off Junior and his mates for picking on younger kids. Don't mess with the Princes!

A couple months later, me and Junior were on the way to school and I got into an argument with four boys outside St Michael's school, which I had to pass to get to my school. Junior leant back against the wall and watched as if he was taking a ringside position, maybe because I was doing all the arguing. It went from a dispute to a fight pretty quick, but that's what they were looking for, because there were more of them than us. I walked over and punched the biggest of them in the gut and he doubled over. It looked like he was vomiting, but nothing was coming out.

The good thing back then was that there was fairness in fighting. They didn't all try jump me at the same time, which happens a lot now. There was some integrity on the streets.

Next up was this tall guy. I don't remember the exact combination I threw, but it was all one-way traffic.

The next was a stiff, upright looking kid and he didn't want to know. He stayed behind a set of railings. I turned to Junior and said "Come on bruv" and we walked to school as if nothing had happened.

These days, guaranteed someone would have recorded it and that fight would have gone viral on YouTube, entitled 'MUST WATCH. Little boy beats up older bullies!' We never saw those guys hanging outside the school gates after that and if I have to be honest, I loved that moment. It gave me significance.

As I moved into my early teens, I started to love boxing a lot more. I still wasn't a big fan of the training, but I loved the sport. I read all Dad's old boxing magazines over and over, and learned about Jack Johnson, Henry Armstrong, Sonny Liston, Floyd Patterson, Ali, all those greats.

At school, hardly anyone was into boxing apart from me. The thing is, it ain't like no other sport. You can't say "Let's play boxing," like you can football or tennis.

I always looked at football as this dirty, muddy game. Why? Because if you watched *Match of the Day* back in the 1970s, you'll know what I mean. That said, I did play football every day at school. I loved being in goal.

I used to dive across the concrete playground to save shots.

Everyone thought I was mad, but I didn't care. I was willing to do anything to stop the ball.

The thing about football was that I knew my limitations. Determination or not, there was only so far I could go. For my mate Paul Furlong, on the other hand, football was his talent. He was keen on boxing and used to go to the club opposite Tottenham Hotspur football ground, but when Spurs started showing an interest in him, he knew where his future was.

Paul was such a humble and blessed guy and I never saw him get into drama or fights in the five years we were at school together. Despite being a standout striker, you'd never once hear him saying: "I'm playing football for this club or that club."

I just remember how we all wanted him on our side when we were picking teams!

I also admired his BMX which had all the bits on the back wheels that you could stand on, a wicked paint job and all the race kit. His parents must have been doing alright.

When we finished school at 16, we kind of lost touch. And when we did speak again 21 years later, it would be under much darker circumstances.

★★★★★★★★★★★★★★★★★

Despite school being a place of learning, the biggest education for me as a child was from God. Going to church and learning about the value of my life and my purpose. How I should treat people with love, forgiveness, caring for others regardless of who they were. I also gained inspiration from the people of faith that trusted in God through adversity and saw them as my role models. The likes of King David, Job, Joseph, Moses,

Abraham, Elijah and Daniel. David at 17 faced a giant in the name of the almighty God when all the other seasoned soldiers were afraid and he was victorious.

Daniel got unjustly set up, thrown in a lions' den and came out unharmed. Joseph got jacked by his 10 jealous brothers and sold into slavery, then falsely accused of rape but still ended up becoming assistant prime minister in Egypt.

If this God could do that for them I wanted to know more, so I started to read a lot about him. It got to the point where Mum would catch me trying to use the moonlight through the window to continue reading in the night. She'd say: "You're gonna ruin your eyes. How can you see in the dark! Go to bed!"

At 13 I decided I wanted to give my life to Jesus and I got baptised, with my brothers and sister, in Islington, by a guy named Dick Barron. I got goosebumps listening to him talk about how much God loved all his children and that he'd sent his son to take our punishment on the cross.

I liked the thought that all the terrible things on earth, like death, greed, sickness, murder, rape, beatings, poverty and the devil, would finally be destroyed forever. I kept thinking I wanted to be with Jesus when he came back. I wanted to meet my creator one day. I wanted God to use me in this life.

I just knew I was doing the right thing. Children need training to shape their character as they grow and I was willing to allow God to train and shape me into his likeness.

The psychology of the Biblical figures who had faced such trying tests would be a strong theme of my adult life. Unfortunately, it would also become a big part of my childhood.

2

'Dem Beatings

"I couldn't manage him when he was beating them. I used to scream at him, 'Just control yourself. That's enough, that's enough.' I kept shouting to him but he wouldn't hear. He wouldn't stop. I pleaded with him."
Marva Prince, 2017 (Mark's mother)

Dad loved to sing in church, but also enjoyed every kind of music, from Johnny Cash to Motown, Calypso, you name it. He was very proud of his record collection and I loved sitting on the stairs listening to him playing his music and singing along.

He also used to talk about how good he was at dancing and how he'd be winning competitions all the time when he was back in Guyana. He used to get us up to dance and say: "Show me your whining [a type of Caribbean dance]," and you'd do it and he'd be wetting himself laughing, with his big echoing voice. Junior and Chris especially were always under the spotlight. Dad would show them how to dance and say: "Now come on. You must hold a woman so. Dat's how you whine."

Chris used to have her chin on Junior's shoulder, so much so that to this day, Junior still maintains he can't have a woman put her chin on his shoulder!

Another passion of his was cricket. I loved playing it, but what a dead game to watch. He'd be on it 24/7 and you couldn't talk or play around in the room when cricket was on. I have great memories of him taking me to play down the park. Because of my goalkeeping at school, I used to love being wicketkeeper as my reactions were really quick and I used to like diving.

Dad liked to see us compete against each other, but not always in a serious way. Arm wrestling competitions were a regular thing in our house and Chris was the don. It would be close between her and Junior, but she would always win.

Same with running. It was neck and neck in the 100 metres. I couldn't beat her. Chris was tough and fiery. Dad never brought her up all girly. Even boys were scared of her.

I looked up to Dad and was always trying to prove myself to him. We'd be walking back with the shopping and I'd carry six bags, insisting I could manage. I could hear Mum telling Dad: "Prince. Tek some a de bag arf de bwoy. Man him a struggle." Dad would laugh: "Leave him. He's OK!"

That made me more determined. As I looked at our house at the end of the road, I'd think: "Come on. Do this. You can make it." My arms felt like they were torn out of their sockets and my fingers turned white because all the blood had been cut off from the bag handles denting my fingers.

Another time, I did 300 press-ups for a piece of pudding. I was 13 and did it right next to his bed. If I stopped, I had to lock the position in a plank then carry on. If I went on my knees, I wouldn't get the pudding.

I used to love to see that smile on his face when I did it. I wanted to make him feel proud, because he was Da Man for me. He was the toughest and I wanted to be like that.

Probably the craziest thing we did was this ridiculous run. There was me, my brothers and Mark Christian, a close friend I knew from church. Christian was a couple of years older than me and said to everyone: "You lot want to go for a jog?"

"Yeah," we says.

"Cool. I'll pick you up tomorrow and we're gonna run to Battersea Bridge."

"Where's that?" we asked.

"It's quite far, but we'll be able to do it," Christian said. I was 13 at the time.

We didn't know where Battersea Bridge was. We started this flippin' run and when we get to Palmers Green I asked when we were going to stop.

"We're nowhere near Battersea Bridge yet," Christian replied.

It's not like we were wearing proper jogging trainers that you see people running with these days – we had some dead trainers with no cushion for impact.

We got to Islington and I'm wondering when the hell we were going to stop. We kept running and running. My brother Colin couldn't run anymore, so we told him: "Stay here. Don't move from this lamppost and on the way back, we'll pick you up."

It probably wasn't a great idea leaving a young child standing on his own in the street for a couple of hours. We made it to Battersea Bridge and Junior turned to me and said: "What the hell man? We're on the other side of the world. What now?"

"Let's go back," Christian said. We didn't even get time to recover. We started running back, picked up Colin where we'd left him and got home.

I worked out that we'd just ran a marathon. For the next 72 hours, I'd never experienced my body like this. It was ruined. It's not like we were in training. We were just a bunch of kids who banged out a marathon. When you're a kid, you think you can do anything. Dad laughed when he saw us stiff as boards.

It was one thing for us to be in pain from running a marathon, but if anyone laid a finger on us, God help them.

My sister used to suffer really badly with earache and one day this teacher pulled her ear. She came home that night and had a big blood patch on her pillow. She told Dad what had happened and in the morning he came into school. When we got inside, he told Chris: "Point the teacher that pull your ear."

Dad saw the teacher and with a stern face looked at him, then motioned for him to come over.

"Look man. All four of my Pickney 'dem. Don't ever put a hand on my kid again," he said.

The teacher looked petrified and never touched her again.

That was funny, but for years Chris had trouble finding a date because all the boys in the area were terrified of Dad.

Another time, a teacher pushed Junior at school and he nearly fell down the stairs. Junior was only seven at the time. He told Dad and he came down to school. Dad went straight up to the teacher and his exact words were: "You touch him again and I'm going to turn you into a cabbage."

Funnily enough, that teacher never came near Junior again.

It was one thing sorting out a few teachers at school, but his actions beyond that were what led to him being a feared man. Very feared. Boxing was something he used to practise like a religion. It was a strict discipline he preached to us, but when it came to street fights, Dad was ruthless. It was all about winning at any cost. He would talk about biting and sticking two fingers in the person's eyes to end things. He wouldn't stand there and box to show that he had skills.

In the 1970s, Dad used to work the doors of the clubs up in the West End of London as a bouncer in the evenings. He used to dress up in his suit and there would almost always be a story to follow from the night before. One night some guy wanted to get in and Dad told him he couldn't. The guy came back with a knife and Dad smashed him up really bad. In the morning, you saw blood all over his clothes. None of it his.

Although Dad had weapons at home, he would never have used them in a street fight as he saw it as cowardly. Either fight with your fists, or don't fight at all.

He kept three weapons under his bed; a hunting knife, a flick knife and a machete. Machetes were a must-have in all West Indian homes – when I spoke with my black friends back then, many of their parents had one. He also had a metal bat with black tape around it. These were for protection against any intruders.

I was intrigued with throwing knives and stars, because martial arts was in and everybody wanted to be Bruce Lee. I used to take Dad's flick knife and throw it against a tree at the end of my road, but didn't realise it was only special types of knives which were weighted to be thrown. I was always baffled why everyone else's knife would stick, but not mine. I still practised anyway, but I threw it like a javelin.

Although I sometimes carried that knife with me over the next few years, looking back, that was stupid. Especially as a kid was stabbed in our neighbourhood a few years later.

That was the first time I'd heard anyone killed in the local area. I was about 13 or 14, when Aunty Duffus came round to my mum's crying. I overheard her say: "Tyrone is dead."

Tyrone was a couple of years older than me at school and was a tough mixed race guy who was known for fighting. I even had a run in with him but it turned out to be a stand-off and neither of us made the first move.

I always wondered how that fight would have turned out – he was tough. From that day on, we were always cool with each other.

Unfortunately, it didn't end so well for Tyrone one day. I cried as I heard Aunty Duffus spill all the horrible details. Three boys from West London came down to Commerce Road and approached him. Rumour has it that it was over a girl and the boys thought Tyrone would have been scared of them.

Three-on-one is an easy beatdown but I heard Tyrone was getting the better of them until one of them pulled out a sword and pushed it inside his body. That's a really horrible death.

When you're young, you don't fully understand grief. It has to hit real close for you to feel it properly, so I just stared in shock seeing Mum and Aunty Duffus both crying. Little did I know I would have a much deeper understanding of this pain many years later.

Anyway, back to Dad. The fights didn't always need to be in a nightclub. Another time, Chris opened the door to see him holding a shopping bag and covered in blood.

It turned out Dad had left about six bags of shopping on the floor of the bus. When he went to pick up his bags, this woman next to him shouted: "You're trying to get into my bag."

"No. I was just picking up my mine," he said.

This big man stood up and said: "Oi. Leave her alone,"

thinking he was saving this poor woman from being robbed and that he'd teach Dad a lesson. Instead, Dad ironed this guy out. People on the bus were telling the driver to call the police.

As a black guy in the 1970s, Dad didn't stand a chance, so he made a run for it without his shopping bags. Those were the days when buses had the back open, so you could jump off. Apparently he jumped while it was moving pretty quick.

I wonder if someone had a go at frying sprats, making rice and peas, ackee and salt fish from Dad's shopping...

A few months later, he was on the train and this group of mods began to give him a hard time. He went into another carriage. If they'd have known he was a boxer, they wouldn't have started in the first place. But the moral of the story was to try and avoid trouble when possible.

Dad was a 'do as I say' sort of person, not 'do as I do'. He once told us how he won a bottle of rum at a dance competition, drunk it and didn't remember how he got home.

The story was told with a good sense of humour, but after he came home drunk another time and Chris saw him, he never did it again. He didn't want us to see that darker side. Although his darker side went far beyond coming back a bit tipsy.

★★★★★★★★★★★★★★★★★

Dad loved his family and being with them. He was proud to walk down the street with us and he loved holding Mum's hand walking down the road. Unfortunately, what happened behind closed doors at the Prince household won't leave us until the day we die. To say we walked on eggshells was an understatement.

As kids, we never used to call him 'Dad' – we used to call him

'Power'. I'm not sure who came up with the name, but it was obvious why.

Dad would make us do spelling and times tables tests. He would sit there with the Bible and he'd choose a word. If you got it wrong, he'd go on to the next person. But when it came to the times tables, we were frightened, because if you got them wrong, you'd get your ass whooped.

You'd be standing there saying: "One times one is one, one times two is two," but all the time you were looking at Dad with this belt in his hand. You'd forget, stutter and stall out of fear. Then you'd get it wrong and you'd get beats.

He had a real Jekyll and Hyde personality and Mum picked up on our reactions when he used to come home. She'd be working on her sewing machine when all of a sudden you'd hear Dad's key in the lock and she'd spot the look of fear on our faces. As soon as he opened the door, we'd all stand to attention.

We'd rush over to take his bag from him, then he'd get his plate of food, sit on his bed and we'd dive at his feet to take his shoes off. It didn't matter if those shoes and socks were wet and muddy – that's what you did.

We basically wanted to do anything to appease him before he'd get upset and angry. We did it out of fear, not love, because we knew he'd kick off over something as minor as bread being eaten without his permission.

At the time, Mum used to go to evening classes at some place near the North Circular. Her last words to Dad were always: "Don't touch 'dem Pickneys when I'm gone. I'll be back soon."

That night, we had dinner and Chris felt really tired and wanted to go to sleep. "Can I go to bed?" she asked. Dad looked at her funny. She was only eight years old.

She went off to bed and then about 10 minutes later, Dad told Junior to go and check if she was asleep. Chris was lying down, but hadn't quite fallen asleep yet.

She should have pretended she was sleeping, but instead she popped her head up to look. Junior told Dad: "She's not sleeping yet."

Dad came in with a raging temper and started beating her with this belt. He was hitting her so much that she pushed herself against the wall, hoping she could fall between the bed and the wall. But she didn't manage to and he just carried on.

As he was lashing away, the belt hit her eye. Chris covered it with her hand and was screaming: "My eye, my eye." He carried on beating her, but when she pulled her hand away, he could see the blood.

It was like he sobered up instantly. He didn't know what to do. He took her into the bathroom and bathed her eye in hot water. She was screaming even more now as the blood gushed out like crazy. She was telling him to use cold water and he just kept apologising. She went to bed with a tissue on her eye.

When Mum drew the curtains and saw Chris the next morning, she screamed and almost collapsed in shock. My sister's eye was closed, cut and badly swollen.

Mum shouted at Dad then took Chris to the doctor, who just asked: "Is he mad? Is he mad?" Mum pleaded with him not to say anything to the police, because she didn't want to lose her children.

The GP eventually said: "If I didn't know your family so well, I would have reported your husband. Don't let me see this again."

There was another close shave for Dad shortly afterwards,

when Chris had her general medical at school. The teacher asked Mum: "What are all those scars on her body?"

She didn't say anything. The teacher asked again and Mum pointed to Chris and said: "You ask her."

"That's where my dad beat me," Chris said.

The school reported it. Social services came to our house and even though nobody got taken into care, Dad didn't speak to us for weeks.

Unfortunately this scare had no effect on Dad – his ways of dishing out discipline got a lot worse over the next few years.

Another time, I got beaten in the early hours of the morning after being caught going downstairs to get something to munch on. As I slowly made my way back up the stairs, I shook with fear when I heard my parents' bedroom door open.

I pressed up against the stairs and prayed that Dad wouldn't see me, but he spotted me from the landing straight away and said: "What you doing, boy?"

My dad's favourite tool was a leather skipping rope and that's what I got for my reward. The skipping ropes back then weren't the silly little things you see now. These had serious weight to them and he always had two, in case you tried to hide one.

As he was lashing out, I must have got my hand in the way. Maybe the handle hit me. My finger was so badly swollen I think it was broken. I never went hospital – it stayed bent and healed in a different shape to the other fingers.

Yet another reminder of how badly hurt you could end up over misdemeanours at 13 Northcott Avenue. But it didn't stop there. The beatings seemed to come out of nowhere. Dad might start calm, but he'd suddenly wild-out. Mum might try to help us, and her presence was always comforting, but the end result was always the same.

On one occasion, we were doing our writing practice. We'd be told to pick a book and copy it, but after about three hours, we were tired and started messing around. Dad had fallen asleep, but when he woke, he asked Chris to check on us.

When she told him we weren't writing, he ran in, held me upside down by my foot and started beating me like mad with his other hand as I dangled, screaming and jerking around.

Suddenly he got dizzy and Mum screamed: "Get the chair and get some water." Junior got the chair and Dad collapsed into it unconscious, dropping me to the floor like a doll.

As everyone helped him, I didn't move. Not because I was in shock, but because I didn't want to help him. That glass of water was never going to come from me after those beats. I was really beginning to resent my dad and the way he beat us. I was even annoyed that anyone got any water for him.

If you got hit hard enough and fast enough with that rope, your skin was going to tear. We used to call it 'the horseshoe,' because you'd be left with this red bloody curve shape, where your brown skin had been ripped off. After that beatdown I had horseshoes all over my back. I never forgot how my t-shirt dried up and stuck to the cuts. Then when I tried to pull it off, I cried out as I was pulling the t-shirt off the wounds.

That was pretty wild, but the most traumatic beating I witnessed happened to my brother. Me and Junior had come home late and Mum said she was going to smack us. Mum's smack was a smack. That's how you're supposed to get smacked as a kid. There wasn't any fear involved when she hit you. You weren't scared for your life. Mum would say: "Put your hand out," then she might use the same skipping rope my Dad had, take a few inches from the end and smack it on the palm of your hand. Yeah, it stung, but you weren't left with any physical or mental scars.

Problem was, Junior was a real scaredy-cat. He wouldn't come in because he was knew he was going to get a smack. He stayed at the front door and I went over to him and said: "Are you nuts? Just come inside and get smacked."

But he wasn't listening.

"You gonna let Dad come in and see you at the door? He's gonna go wild," I said. "Dad won't be aiming for anywhere. He'll just go wild and beat you anywhere. How can you take that risk?" But he still didn't move.

Junior told me: "Getting hit on the hands and feet is more painful than getting whacked on the arse. I hate it! Dad's gonna beat my arse, so I'll take his beatings."

He even told me to count how many licks he got. As it started to get dark I knew Dad would be on his way home.

When he got back, he looked surprised to see Junior at the front door. He took him inside and questioned my mum about what had happened. Dad then took him into the sitting room and locked the door. Junior was running all over the room trying not to get hit, but there was nowhere to run because the room was locked.

I was scared and emotional as I listened to the screaming, begging and banging of furniture. I heard the sound of the skipping rope whizzing through the air and hitting Junior's flesh as he tried desperately to escape.

Eventually the door opened and Junior, sweating and barely able to walk, looked like a slave from one of the scenes from

Roots after being beaten by one of the masters. He'd counted up to 30-something lashes with the rope and then stopped keeping track as the beatings kept coming. That was a bad one.

Junior was a sorry sight as he staggered out. Mum took him upstairs and stripped him naked so he could stand in the bath while she ran cold water on his body, which was covered in cuts and bloody welts. He just stood there sobbing his eyes out, with blood pouring down him.

That's not something I like to revisit in my head. It still makes me cry when I think about it. It bothered me a great deal.

I really don't know why my mum let Junior stay outside that night, knowing my dad's history. I can't judge Mum on that stuff now, but I know she must have regretted it afterwards.

We never saw Mum getting beaten by Dad, although we knew it had happened a few times. She told us how after being hit she used to run to the bathroom and lock herself inside.

And like with us, he'd lose it with her out of the blue. Once she picked up the phone in the living room and Dad got up, walked away, came back in and bang, bang, started slapping her. He then tore the phone off the wall. He never said why.

He didn't beat Mum regularly and he didn't want us seeing it. It was as if hitting us was a way of life, but hitting Mum wasn't.

There's no justification for a grown man to hit small children, but the only understanding we got was from Mum, many years later, when she shared something with us.

"For years, I thought something was wrong with my husband," she said. "Then one day his mother came here in the 1970s and told me about him. She said he was very stubborn as a little child and wouldn't listen, so she beat him a lot when he was in Guyana. She used to beat him bloody and then tell him to go into the river, which was full of alligators and piranhas. She thought that was the way to bring up children. Maybe that's why it was in him. Maybe that's why he kept beating you."

I guess we are all products of our environment. That was a good enough example of why the cycle needed to be broken.

3

Runaway

"Adventure must start by running away from home." **William Bolitho**

Enough was enough. I loved my family and believe it or not, I still loved Dad, but I couldn't deal with the beatings anymore. At the age of 13, I packed a bag and decided to run away.

The first night I tried to stay at my mate's from school, Andrew Hilton. He said his mum would never know if I stayed overnight, because she worked late as a nurse and whenever she came in, she went straight to her room. I thought it was strange that she wouldn't check to see if her little son was OK, but I took his word for it.

I went to his house after school and felt safe because he only lived two roads away. We played Marvin Gaye for hours and joked and laughed with no stress or fear. It was like I was tasting a form of freedom. As it started to near 2am, he said his mum would be coming home soon, so we went up to his room and turned off the light. I couldn't sleep because I needed to hear his mum go into her room to know I was in the clear.

His house was a similar set-up to mine. She came through the door and as her footsteps came up the stairs I was holding my breath. I waited for her to pass so I could exhale, when bam, his door burst wide open. "Andrew! Who is this?"

Then she shouted at me: "Get out. Get out."

So there I was, walking the streets all night. I didn't sleep a wink. I was scared of strangers. I walked about in a park near our house, sat on benches, walked about, sat on benches, then when school opened I went straight over there.

Later that morning, I was sitting in a lesson and someone came to the classroom door and started whispering to the teacher. I had this feeling it was something to do with me. Next thing, the teacher said: "Prince. Can you come to the front please."

It was social services.

They wanted to be the mediator, mainly because they wanted me to stay at home instead of putting me into a care home. I wasn't interested and wanted to go with them, because I knew I was coming back to a beating.

That's exactly what happened. I got busted up bad. I took the beating for my mum, because when I came home, she was crying from worrying where I'd been and I didn't want to see her stressing any more.

Things didn't get any better. Around this time, Dad decided that we were using too much water up at home. Basically, he was being a bit tight.

"You're only supposed to have showers three days a week in the house," he said, so we started to take them at the New River Sports Centre instead. Only thing was, you couldn't just walk in, take a shower and walk out, you had to be seen using the facilities. So we ended up running, playing basketball and doing the high jump. Then one time they had a South London v North London athletics competition, where they brought all the best athletes together. They didn't have enough kids for some of the races, so the officials saw us playing around and asked whether we wanted to make up the numbers. We looked at each other and went: "Yeah. OK. We'll have a go."

Well, we took part in all these races and we smashed the lot. We had all these pictures taken with our awards and medals and were in the local newspapers and everything. What a buzz.

We went home on top of the world, feeling really proud of ourselves.

The thing is, winning stuff like this meant nothing to Mum and Dad. Absolutely nothing. I always used to get A or A+ for PE all the time, but they didn't care.

It wasn't like it is now, where you're encouraged to be an athlete and change your life through sport. Back then, PE was a joke subject. It was all about jobs and getting an education that would lead to those jobs.

We got back home around eight that evening. It was a little bit late, but it was still light as it was summertime. We couldn't wait to tell Mum and Dad what had happened. We had some close family friends over from the Duffus family and they were chatting in the kitchen.

Before we could say a word, Dad said: "You're going to get beaten tonight." Junior replied: "No I'm not," which was the bravest and most stupid thing he'd ever said. The Duffus' eldest daughter Sheila then joked to Dad: "Ohhhhhhhhh. He's taken his eyes past you!" which is what Jamaicans say when someone has been rude to someone else. Jokes like that didn't have happy endings in our house. This just got Dad even more hyped.

Junior wasn't trying to be rude, he just meant he'd explain himself for being late and that Dad wouldn't need to beat him. That's what he meant, because Junior would never be rude to Dad like that.

Dad didn't want to know any stories. He calmly walked over to the cupboard under the stairs to get the skipping rope. He couldn't find it straight away, so Junior got out of his chair slowly and started backing off. As he got up, Dad went to grab him.

I watched as they starting running round the table, worrying about how this would end. Junior ran round the table a couple of times, but he knew it wasn't going to last for long, so he made a beeline for the back door. The lock on that door was unreliable. Sometimes it would open, other times you had to really fiddle around with it to get it to click.

I'm thinking, 'Please make the door open,' but it wouldn't. Junior was that scared he was ready to jump straight through the window, which could have been fatal.

He wrestled with the door handle, desperately trying to open it as Dad steamed round the corner. I was literally praying now, begging for the door to open.

I don't know how Dad didn't grab hold of my brother, but somehow Junior managed to open the door and run to the bottom of the garden. He started jumping over fences, making his getaway.

You could hear one of the neighbours screaming: "Fred! There's a black man in the garden!" Then you heard a dog going for Junior, which would have made him sprint even faster as he's petrified of dogs.

He jumped the last fence and got to the main road, then carried on running. He slept somewhere in the mud that night.

The day after, he went to the YMCA. Junior still has nightmares about that. He dreams of running while Dad chases him. No matter how fast he's running, Dad's always just behind him.

A couple of days later, Junior got called to the YMCA reception. Me and Dad were there waiting for him. We all thought Dad would flip, but it was one of the only times I'd ever seen him remorseful. He wanted my brother home and when he did come back, he didn't beat him.

He might have been sympathetic with Junior that day, but I got no sympathy when I got nicked for the first time soon after. It was lunchtime and I was on the way home from school.

I walked past a bus stop and someone had smashed the advertisement glass panel at the stop, and there were loads of bits on the floor. This was a new type of laminated glass that broke into little square pieces when it smashed.

I was intrigued, so I picked up some pieces and threw them in the road, just to see how they landed. Guess what drove past? A police car.

They rolled up next to me and asked where I lived. I pointed to my house, which was about 60 yards away and to my shock they told me to get in the car because they were taking me home.

When we got to the front door, I said: "Wait there. Let me see who's home," because I didn't want Dad to see them. I walked in, turned left into the sitting room and there was Dad on the phone. As I was about to explain what had happened, the policeman stepped in behind me. "Let me call you back," said Dad, as he put the phone down. His expression said it all. His eyes were like huge marbles. The policeman said he wanted to give me a verbal warning.

I knew I'd be getting a serious beatdown, but the worst part was that I had to go back to school first and then dread going home all afternoon, knowing what was waiting for me.

His line was always: "You're gonna get six of the best." It was never six and it wasn't the best anything to me.

About a year later, in the summer of 1984, Mum went to Jamaica to see her mum. I was now 15. She hadn't seen her mum in over 20 years and even though I knew she had to go, I was thinking, 'Shit, this is going to be a tough one.'

I was always fearful of Dad's moods, especially when Mum wasn't there. She'd had a chat with him before leaving and said: "Prince – leave da Pickney dem alone." But I knew things would kick off and it didn't take long.

A few days after Mum left, Dad said: "I'm gonna pop out. You wanna come with me?" I said I didn't. The thing was, it wasn't a question and I didn't have a choice.

Next minute he came storming into the room, saying I'd disrespected him and started beating me with the skipping rope. When it got to this stage of my life, it wasn't a case of hold your hand out or bend over – the skipping rope was just flying.

As the rope flew towards my face I thought, 'I don't want to grow up with these scars,' so I covered up and backed away. But then I tripped and this massive telly fell off the shelf and landed on my head. This was long before the days of flatscreens.

It felt like it had broken my neck. I remember thinking, 'Surely Dad's gonna stop now the telly's fallen on my head.'

No mate. He just carried on.

Mum leaving was like the straw that broke the camel's back and my mind was now consumed with escaping. That would make me free from fear and from Dad's beatings, which had scared me so much that I was thinking about stabbing him. When I used to think like that, my concern was he probably wouldn't die straight away and he'd turn around and kill me instead. One time I was helping cut veg in the kitchen and turned slowly to look at Dad behind me as I thought about stabbing him with the knife. That's how bad it had got.

After the TV incident, I was angry. I'd taken this beating for no reason and still had to go out with him afterwards.

We went to BHS and Dad told me to pick a pair of boxer shorts. I was thinking, 'You're feeling bad and this is how you're trying to make it up?'

I just went along with it, but I was seriously pissed off. The second I got home, I wrote a letter to Mum saying how much I hated Dad and that she had to come home as soon as possible.

When Mum came home, she cried when she saw the cuts and bruises on my back. I asked if she'd read my letter.

"No. What letter?" she replied.

The letter had arrived in Jamaica while she was travelling home and her family had posted it back to London. Who opened it even though it was addressed to Mum? Dad, of course.

He took that letter to heart and now he really had it in for me. At that very moment, I knew I was going to run away. I was 16 in a few months and about to leave school, so I didn't see the point in staying home and getting beaten pointlessly.

I wasn't the only one to leave though. It got to the point where I cried more for Chris being beaten than I cried for myself, so when I left, I wanted her to come with me.

On this particular day, Dad and Junior were about to go to the airport to pick up Auntie Peggie when Chris said: "I ain't staying here no more. I can't do it anymore. I've had enough."

I told her to come with me. We packed our bags, put them under the stairs and when they left, we slipped out. Chris still makes out it was a big thing, even though she was nearly 20. That's not called running away, that's just leaving home!

We went down to Middleton Road, to the Duffuss family, who looked after us. Within a few hours, my parents came over and tried to get me home, but I was determined I wasn't going back. That really cut my mum up badly. Chris went home after a few days, but I never returned. Soon after, Junior also left.

A few months later, we went out looking for jobs. After going all over Wood Green and finding nothing, we went back to the house about 11pm, but Dad had locked the door.

We looked through the glass and could see Dad standing at the top of the stairs. Mum had her arm round his neck, trying to hold him back, while his eyes were almost popping out of his head with rage. She shouted: "Go, just go."

We walked away from the house and went round to this girl we knew in Tottenham called Wendy, who used to go to our church. She was a lot older than me and had a kid, but she was cool to let us stay. We ended up staying for a couple of weeks.

Dad found out where we were and asked for both of us to come back and chat with him. Junior went and Dad said he was really sorry and all that, but I still refused to come home.

Junior was really gutted as he wanted his brother back. He wanted it to be the way it was, but it would never be like that ever again.

★★★★★★★★★★★★★★★★★★

If anyone tells you leaving home at 15 is a breeze, they're talking crap. I left home with no money, an old blue cardboard suitcase and a black bin bag full of clothes. I was living all over the place. Some nights at a mate's house, other nights on the streets and for a spell I was sleeping in Mark Christian's dad's car. It was an old orange Austin Maxi and it was freezing.

I remember trying to get out in the morning and my knees had seized up. It was like bending metal.

Dad banned me from entering the house. Even when I went round to see Mum, I had to wait outside for her. She would always say I looked well even though I was homeless.

I took pride in my appearance and for a while I still attended church on the Sabbath, because I loved gospel music and used to sing in the choir. I even used to have the solo lead on occasions. It was important to have faith in God taking care of me.

My bredrin on the streets, Mark Smith, knew a social worker. I wasn't keen at all, but Mark said: "No, no, no. This guy's alright. He's a black guy. He'll look after you and tell you about your rights as a tenant and also any money you're eligible for. His name is Will Dowden. Let me bring him over..."

Back in them days, they're weren't a lot of black people in social services, so I said: "Ahhh, mmmm, OK. I'll go on your word." It turned out Will was a really cool guy. A lot of the people who spoke to social workers just wanted to get the money they were entitled to, but that wasn't my mindset. I was more concerned with getting my issues sorted out. Will recognised I was genuine and went above and beyond for me. He said: "You're not like a lot of the kids I see."

He helped me to sign on and also gave me a sub to at least buy the basics like toothpaste, a brush, some food. Then he asked me what I wanted to do with my life.

"I want to be in the army," I replied. I wanted to do something that involved discipline, which probably evolved from what I'd grown up with at home.

I knew the army could give me a good job. I'd be respected and could learn skills. Yeah, the army, that's what I'd do. He looked into that for me, but he also said: "Let's look at getting you a flat, but until we get that sorted you'll stay at a bedsit."

So there I was, staying in this bedsit in Finsbury Park called Pembury House. I was scared stiff. I spent the first night sat on the bed and didn't sleep a wink. The place stunk, it was dirty and there were cockroaches everywhere. That morning, I went down to the room where you made your breakfast and it was full of grown-ups. It felt like everyone was looking at me and I didn't feel comfortable.

I walked out of the door that morning and never returned. I was back to sleeping in cars, the streets and I even lived in a foster home for a while. For 18 months I never settled anywhere.

The problem was I never reported that back to Will, who was still trying to set me up with the flat. I used to see him regularly, but I never told him I'd left the bedsit as I felt like I'd let him down, knowing how much effort he put into getting it.

He'd been trying to contact me, but I wasn't settled and my forwarding address was constantly changing. Then one day, I went round to see him and Will said: "I hear they've sent you a letter about housing. Have you got it? Have you been to see the flat the council have offered?"

"What? I've got a flat? I didn't know," I replied.

That's when I told him that I'd left the bedsit. It was a relief that Will wasn't angry. He understood my reasons and knew that it wasn't exactly five-star accommodation. From my side,

I was so happy and excited. My own place. A couple of days later, I went over to the 14th floor of 108 Oatfield House. Some guy from the council was there to meet me. He opened the door, showed me around a bit and I just said: "I'll take it, mate."

It was small, but cool. But in all honesty, I don't know how bad it would have to have been for me not to accept it. It was my space. It didn't matter what it looked or felt like, I'd make it look great and feel good.

I grew up seeing my mum cleaning our house non-stop and that had a big impact on my own cleanliness and sense of keeping order over my space. I was always close to Mum, helping her in the kitchen, so when I was given the keys to that flat, I thought, 'What would Mum do?'

In no time, I was on my hands and knees as I went to work on the place with bleach and disinfectant. I was wiping everything. The skirting boards, the floors and even the walls.

I loved that flat, so much so that I had dreams about the place for many years after. Mostly good memories, although, at later stages the dreams would involve people knocking on my door and me escaping through a window. More about that later.

So here I was, an independent man. Well a 17-year-old kid with his own flat. I had a level head on my shoulders and some money in my pocket. What could possibly go wrong?

4

Apparently Maturing

"Bruv, what you laughing at? Seriously.
*I am Skeletor." **Mark Prince tripping***
on acid, 1988

Even though I ran away from home, I still finished my schooling.
I did my maths, English and biology exams, but I have no idea
what I got because I didn't go back to the school to check. I
didn't see the point. A year later I knew I wasn't going to be
looking for a career as an accountant or a lawyer.

I had my own flat, but I was on my way to becoming a product
of the street and when the street gets a hold of you, you're at
its mercy.

Although I was scared when I first left home, by the time I was
16, I knew I could handle myself. That was mainly down to Dad
teaching us boxing and me going to karate and judo, but it was
more the mentality that I'd inherited from him. The difference
was, the street mentality was now starting to influence me to act
in ways I wouldn't have normally.

One day I went to the gym where we used to do martial arts every week. I ended up having an argument with this older guy, who was bigger than me. I don't know why, but I decided to bring that stupid knife out with me that day.

Once you have it on you, it's like it has power over you; like it's calling you. I went back to the changing room to get the knife and my friend Manley looked at me like he was really ashamed.

He knew my family, he knew we were all fighters and he knew what I was capable of, even against grown men. Manley turned out to be the voice of reason and gave me a right earful. Something I'd relate to in many years' time. I felt so stupid. I was thinking, 'What am I doing? You don't need this. You can fight. You can bang this guy out.'

There was no thought behind it. I was never going to stab him. I went back into the gym and that was it. I didn't even fight the guy in the end.

What I didn't realise was that I was damaged goods emotionally. There was still a lot of anger in me and I didn't know the correct way to channel that emotion.

Unfortunately, my fighting gene needed to be released and it wasn't long before it became a regular thing. That led to my first court appearance and me being nicked when I was 17.

I was with my mate Darren Cumberbatch and we were leaving Wood Green shopping centre when I threw my half-full McDonald's milkshake on the floor. A bit of the milkshake splashed up onto a lady walking past. I didn't mean to throw it at her, it was just a stupid thing to do.

The second it hit her, she looked at me angrily and called me a black bastard. I said: "Who you calling a black bastard?"

Next thing some guy with glasses walked over, started taking his jacket off and said: "Fight someone your own size." Before he could land the first punch, I threw this straight right karate kick to his head and knocked his glasses clean up over his face. By now, a crowd of people had started to look and Darren said: "Let's go, let's go."

We left the shopping centre and walked up this hill towards Wood Green station. Near the top we saw this policemen with the guy who I'd just kicked in the face. My first thought was, 'How did he get in front of us? I never saw him pass me.'

The policeman then said: "We've been informed you've attacked a man."

"Rubbish. I've defended myself," I replied.

"We're going to arrest you," the policeman said.

In the meantime I'm thinking, 'I've got a knife on me. I need to get rid of it.' Somehow, with all this going on, I've angled myself to Darren and passed him the blade without them seeing it. The second I had got rid of it, my argument changed. I told the policeman: "Cool. Take me. Do what you need to do."

The truth is, I was shitting my pants. I'd never been to a police station before, but it certainly wouldn't be the last time.

They kept me in there for hours and all these things started running through my mind. At the time, a black man had been beaten in a cell not far from where I was and I started to wonder if I might be next.

I spent the next few hours reading all the writing on the wall from previous people who'd been nicked and decided to scrape my name in there with a message and date for the next person. 'Mark Prince was here.'

On 22 June 1987, I ended up in Wood Green Crown Court and was charged with ABH. I was made to pay £100 in costs and £150 in compensation. First notch on the criminal record. No decent brother should be proud to say that.

★★★★★★★★★★★★★★★★★

Not long after running away, I started a job as an apprentice engineer in Putney, making ball bearings. It was a shit job and I had to travel about two hours to get there. Work started at 8.30am, but I never used to get there until about 11. Hard to believe, but I got sacked for bad timekeeping.

Then Junior sorted me out with a job. We started working together in a factory reconditioning gearboxes and axles, and I was there for nearly a year. It was good having some money, but that job was dangerous. Health and safety? Forget it mate.

You had a tub full of a paraffin-like substance that would clean the grease that covered gearboxes. You'd use it to polish the gearbox with this really powerful buffer machine.

This thing had a spinning lump of wire material that would go round at great speed to polish the metal. Somehow, on this occasion, my hand got trapped inside the machine.

Someone saw what happened, ran over and switched the machine off. I could have easily lost my arm – that would have been the end of my boxing career before it had even started.

The turning point in that job wasn't almost losing a limb, it was weed. As a kid, I'd only ever smoked rolled-up paper. Me and my brothers used to roll up a sheet at home, set it alight on the gas stove and then blow it out. I don't know why. But I started smoking weed with a couple of schoolmates Robert and Spencer very soon after running away. At first, I didn't like how it felt at the back of my throat and how dizzy it made me.

Back at the factory, there was this guy that used to sell weed and I used to smoke with him. This stuff was called high grade, which basically meant it was high-quality weed. Not punked.

Everyone on the streets knows it's about proper leaves, not the ones grown in the house with the UV lights. That's called punk on the streets, but everyone knows it as skunk. Real weed smokers will only smoke weed that's grown out of the ground.

Then one day I asked myself how I could make money from it. I wanted to buy and sell my own stock and be my own boss. That's when things started going downhill for me.

My faith in God was strong and I still went to church regularly after I had run away. I'd built up some good relationships with guys from church. There was Blakey, Rodders, Mikey, Clive and a few others. These guys had musical instruments and we even had dreams of forming a band. Clive could play the keyboards well, I could sing and we all had some decent skills.

I was able to travel all over London to other churches, in places like Watford, Reading, Willesden and Stratford, meeting different congregations and socialising with people our age. It was like a warm bond between like-minded people. But when I started smoking, I began to drift from the church and my faith. You can't serve two masters. You either love one or the other.

Now this will come as a shock to everyone who knows me, but before I started smoking weed, my timekeeping was unbelievable. I was always either bang on time or early. When I started with the drugs, my timekeeping went to pot, literally. I started coming in later and later, until eventually I got the sack.

The more I smoked, the more everything sensible in my life started to get affected or disappear. Up to this point, my fear of Dad had always kept me in check.

Now, new friends and influences were guiding me and being in the big bad world on my own meant I'd do anything to survive.

Month by month, the more weed I did, the less I trained. The less I trained, the more trouble I got into. My life started to spiral out of control, big time.

★★★★★★★★★★★★★★★★★★

Growing up in a strict Christian family meant we lived like monks. Running away from home not only introduced me to weed, but also women. Around this time, I was seeing a few girls, but nothing serious. And as most people know, there's a rule between mates – you don't date each other's sisters. The problem is, you can't choose who you fall in love with.

The first time I saw Darren's sister Tracy, I was on a bench by a bus stop. Tracy and Darren had a cousin over from Texas and they were getting ready to take her back on the bus to Hackney.

As they walked past, Darren said hello to me. Tracy looked over at me and said to her brother: "He's nice."

"You're never gonna get him, he's got too many women," Darren replied. Tracy shrugged her shoulders.

About three months later, around 11pm, I was round at Darren's house when Tracy walked in, having just come back from a party. Her mum apparently told her: "There's this really lovely boy upstairs!"

She came upstairs and walked straight into Darren's room to check out who it was. It all went from there. Thankfully Darren was really cool about us and we're still best mates to this very day. His mum, on the other hand, kicked off and we had a rocky start.

Shortly after we started going out, I was round their house, when Tracy and her mum started having this blazing argument. I was just standing there saying nothing, when suddenly her mum looked at me and said: "And you – you home-breaker."

Whoosh. She slapped me around the face. Not a little tap, but a proper strike, like I'd been hit by a 20oz steak across the face.

Darren knew I was holding my anger in. He'd seen me lose it before for much less and said: "Mark. Let's go, let's go."

It was purely my love for Darren and Tracy that got me out that door without any issues.

Me and Tracy hit it off straight away and within a couple of months, she announced: "I'd love to have a child with you." I was only 17.

A matter of weeks later she fell pregnant. Nine months later, Tracy gave birth to our beautiful daughter, Tannisa.

Becoming a dad at 18 was weird. I was still a kid myself and was just trying to work out what to do with my life when Tannisa came into mine. There were two stages to the reaction. Oh shit, then excitement for being a dad.

I loved my daughter to bits and just wanted to take care of her. The only problem was, by now I was starting to go off the rails a bit. I was hoping the responsibility would help me with my own issues. Unfortunately, it didn't. Although it wasn't always my recklessness that was getting me into trouble.

A few months after Tannisa was born, I was out with Darren, a mate called Sammy and a girl he was seeing at the time. Sammy had a Renault 5 GT Turbo, which back in the day was a top car with a lot of power and only two doors.

This particular night we'd gone for a drive in it. Darren and I were sat in the back, with Sammy and his girl in the front. None of us were wearing seatbelts. The problem was Sammy couldn't handle that car, especially at high speeds and especially when we were all red. The expression 'red' comes from when you get high or drunk. You get the red eyes.

Anyway, after cruising for a bit, this car came the other way and I recognised the guys inside. They were a group of bad boys, but they had no beef with me. However, they did with Sammy. They spotted him, he spotted them and this other car immediately turned round and started coming after us. Sammy started speeding up and driving like a madman.

I was like: "Listen bruv. Stop the car and let me out."

If you're familiar with Hornsey Lane, you'll know that certain parts are narrow and just not meant for doing that Brands Hatch shit he was doing. So I'm looking at the speedometer, and seeing 50 miles an hour, 60, 70 and I said again: "You don't do 70 down this road bruv! Let me out the car."

He replied: "Nah. If I'm gonna die, I'm taking everyone with me." That really pissed me off, but I didn't have time to dwell on it. The only thing I did do was say a quick prayer to God, because I honestly thought I was going to die.

Boom. He clipped a kerb and lost control of the car. I closed my eyes and next thing I remember is my head crashing into the roof of the car as it started to roll, over and over again.

I don't remember how I got out, but when I did, I called for Darren, helped him out of the car and started walking away in a daze. We cut through 'Ally Pally' [Alexandra Palace], which was pitch black at this point.

We came out the other side, walked over a bridge, came to another main road thinking, 'Brilliant, we're safe,' when out of nowhere this undercover police car rolled up next to us.

We must have looked a bit dishevelled, but played it cool.

"Why you stopping us for?" They started to explain about this car down the road that had been involved in an accident and said a girl had been injured and taken to hospital. "We weren't there. We've just come from 7-Eleven," we told them.

They could tell we were lying, popped the handcuffs on and put us in their car. One of the policemen said: "We don't know how you survived that accident. The girl is in hospital."

Sammy had got away and they had no evidence on us, so all they could do was keep us back to the cells for the night then let us go in the morning. Close call, on many fronts.

★★★★★★★★★★★★★★★★★★

My progression to harder drugs was all down to the company I kept and what they brought to the table. The first time I took an acid (LSD) tab was at 19, at Tracy's mum's house.

The guy who gave me it was convinced that the first one didn't affect me, so he gave me another straight away. He told me: "Just remember; once you've taken it, you're on the trip. People have gone a bit funny, so try and keep yourself together."

Easier said than done as I was now seeing all sorts. I looked in the mirror and, oh my goodness, I was Skeletor. Massively ripped body and seriously scary. When I looked away from the mirror, paint was dripping down the wall. This was messed up.

I then went to the pictures with my mates Dean, Darren and Raymond. I was cracking up so loud, everyone could hear me. What the hell was I laughing at? I have no idea.

We came out of the pictures and decided to go to a nightclub in Hackney where this crazy new music called acid house was being played. We got in and I started dancing like I was nuts, jumping around like mad and dripping in sweat. I was even thinking to myself, 'I don't dance like this. What's going on?'

That's when my mate looked over and said: "Now I know you're on it!" When I looked around, I realised everyone else was dancing like me. That's when it hit me — everyone else was flippin' tripping on acid.

It wasn't just dancing. Girls looked beeeeeeeauuuuuutiful. This drug made the ugliest girls look amazing. I remember Hollywood films used to have this soft-focus look to showcase their beautiful actresses and this night in Hackney, every girl had that same look. You just wanted to chat to all of them.

I decided to have a walk around the club. As I walked past the bar I saw this woman turning slowly to look at me. She had two horns, the devil's head, but her body was normal from the neck down. She just kept staring at me. It seemed that when I moved, she moved her head to keep watching me. I was so scared. I walked off, then came back. I needed to see that face. Why did the devil's head keep looking at me?

Eventually, I got home and the paint was still dripping down the walls. I looked in the mirror and I was still Skeletor. I kept touching my face and body, wondering, 'What the hell is this?'

I walked into Tannisa's room and as my criminal activities were doing well, it meant she had loads of toys. As I walked in, all these toy cars were driving themselves around the room on their own. I was standing there smiling, thinking, 'When I bought these, I never knew they could do that. That's amazing.'

The other thing that was incredible when I was tripping was the amount I could drink. Back then we used to have this strong drink called Thunderbird. It was popular with alcoholics and people who didn't want to spend a lot of money on brandy.

Most people would share a 250ml or 500ml bottle, but I used to drink this massive bottle shaped like a freakin' barrel.

By now I was ready to come off this trip and you can imagine the comedown that came with the Thunderbird and this drug. About seven in the morning, all of a sudden I got so depressed.

The comedown from acid is disgusting. You could seriously hurt someone in that state. You got so moany, miserable and angry. Thankfully nobody crossed my path on this particular comedown, but that wasn't to be the case in the coming months. Drugs brought out a really mean side to me.

There was this mate of mine in our area, who I'm not going to name because I'm embarrassed about how I used to treat him on occasions. I apologised to him years later. As bad as I felt, I've got to say he had what you'd call a hygiene problem. He never used to wash and his place had crap all over it.

When I used to go round to his flat, whether it be to get some drugs, whatever it was, my routine was the same. I'd knock on his door, wake him up and I'd run straight to the window and take a deep breath, because his flat would stink that bad.

In between breaths I'd be like: "Bruv. Get the fuck out of bed. Get ready, this place stinks. I'm dying here."

There was one occasion involving this guy when things got out of control. When I was red, as my mate Kevin would say: "Mark could make a room go dark very quickly."

Someone wanted some coke. I didn't have any, but the mate I was with had some. This guy suddenly became paranoid and convinced me my other mate from the stinky flat was trying to set me up, maybe rob me of my stash. I stupidly believed him. I called this mate from the stinky flat and said: "Come down to the house." He didn't really have much choice. He came over and I invited him into the spare room, which had started to become known as 'The Beatdown Room'. I said: "You trying to set me up?" He looked scared and denied it.

My other mate was a big guy. Not muscular, but heavy. He started to lay into him, then I joined in and banged him in his mouth so hard that his tooth went into my knuckle. You could stuff a tissue into the gap it left. I've still got a scar there now.

We dragged him into the bathroom and the big guy pulled out this massive thing of bicarbonate of soda. Kevin and Darren were telling me to calm down, but I wasn't listening.

My mate wanted him to sniff all the bicarb. It was like a scene from a gangster movie. He knew the ramifications of sniffing large amounts of bicarb and started begging for his life. He was screaming: "Pleeeeaasse. Nooo. Don't make me do that."

Then I suddenly had a sober moment. That's when I realised, I ain't no gangster. I could feel it in my heart every time this guy was pleading. I could feel that this guy was seriously scared for his life and we'd busted him up enough. I had to put a stop to it. I told him to get up and kicked him out of the house.

This is what drugs can do to you. Looking back it makes me cringe, thinking I used to behave like this.

As much as I beat this guy up, I also saved him a few times. This was someone who'd done a lot of bird and was connected to some big people. One time there was about 15 youths that saw him in the street and wanted to smash him up as repayment for a deal he'd been involved with. I didn't let that happen. I ran over and let them know that if they started on him, then they had beef with me.

That sort of things happened a lot when he asked me to meet him. It was like I was coincidentally there whenever he was going to be outnumbered. Or maybe it wasn't a coincidence. I kind of looked at him like my investment. I needed him to make money. He had connections to get me stuff that I could sell on for the best deals. And if I ever needed some money, he'd never let me down. He'd walk into a building and come out with cheques, cards, cash, whatever. I don't know how.

I never forget the time we were walking next to some industrial estate. He owed me some cash and I said: "Let's go get me some money bruv." He went into this building and came out with the lot. I don't know if he'd seen stuff in some handbags, if he'd stolen someone's wallet, I don't know. I never asked.

His version of robbing was different to mine though. He also used to do 'creepers'. Creeping into people's houses when they were sleeping. I used to say: "You're a punk man. How can you creep into their house and rob them when they're asleep?"

He used to tell me about how he'd break in, see them move and he'd keep still in case they woke. Then he'd go through their drawers as they were asleep next to him and steal everything.

The big guy who beat up my stinky flat mate was also the one who introduced me to coke and acid. He was a really bad influence. Once he came round with a pile of coke which he'd washed and turned into rocks [crack cocaine]. We piped it, then afterwards he hit me with a £300 bill. I had to rob to pay him back.

I had never robbed as a kid, but now it was becoming habitual. One time, after a long night out, me and Darren got a cab home. I was sitting up front and Darren was in the back seat. When we got to Oatfield House I pulled out a weapon and told the driver to give me his money. The guy was pleading, telling me he had a family. I took the money, which was literally a few quid. We got up to the 14th floor and I suddenly remembered I'd left a glove in the taxi.

Darren was telling me not to go back, saying the taxi would be long gone and the police might be on their way. I said: "I don't care, I'm getting it."

I ran downstairs and the guy was still there, drooped over the steering wheel in shock. I opened the door and said: "I left my glove." He stared at me with a glazed look, not saying a word. I calmly leaned in, grabbed the glove and walked off.

It was all to do with choices at that stage of my life and I was making bad choice after bad choice. However, one positive decision I did consciously make was about my daughter Tannisa.

As she started to grow up, I had this thing where I could see bits of my dad in me. Where I was a bit too firm. Whatever it was; not eating her food, messing around, like I'd do when I was a kid with my parents.

I'd get annoyed and smack her bum. The second I did it, a horrible feeling went through me, like when I was little. It was like a voice said to me, 'Don't do what your dad's done. Don't let this develop. Don't let this be you as a dad.'

As crazy as my life was at that time, I still had a clear enough head to realise I needed to break the cycle. That message was very, very clear. My aim from then on was for my daughter to see me as fun and firm, not feared.

It's just a shame the rest of my life was lacking that self-reflection, because I was about to raise the bar in terms of madness.

5

Don't Bank
On It

*"The first and worst of all frauds is to
cheat one's self. All sin is easy after that."*
Pearl Bailey, American actress

I'd gone from soft to hard drugs and from not stealing to doing
inside jobs. My temperament, even when I was doing bad
things, was to work hard, be focused and constantly improve
my game.

By now, my appetite had gone way beyond a few hundred
quid. A guy I knew told me about this group and how they'd
made a lot of money from fraud. If you did armed robbery, you
could get up to 10 years in prison, but with fraud it was a lot less
and you could make way more money.

The idea was to go in there wearing a cheap suit, use fake ID
and walk away with 80 grand. I thought, 'I can do that. I like
acting.' These guys said: "If it goes down, we'll look after your
missus and your kid. But don't grass."

I was cool with that. My cut was about 10 or 20 grand.

So there I was, 19 years old, dressed in a suit, sat in this little room in NatWest bank, Hackney. I was there as Mr Whatever and had all the paperwork I needed to prove who I wasn't, trying to look like this businessman.

The guy from the bank took a look at my paperwork, had a little chat with me and said: "Everything looks good. We just need to get you the money sorted out now."

I was surprised how easy it seemed, and already started to think of the next fraud job I could do and what I would be buying with the dough. Cars, jewellery, fancy clothes.

Then another guy from the bank walked in; but this one was black. For me, another black guy in Hackney was not good news. He could see through me.

I felt uneasy and my confidence drained away. He sat down, asked me a few more questions and then he said: "Let's get this money for you."

As he walked out, I felt nervous. I started thinking, 'He's black. He can spot street guys.'

I was sitting in this room on my own waiting for what felt like forever. I had beads of sweat pouring from me and a voice inside my head saying, 'He's taking too long. Get out of here.'

On the other hand, the more confident side of me thought, 'This length of time? Don't worry, because this is how long it takes to get 80 grand approved.' I stayed and took the risk.

Minutes later, four policemen walked in cool as day. Oh shit. They told me: "We're arresting you on suspicion of fraud, you don't have to say anything…" Then they handcuffed me and took me out. It was so embarrassing. Everyone in the queue was looking at me, wondering what I'd done. I felt so ashamed.

When they took me down the station I knew I was screwed.

However, my acting never stopped. They started saying: "We know it's not you. We know you're a mule. We know there are big boys behind this. Who are they?"

I started crying, pretending someone had put me up to this and my kid would be in fear of her life if I grassed. One policeman took to me and said to the others: "This guy is genuine."

They kept going on about the Yardies. "It's the Yardies isn't it?", trying to get me to admit something that wasn't true. Back then, they tried to pin everything on the Yardies. They kept pushing: "We know it's them. We know they're organised. Don't worry, we'll look after your kid. We'll take care of you."

But it wasn't the Yardies! I wasn't saying anything.

On 3 February 1989, I was charged at Inner London Crown Court with conspiring/obtaining property by deception. I was warned I'd most likely be going down for a two-year stretch, but one of the policeman went on the stand, saying I wanted to cooperate and my family was under threat.

That really helped me out. In the end I received 12 months' probation. Close call.

I learnt absolutely nothing from that experience. I walked straight out of the courtroom and committed another criminal offence that same afternoon. How stupid was I?

My sister Chris called me, saying that money kept going missing in her house. Then she mentioned who she thought it was. It was just a friend, not a boyfriend.

One time she'd left some money out deliberately to set him up and when he was gone, the money was gone too. Now it had happened again.

I was studying electrical engineering at college at the time, so I left the courtroom and went straight to the college to get this guy. But I was shitting myself. I was going to face someone who was quite threatening. He was no pussy by any means.

This guy was known for banging people out and bullying younger and smaller guys. He was about 6ft 5in, in his mid 20s. I hadn't even hit 20 yet. All I kept thinking was, 'I need to let this guy know that he can't be thieving from my sister.'

I bumped into some guys I knew at the college and they told me he was playing on the basketball court. There was this balcony in the basketball arena and I sat down. My heart was thumping as I watched him. He looked daunting, pushing people over and doing what he wanted on that court.

As the match came to a close, I went and spoke to my mate Slider [Mark Grant] and he said: "He's in the common room." Over I went and there he was.

"You been coming to my sister's house and you been teefing money?" I said. He got aggressive, defensive and denied everything. I hadn't come to talk. I started swinging.

I've got this thing that I start and end fights quickly, so my first swing is important. I missed and now I was even more scared, as he knew it was on.

After I missed, I began this onslaught borne out of the fear of being beaten. I was so vicious that as he tried to escape from me, I did this flying kick and he went into this door. It flew off the hinges. He and the door landed in a pile.

He ran off, leaving a trail of blood. This teacher came in and said: "He's called the police. There's blood all over the phone and wherever he's walked he's left a trail. Where's the knife?"

I said I didn't have a knife, but the teacher said: "You must have used a knife on him. This guy is really hurt."

Next thing Slider came in and shouted: "Police are coming."

We all ran out of this fire exit and headed straight for my house. That was college over for me. It was my first and last year.

★★★★★★★★★★★★★★★★★★

I reckon I would have been behind bars for many years if things had turned out differently.

One time, stupid me, I decided to swap jobs. I was always the guy who took the money. My mate was always the driver. But on this occasion I turned to him and said: "Can you take care of that today and I'll drive?"

We had a connection with this guy in Whitechapel and he used to give us information about who we could get some money from. Me and my mate had been hanging around for a couple of days, waiting for a beep on my pager. These were the days before mobiles. So there we were, waiting for the pager to beep with a registration of a car we were supposed to follow.

It was the third day in that I decided I wanted to drive. We were in my mate's girlfriend's car, this shitty old Nissan Micra. After we got the beep, we followed this guy right into the City, near the Bank of England.

My mate jumped out and went for the guy, but he ran off, dropping a bag along the way. My mate jumped back into the car and I screeched off. As we drove off, I kept asking him: "What's in the bag? What's in the bag?"

My mate opened it and next thing, bang, we hit this car in front. Then this car crashed into some guy on a bike, who went flying up into the air and landed about 10 feet away.

The driver I smashed into came out petrified, like he expected us to do something next, whereas normally the person would come out mad, wanting to know why you've rear-ended them. I found out later that he had seven grand on him and he thought we were about to rob him.

My mate had hit his head on the windscreen. I checked to see if he was bleeding, then we pulled the car round some side road, ran to Moorgate tube station and legged it.

My mate phoned his girlfriend and told her to report the car as stolen. He went home, then at 6.30 the next morning, the CID were knocking at his door.

Apparently the barrel of the car in the ignition was fine, so they knew a key had been used and it hadn't been hot wired. Instead of keeping quiet, she'd grassed us up and said we'd borrowed her car.

Next thing, there was a knock on my door. Usually the concierge would buzz me if the police were coming up to my flat so I could do a runner, but not this time.

Silly me, I went to the door instead of leaving it. Two undercover policemen were there with a warrant, saying they were going to search my flat. They asked if they could come in. On the outside I was calm as you like, but inside I was nervous.

I just sat there watching them going through everything in my flat. Thank God I kept my place fairly clean and the only thing they found was a driving licence.

While all this is going on, I had about two grand of fake 'Georges' (that's what we used to call Giros) in my sock, because I was just about to go out and do my work for the day. Giros back then were easy as you could cash them at any Post Office.

I also had some weed hidden in my pants. If they'd have come 10 minutes earlier, they would have found everything.

One of the police pointed to a woman's driving licence and

said: "What's this then?" They knew I'd been done for fraud already and you could see them thinking they'd nailed me.

I told them the licence belonged to some girl who'd stayed round the other night. They kept the licence, nicked me, took me down the station and kept me there for hours.

They charged me for robbery and gave me a slip to say I had to come back for an ID parade, because there were witnesses who'd seen me and my mate and they wanted to identify us.

On the day of the parade, I went to the barbers and got everything shaved off. The hair on my head and every little hair on my face. I knew the only way I was going to get out of this was to look different from on the day of the robbery.

One of the policemen looked at me closely and said: "You've done that on purpose."

I replied: "I don't know what you're talking about."

He stared at me and then said: "Alright. If that's how you want to play it." He told me to sit down and wait. I was there for hours. When he came back, they'd scrapped the ID parade. He said: "We'll call you back another day. This isn't over."

"Cool," I said, and walked away. I heard nothing about that charge ever again. It was a serious case they were building up and it just disappeared. Very strange.

By now, my respect for the police had dropped to nearly nothing. It wasn't that they were doing anything wrong, it was that they were trying to stop me from what I thought was right.

In my mind, violence, drugs and theft were a natural way of life. Why were they stopping me enjoying myself? So when the opportunity came up to aggravate them at the Notting Hill Carnival in 1989, I was right in there.

It started off as a gathering of people, then the police started to form a group. Maybe 15 people each. We hadn't intended on doing anything, but they stood there in front of us like a stand-off and when the mood got a bit warm, they arrested one of our guys and dashed him to their van.

We shouted: "Let him go, he ain't done nothing," but they didn't listen. I thought, 'OK. Let's see what you're made of.' There was loads of rubbish on the floor, so I picked up a bottle, said to my lot: "Let's get them," then threw it. Bam. It hit this copper on the head. Home run. He shouted out in pain.

It then went silent, when I was expecting the guys I was with to be geeing me on. When I turned around, they'd all done a runner. Then the police did a runner and I was left there on my own thinking, 'What the frigging hell was that about?'

★★★★★★★★★★★★★★★★★

The last piece of my messed up jigsaw at the time was street fighting. All those years training in boxing and martial arts went totally against what I was now doing on the roads. I didn't think twice about fighting with anyone over anything. I'd like to say that trouble came to me, but I knew I played my part.

Around Christmas 1989, I got on the bus with Darren, heading towards Muswell Hill. We were already stoned and were in such a good mellow mood that night, just laughing, joking, smoking and drinking.

We were sat at the back on the top deck. Me on the left side of the bus and Darren on the right.

Back then I used to get on the bus and build a spliff nearly every bus ride. I even used to challenge myself to see how quickly I could build a spliff in between stops.

When you start getting too red, you start getting hot, so I opened one of the windows. It was Christmas time, so obviously it was quite cold outside, but I was grateful for the breeze.

Next thing, this big black stocky guy sat down a couple of rows in front of us. He closed the window, because he was cold. I was red and needed to cool down, so I opened it again.

He went over and closed the window and when I've opened it this time, he said: "Hey. Close the window. It's cold."

Darren looked worried, knowing where this was heading.

I said: "Look. I'll tell you what. Let's do it half way, because I need some breeze."

"Fuck you. I know about you. You think you're hard don't you?" he said.

He got up and we walked towards each other. As he got closer, he put his hand into his jacket to pull out this knife. I knew I couldn't let him pull that blade out, because I'd be in trouble, so I let off some speed combination and dropped him.

He ended up on his seat and I got behind him, put my arm around his neck, pushed my knee in his back and pulled his neck back onto the bar of the seat. I wanted to really hurt him.

He was now panicking like mad, as he was choking. Darren tried to pull me off, shouting: "Mark, you're killing him. You're breaking his neck. Let him go."

Just like that I snapped out of it. He dropped down on the floor spluttering and I just sat back down as if nothing had happened, while he staggered back to his seat.

Hearing someone say "You're killing him" is different to actually thinking you've killed someone. Not long after, I crossed paths with that reality check too.

This guy was telling me about someone who was selling some

weed at a house party rave in Hornsey and thought I might be interested to come along.

"Don't waste my time bruv. I'm warning you," was my first reaction. Anyway, I drove us down there and he came back to the car and said: "He ain't got it today."

I was thinking that he'd basically just got me to drop him off at this rave like a free taxi. Not happening. We got into this argument and I told him that he'd mugged me off. Next thing I banged him. One crack. He fell to the floor hard.

Now when I tell you I got scared, I mean proper scared. When he got dropped, he never moved. I got the hell out of there. Some neighbour had seen this guy lying on the floor and must have also thought he was dead, so she called the police.

I ran into this rave to get a bit of cover from all the people in there, but next thing, they all started going to the door as they heard the police coming. The officers started questioning everyone, asking if they had a description of the suspect, which meant one thing; I needed to get out of there quickly.

They also started to get everybody who was hanging around outside to get back in to see if they could match the description of the person the neighbour had seen. The second the police had their backs turned, I shot off.

I found out later that week that he was fine. Thank God.

I knew deep down that if I didn't change my lifestyle, I'd soon run out of chances. I'd be behind bars for murder, robbery or something drug-related. The way I was living was like a time bomb ticking away. How, what or who could get me that positive focus I so badly needed? That was now the big question.

6

New Dawn

"You raze the old to raise the new."
Justina Chen

After all the wake-up calls, brushes with the police, court cases and near-death experiences, in the end it was a session with a crack pipe which showed me the light.

One of my mates' dad was a big G [gangster] in the game and he used to sort us out with some gear for nothing. We'd go down and see him in Chatsworth Road, Hackney to pick up some stones, put them on a piece of foil that went on top of the pipe, then light it and suck.

Now I look back, that's insane. What kind of world are you living in when your dad's giving you a drug that ruins people's lives, instead of telling you: "Son. I've gotta make my money, but you don't ever take this."

You'd see girls coming in looking for that stone and they'd do anything to get it. They were degrading themselves doing all kinds of things, like sucking dirty dicks and sticking their tongues in places they shouldn't have.

That's the world his dad was in and he was hooking him up.

But when we were young, we didn't really get that. We just thought it was all cool.

One day we went down to Hackney and got some, then we went down to Tottenham to someone's house where everyone was taking it in turns to get their blast. Then something happened while I was high. Somebody was on it and I watched the way this smoke came out of the pipe as he blew it out. It looked like a demonic spirit.

I felt like I was sucking this spirit into me and it was taking control of me. This feeling wasn't strong enough for me to stop, because when my turn came, I still took my hit. But I did have a moment where I thought, 'Why are you doing this? Seriously – look around.'

The next day, after an all-night piping session, I went home when it was dark and slept the whole day. That's what crackheads do and that's how I felt. When I woke up, it was dark again and I thought, 'What kind of shit life is this you're living?'

At that time, I didn't think of the future, it was always about now. Whatever I needed at that time, I'd get it straight away. An ounce of weed to smoke? I could get it. Clothes for my kid? I could get them. I had my little car and I even had a mobile phone. It was a massive Motorola, but back then you were a G if you had a mobile phone. Only businessmen had them.

But then I stopped and questioned myself. 'What do I have? What do I really have? What is this that I've built up? What is this reputation I have? In years to come, what will I tell my kids when they ask me how I make a living?'

All these things started going through my head, but it was the question about my kids that really got me. I wasn't doing anything I could be proud of to share with them. I asked myself,

'When you ran away aged 15, did you think this is how it would end up?'

For the first time in my life, I also started thinking about doing a bird. What exactly would prison do to me? How would having my freedom affect me? I started thinking what it would actually be like behind bars and I realised there was no way I could have someone walking behind me shutting my door, sharing a room with someone I didn't know and putting on boxer shorts that God knows how many other prisoners had shat in. Nope. I needed to straighten myself up.

As the days ticked on, I started to think about what I could do. I thought about uni, I thought about getting a job, but none of it appealed to me. I wanted something that marked who I was. I needed something which would help me find myself.

Then I started to think about my dad and the offer he'd been giving me over the years.

"Why don't you come training with me. Come running."

For years I used to think. 'I don't need your training. Why should I run? It's a waste of time. While I'm out running I could be making cash. Do you know how much money I'm making? You don't even know what I'm doing in my life.'

But now, training to be a boxer appealed to me.

I started thinking about these top fighters, thinking that if I trained really hard, I could challenge them. I thought, 'You've got a reputation on the road that you can fight. Why not do the same thing in the ring?'

That was my logic. It was raw. It was a street mentality. I didn't take into account, as a professional, how much work would need to go into it. Although I didn't have a detailed plan, my belief was so solid because failure wasn't an option. Little did I realise that failure would be an essential part of the journey for me to become who I was. I had to taste that along the way to become a good fighter. But for now, I needed to work out where that journey started.

About a week after putting the crack pipe down, here I was at my parents' house, knocking on the door. Dad opened it and just looked at me. Bearing in mind I'd thrown the offer of training back in his face for years because we'd fallen out, I didn't know how he would react.

I had nothing to worry about though. He didn't care why I wanted to train, because he'd do anything for his kids. Or should I say, he'd do anything for his kids, as long as it was to do with training! He was happy I was up for it and knew something had changed for the better.

"You know you've been talking about running," I said. "I want to start coming in the mornings and train with you. Is that OK? I want to become a boxer. I want to do something with my life."

Dad smiled, nodded and with no fuss said "Come, come" and ushered me in. There was no long conversation. I spoke, he listened and the morning after I was there.

The thing is, when we were young, he never once talked to us about competing in boxing. He just wanted us to be fit and be able to protect ourselves. Mum used to say about Dad back in the day: "When Prince fight professionally, for the first round he would kill you. But after that he run out of breath."

Maybe that's why he used to put us through the stamina routines he did when we were young, so we didn't have to experience what he did. Either way, when I needed his help, he stepped up. I'll always give Dad massive credit for being there for me each morning and setting an example. He didn't need to come out with me. He could have just said "Go on" and left me to it, but he didn't.

We were both very proud people, but this helped us get closer again. I'd get up at six in the morning, take the 67 bus from Seven Sisters, Tottenham and it would stop near Wood Green station.

I'd then run the rest of the way to make sure I wasn't late, as my dad was hot on punctuality. I'd be at his house by seven in the morning, knock on his door and we'd be off running.

There used to be an old horse track around Ally Pally and we'd run around that. I will never forget that first run. We left Mum and Dad's house, went round the back streets all the way through to the Palace, got to the end then went round the horse track. I was absolutely messed up.

I then realised the way I'd been living over the last few years had taken a serious toll on my body, because my chest was in a right state and my fitness was non-existent.

That's when questions and doubts started creeping into my head. 'What are you doing? The training is too tough for you. You've done too many drugs. You can't do this. You don't need it. Make it easy on yourself. Get back to the streets and do what you know.'

What was strange was that no matter how much I tried to convince myself to stop training, I knew that I had to keep going and come back the next day. And that's exactly what I did. I never took no days off. The next day I was there knocking on Dad's door and the next day, and the one after that.

I started recognising that there was this guy in me who was very competitive. But the person I was competing against was me. I was now questioning myself, but in a different way. "I've just finished a run, I've done enough today, but don't stop there."

When I got back to Tottenham, I'd always sprint up the 14 flights of stairs to my flat instead of taking the lift. By the fourth floor it didn't seem like a great plan. My legs were like jelly, but I didn't want to stop. I was absolutely finished when I got to the top, but I always got to the top.

The runs became longer. After a few weeks, one lap became two and two became three.

I'd been doing a lot of drugs over the previous five years, so I needed to make some decisions. On one hand, here was my chance to become a champion. On the other, there was this stupid little spliff that I wanted so badly.

I asked myself, 'You going to let this spliff stop you becoming what you want?' Every time I wanted to smoke a spliff, I kept having to think like that. I had to have a strategy for my habits.

I was smoking 10 spliffs a day, so I tried to get down to one. Then when I got down to one, I managed to cut it to half. As long as I had a taste of something, then I'd put it down and come back later to it and take a hit.

Anyone knows that when you start a spliff, it's hard to put down, but I kept telling myself, 'At least you've had some.'

This was the discipline that helped me get over my drug habit.

As I smoked less, I was building my fitness and getting down to boxing training. I hadn't forgotten what my dad had been teaching me from eight years old.

He'd lit that fire in me again, but this time round I'd become a great student. I listened to every word he was telling me. My dad had great foundation skills in boxing and would be watching me like a hawk on those heavy bags. He wasn't trying to develop a style for me – it was all about the technique. He was helping me perfect my feet, my jab and the fundamentals. He wanted those to be solid.

He helped me develop the understanding and gave me the ability to throw that jab. I'd throw it with such force and speed that my opponents would struggle to read it. And when it hit, it did damage straight away.

Everything was old school, guided by my dad. It worked well. And on the food front, it was proper old school. No protein shakes or any of that nonsense, we're talking back to basics.

There's this thing in Jamaica called Guinness Punch, but Dad called it Kick. It would be full of stuff like stout, condensed milk, vanilla, and my dad would top it off with eggs. Trust me; you have a glass of that and you are fuelled.

Then after my runs in the morning, it was like a scene out of *Rocky* as Dad would have me drinking raw eggs. I hate anything slimy, but I was willing to deal with the sliminess if it was going to help me reach my goals.

After a couple of months of training, Dad said: "You running good. Now it's time to compete at the boxing gym."

He took me to Tottenham Enterprise, my first proper boxing gym. Well, technically, it was my second. When I was 16, my social worker, Will, had introduced me to a foster family and I stayed with them for a few months.

What was amazing, was that the lady's son was a boxing trainer at Islington Boys Amateur Boxing Club [ABC]. He looked at me and saw this wayward kid staying at his house and wanted to help him. "Come down to the gym," he said. I was like all enthusiastic: "Yeah! My dad's taught me boxing."

I went there a few times, then one day my mind wasn't really focused and I walked in with a can of Tennent's Super lager. What a halfwit. How could I go to a boxing gym drinking a tin of strong ass beer?!

"Naaaaah bruv. Can't be coming in here with that. That's not how we do things around here," they said. I must have looked like I was wasted. That was the last time Islington ABC saw me for a long time.

Six years later, and I was at Tottenham Enterprise without the Tennent's Super, giving it a proper go. I'll never forget that place. It was a real throwback gym. George Martin was the head coach and had this cool cockney way about him, but he knew what he was doing.

You looked around and it was full of good hungry amateurs working hard, from all weight divisions. You'd see loads of seasoned pros coming in to spar with amateurs, because they'd give them all the trouble they could handle.

From the moment I walked into that place I was like a sponge. I was looking at little things that impressed me about a fighter and I'd start replicating them. My schedule became; go running with Dad, go home, get some rest, have something to eat and then go to the gym. I was now living the life I'd dreamt of.

It wasn't just the boxing that had given me a sense of self-esteem and responsibility though.

On 25 November 1990, my second child was born. In addition to my beautiful daughter Tannisa, me and Tracy now had a gorgeous little son named Kiyan.

I remember how warm he made me feel when he started toddling and walking. I kept thinking that one day, he'd grow up and be like me.

In fact, as he started to grow, he looked a lot like me and he was proud of that, which is exactly the way I used to be with my dad.

However, it wasn't all plain sailing at the beginning. Despite turning into a real athlete, when Kiyan was only four weeks old, he had to go back to hospital because his lungs weren't working properly. He had this thing called bronchiolitis, which basically led to him being asthmatic.

Kiyan being Kiyan, didn't let that stop him. From the moment he could walk, he started playing football. He absolutely loved it. He was an active kid, and always happy. Watching him and his sister Tannisa together filled my heart with joy.

★★★★★★★★★★★★★★★★★★

In those first few weeks at the boxing gym, it became apparent that me and Dad couldn't work together long term, because Dad was still trying to be Dad. He couldn't get his head around me swearing in the gym, but that's who I'd matured into now.

I would have loved for him to have been in my corner, but it was never going to work. Thankfully, he still came along when I was training and there were no hard feelings. He just wasn't my trainer anymore.

About six weeks after stepping through the doors, a pro boxing trainer called Eric Seecombe came in looking for someone of a good size for Michael Watson to spar with.

Eric looked at me and said to George: "Can he do some sparring with Michael?" George asked me and I agreed.

I'd never sparred with anyone apart from my own brothers and my dad at that point, but from what George had seen of me, he'd assumed I'd sparred before. At the time, I knew

Michael Watson was someone, but not to what level. As I was putting on the gloves and George was putting on my head gear, I was thinking, 'Why did you say yes?'

But the second we got cracking, the nerves drained out of me. We sparred four, three minute rounds and for the first couple, I was boxing Watson really well behind my jab.

I tell you how he got to me – by going to the body. As he started to drop these hooks around my ribs, I distinctly remember thinking, 'Why aren't my legs moving as much as they want to? Why do I feel tired like this?'

Michael was one of the good guys. He didn't take any liberties, but he also wanted to make sure I got something out of the spar. I learned that I needed to work on defence and I also wanted to plant body shots the way he did, because I was a head hunter in the ring at that point.

After the fourth round, Watson came over and said: "You're a really good fighter. For two rounds I couldn't get to you, but you were getting to me. You'll become a champion one day."

Hearing that from him and then later realising who he was really encouraged me to give myself to the sport. I was really excited that I could genuinely do something with boxing. For now, this is where I saw my life.

After that spar, Eric started watching me and even used to take me for lunch after at the café across the road from the gym and I'd sit there and eat with these pros.

Then it developed where he picked me up and started taking me running. That was a bit of a game-changer, because I knew if someone picked you up at 4.30 in the morning to go running with the other pros, he must have seen something promising. He used to pick me up in his taxi and take me to Hampstead

Heath, where all the other fighters were waiting and ready to go. He'd tell me: "This is where Frank Bruno does his runs," and that would give me a boost.

I was very competitive at those runs. I wanted to be first at everything, but I didn't realise I was up against welterweights, featherweights – guys much lighter than me. I always came in the first three, but trust me, these lighter guys could run.

Even though I was an amateur, I always looked ahead. I wanted to train as a pro, because I knew that's what I wanted to be. What I noticed about the amateurs I was training with back then was that they did a run and then came into the gym and trained.

The pros on the other hand got up early in the morning, ran, rested, ate, then went to their next training session, trained hard and then fitted in another session. That was now my routine.

Within a couple of weeks of sparring Michael Watson, George Martin told me: "I think you're ready for your first amateur contest. Are you ready to fight?"

I said: "Yeah. I wanna fight."

After having a crack pipe in my mouth just nine months earlier, here I was now, replacing that pipe with a gumshield and getting ready for my first fight. Boy was I scared.

7

Fight Or Flight

"Everything you want is on the other side of fear." **Jack Canfield**

What a terrible way to lose my boxing virginity. My first amateur fight was at the Irish Centre in Islington, which had a really low ceiling, where the ring lights were literally beaming a few inches over your head.

People were drinking and smoking to the point you could barely see the crowd. And this wasn't a big place. I felt like I was fighting in a dungeon that smelt like death.

I remember thinking, 'I've been smoking for the last six years and now you're trying to come away from it. What's the point in training so hard in the fresh air when I'm now in this den?'

If that wasn't enough, my nerves were killing me. I never ate the night before. I kept shitting myself, literally. Nothing would stay down. I also had this reputation on the street and loads of people were turning up to see if I could actually fight or if I had delusions of grandeur, so the pressure to win was big.

To top it off, I couldn't sleep, which meant I ended up doing something I'd been told not to do. I'd followed all the instructions from my coach, did all the training, but the one thing I was asked to do the night before the fight, I couldn't do. Have no pussy. I couldn't resist it. Bad move. When you fight you're gonna need your legs. Adrenaline and nerves are gonna take them away from you anyway, so the last thing you need is to be battling wobbly legs.

Thankfully I had really good support. Colin, Junior, my dad, Tracy, my sister, my mates were all there to support me. The only person who didn't come was Mum. She never attended any of Dad's professional fights and wasn't going to break tradition with me.

Although I was really nervous, when the bell went, the warrior came out and I went to work. I went on the attack straight away against this guy from Finchley boxing club, who had a good record with a number of wins.

He was also taller and bigger built, so he wanted me to get into a proper ruck with him. Instead, I leant back on the ropes and let off combinations. This was stuff that I'd learnt watching footage of Ali. Bam, bam, slip, bang, lean back, right hand.

I just kept throwing punches and whenever we got in a clinch, I'd be the first to start throwing punches again. Everyone must have thought I was spent. And you know what – I was.

I walked back to the corner at the end of the round and my legs were shaking so much I almost tripped over them. As I sat down on the stool I thought, 'How am I gonna get through another two rounds?'

My corner said: "Suck it in," referring to getting my lungs full of air.

"Suck what in? Cigars?"

It was pure heart that got me out for that second round.

Technique went out the window. I didn't want him to take over and think he was leading or hurting me.

Every time he started coming forward, I leant on him and he'd let his shots go. I then started responding with my own. At one point I let this 20-punch flurry go. Proper windmilling. I wanted to let the referee see that I was winning this fight, because I was the one throwing more punches.

At the end I was standing in the middle of the ring with the ref and the other guy. The decision was announced: "It's a unanimous decision....... Prince..."

I ripped my hand out of the referee's grip and just shouted: "Yeeaaaaaaahhhhh!" That feeling was so amazing. I'd won. That was a massive, massive victory for me, because I knew what I'd gone through to get to that point.

★★★★★★★★★★★★★★★★★

Soon after my first amateur fight, I broke up with Tracy. That was quite disturbing. My main thing was that I just wanted to see my kids. Because I was young and had something to focus on with the boxing, that made it a bit easier.

My life with my kids was now different. I was going through a new experience of not living with them, but instead picking them up. I was taking on a new role as a weekend dad.

A couple of weeks after my first fight, I clocked up another victory. That's when George Martin said: "Listen. The ABAs [Amateur Boxing Association championships] are coming up. I think you can do something in this. Would you go in for it?"

I agreed straight away. What did I have to lose? This was the perfect opportunity to find out what I was made of, because this competition was made up from the best guys in the country. The only problem was I'd only had a couple of fights and I needed at least four to enter. George said: "I tell you what. There's a competition between London and Sweden and I'm going to see if I can get you another fight on this, then I'll get you one soon after." That was a big thing for me.

So here I was lined up, standing against the Swedish team. This was also the first time I'd fought at the York Hall. What an atmosphere. I loved the place. The changing rooms, the balcony at the top, it just breathed boxing history.

I was looking around, wondering which of the Swedish squad my light heavyweight opponent would be. I started going down the line of boxers thinking, 'It can't be him, he's too small, or him, or him, and definitely not him, because he's massive. Like 6ft 4in big.'

The guy I thought I was fighting got called out to fight at middleweight and I suddenly realised I was up against the massive guy. Shiiiiiiiiit. I was so nervous.

This boxer was so well schooled. He was a traditional European fighter with a poleaxe jab, tracking me down, throwing bombs and hurting me. But it didn't matter. Determination. It didn't matter who was in front of me, determination would always get me through. I knew I needed a defining moment to get me the win, because as the fight progressed, it was close.

I also knew that if I was going to be recognised for the ABAs, I needed to do something special. On top of that, whoever won this fight made it 3-2 for either London or Sweden. No pressure.

The first round was close, second round I rocked him and third round I eventually nailed him with a massive overhand right. I didn't stop him, but he got up on wobbly legs like a new-born giraffe and had to take an eight count. That's what tipped it for me. This fight got me a lot of attention amongst the British contingent of amateurs.

Despite the boxing going well, outside of the ring, I still needed money to live. I didn't want to get that from the streets anymore and decided to do it the right way by getting a job.

An old mate of mine told me about working for a security firm called Scorpion. He said: "You can take care of yourself. Why not do some work with them?"

It sounded good. I started working at this old Irish pub in Archway, North London. I also did the doors in some nightclubs and bars, but it was that pub where I spent most of my time and that's where the majority of the action happened.

Aside from just fights, we even had someone trying to drive their car through the front entrance one day to crush us, as a revenge attack. That was the sort of place it was.

Despite a lot of drunk and angry customers, I was able to get on with my job without having to use the hard-man tactics, because I had this way of getting on with people. I was usually able to talk people out of a fight. As expected, there were one or two occasions where I had to take people out because they were about to hit me, but otherwise I never fought on the doors.

The calmness of the older security guys I worked with was rubbing off on me. They'd say: "Prince, you just want to do the job and go home safe.

"Every week there's a guy who's on drugs or drunk who wants a fight and you can't fight them all. You need to ignore racism and be patient when you're calling last orders."

If I'd had that street mentality from a few months earlier, I would have been fighting every week without a doubt. The timing of their advice was perfect, because while they were helping with my street mentality, I was developing in my boxing training and becoming a more rounded, level-headed person. I learned a lot working with these guys.

With all that was going on, I was getting some decent sleep, although I almost killed myself in bed with my creative talents. I tried to pimp out my bedroom and bought some of those sticky mirror tiles, which are meant for the walls. These were glass tiles without safe edges – we're talking sharp.

Well, I decided to stick them on my bedroom ceiling, so I'd have this pimped out bedroom. I wanted to be like this big don, so I could look up and see myself putting in the work with girls on my bed.

The night after I stuck those tiles on, about five of them fell off while I was asleep.

When I woke up in the morning and saw these tiles all over the duvet, I shat myself. First thing I did was get rid of the rest and count my blessings.

Back to the boxing. A month later, I clocked up another stoppage victory and was 4-0. I was now in the 1992 ABAs North West Divs [Divisional finals], which wasn't bad considering I'd only been fighting a couple of months.

I hadn't stopped training since the last fight, which kept me focused, busy and out of trouble. I'll never forget walking into this hall with so many good fighters that I'd heard of, seen or read about. Now I was in there with them.

What I didn't realise was that after the preliminary fights you had the semis, then the finals. I asked my trainer: "When do the semis and finals happen if I win the first fight?"

"It's all tonight," he replied.

"What?? You kidding me? After one fight I'll be finished! I won't be able to fight again."

Oh my days. This fighting more than once business was a revelation to me.

First round I was up against a guy fighting for Trojan Police Sports and Boxing Club. I was thinking, 'He's from the police?' I thought he was probably tough from all the training and that, but it turns out the club had nothing to do with the police.

I started boxing this guy all confident and next thing I was looking down thinking, 'What's this? It's the ring apron. I'm on the canvas. Oh shit!'

The guy dropped me in the first round and I didn't even know which punch did it. This was the first time I'd ever been knocked down and I was genuinely hurt. As I was taking the eight count, I was thinking, 'Wow. This can't be happening. You've got to get this guy.'

I didn't have no pussy the night before, so by the time the count finished, I had my legs back. Second round I went out and whooped his ass. Dropped him and stopped him.

The only problem was, I'd done my right hand in. It was that badly swollen it looked like a pillow. I just had to get on with it. I didn't report my hand to anyone because I knew they wouldn't let me fight on. My dad and brothers knew, but that was it.

Who told me to sit at ringside and watch the other fights? What a bad idea. There I was with my brothers, watching the competition when this guy walked out called Kenny Nevers.

Ding, the bell goes. Kenny Nevers was the smaller fighter and went hunting his opponent, who was giving him jabs, right hands, hooks and uppercuts.

Next minute I saw Kenny slip a jab and boom, his opponent

hit the canvas. I turned and looked at Junior and he had this 'ohhhhhh no' look on his face. Kenny's opponent walked past us and said: "He can bang. He can really bang." Great.

I now knew that if me and Kenny won our next fights, we were going to meet. Kenny had won the North West Divs four years running, so he was expected to win it again. Who was I to fight him after only five fights?

I was now getting ready for my next fight when I was suddenly told I had a bye. Whether my opponent got injured, I don't know, but I was now through to the final. Kenny won his, so things turned out as predicted.

My right hand was still a problem. I was in the changing room with my dad having a massive struggle to get my hand in the glove because it was that swollen out.

Dad then started giving me some advice about Kenny Nevers: "He's a one-handed fighter. He only knocks people out with the same hand, the left. Go the other way. Circle to his right all the time so you don't go into his left hook. That's the punch he wants to throw. You need to keep the jab in his face and turn it into a left hook, but don't use the right hand."

I now had my strategy. I went in scared, but the adrenaline helped me to put on a great display of boxing with my left jab. Come the third round, I looked at Kenny and could see I was breaking him down mentally, frustrating him and hurting him. I remember thinking, 'I've got you mate. I've got you.'

I forgot about not using the right and just went for it. I started throwing lefts and rights, hooks and uppercuts until the ref jumped in. When the announcement was made that I was the North West Divs champion I was over the moon. I was so excited that I dropped to my knees heavily and damaged the right one. That same knee would play a big part in my boxing later down the line, but for now it was back to the gym.

I really knuckled down. The chance to prove myself as the best light heavyweight in the country was there for the taking.

The thing about that boxing gym in Tottenham was it was very competitive and the action wasn't always inside the ring or within the Queensberry Rules.

One day, I was on the punchbags and all the other bags were full. There was this other pro named Paul something or other, who was quite decent and he wanted to go on the bags, but didn't want to wait. Because I was younger than him and he was a pro, he just wanted me to move over.

He started a fight with me in the gym and I smashed him up, then he went for a grapple. I put him in a headlock and all of a sudden I felt this massive pain in my rib and I looked down and there he was trying to bite a chunk out of my freakin' ribs. I've still got the scar from where his teeth went into my flesh.

Not long after, I was sparring with cruiserweight Chris Henry, who'd won the London ABA championships. He was known for running with bricks in his hand when he trained. I was totally out-boxing him and when we finished the last round, I walked back to my corner, he banged me in the back of the head and knocked me out cold [with a glove that is, no bricks!].

I woke up to mayhem and saw Dad attacking him. About 10 people were trying to pull him off Chris, while he was apologising to Dad. I'm still mates with Chris now, funnily enough.

★★★★★★★★★★★★★★★★★

Around this time, my brother Junior was also boxing. He'd

had four amateur fights. One win, one loss, one draw and one disqualification. The full range of results. In terms of that disqualification; his opponent threw a barrage of punches which Junior was blocking, but about a second after the bell went, he went 'whack,' out of frustration with a big right hand and smashed the other guy. That was that.

He decided to hang the gloves up, which was a real shame as his speed, accuracy and technique were unbelievable. He was without a doubt the most under-spent talent of our family.

He could have been one of the most talented boxers to ever come out of this country. You could have compared his hands to Sugar Ray Leonard at the time. The problem was he couldn't maintain the pace during a fight.

Another issue was that his nerves meant he'd get tired really quickly. One opponent even asked him after a fight: "Do you smoke weed?" because he'd got so knackered. So it was all down to me now to carry the Prince family banner for boxing.

Four weeks after my last fight, I was back in the ring at the York Hall in the London ABA semis.

Not enough time for my hand to repair, but enough for me to feel confident to fight. In terms of opponents, I didn't get a break. Every fight I won, the next was even tougher. I always went in as the underdog.

Next up was Monty Wright, who was tipped to win the competition. The fight generated a lot of attention in London and was well anticipated. So well anticipated that one day I was doing my skipping at Tottenham Enterprise gym and three guys walk in who I didn't know. They knew me though and just stood there watching me do my routine.

"You're alright you are. You're that new kid aren't you?" one of them suddenly said. I stopped what I was doing, but didn't say anything. I just looked at them.

"Your next fight against Monty; you're not gonna win that. Maybe next year when you have a few more fights under your belt," this guy said. "Monty is one of the best in England and will be too much for you. He's gonna win the ABAs."

"Yeah. But he ain't met me, has he?" I replied. Then I carried on skipping and they walked off.

Come fight night, the atmosphere was incredible, the place was packed and the temperature roasting hot.

Round one I was dancing backwards, staying out of reach and totally took the round. Boom, boom, boom, jabs, moving, boom, boom, boom, slipping, left hook, right hand and all at my range. When I wasn't firing shots I made sure his range was always short of nailing me. However, I could sense he was starting to get closer in that last minute.

He was inching his way in and by the end of the first, even though I had the better of the round, we started having a few exchanges. Everyone was probably thinking that as soon as Monty got close to me, it would be goodnight.

When I got back to my corner at the end of the first round, George said: "You looked good. You kept him off with the jab, but he's getting closer and cutting the ring off. As soon as he gets close, it's dangerous. Keep him at the end of the jab."

But as soon as he got close in that second round, he was done. As he came into range, I started throwing more uppercuts and left hooks. Then I let loose with a beautiful flowing combination. Jab, uppercut, left hook, then the big punch, straight right. Bam, bam, bam, every shot caught him.

When that right hand connected, he hit the canvas out cold,

in a star shape. Motionless. He was a worst and best knockout. Worst for him, best for me. I'd earned the right to fight in the London ABA finals.

Shortly after I was reading a boxing mag and saw my name in the top amateur 10 light heavyweights. Yes! Get in. I was now a nationally recognised fighter. The headline in the local paper was 'Prince is Marked for the top.'

Two months later, I was back at the York Hall and my opponent was Chris Okoh, who was ranked No.3 amongst the light heavies in the UK at time. Chris was a very competent boxer, but when that bell rang, I just laid into him. I really wanted to do him some damage. No dancing around on the backfoot this time, I went for him.

At the end of the round, I looked over and could tell Chris didn't want to come out for the next one. I knew he was hurt. Second round, I wrapped him up. I let loose with a flurry and the referee stepped in. I was now London ABA champion after eight fights. I was ecstatic.

One of the boxing magazines used the word 'enigmatic' to describe me. 'What the hell does enigmatic mean?' I thought. All the local papers had something about my win in there.

I was now at the semi-finals of the national ABAs somewhere in the countryside. I did this interview with Steve Bunce, who was just one of the nicest, most down-to-earth journalists I'd ever met. He genuinely seemed to respect and be pleased with the achievements in my amateur career so far.

I was starting to feel like a guy who could really go somewhere with boxing. Then I did something stupid. I changed my game. Why? Maybe I was paranoid that I didn't think I'd get the nod from the judges and went for the knockout. Who knows.

The way I performed in that semi-final fight was embarrassing. My opponent was expecting to have a guy in front of him with skills and movement, but all he had to do was wait for me to walk in and bang, he'd tag me with a counter-punch. It was an easy fight for him. I walked into punches trying to knock him out. I'd never done that before.

Second round, the ref stepped in after he thought I was receiving punishment. He gave me an eight count and then waved it off. I was no longer that guy with the boxing skills and punching power that impressed people.

I was an embarrassment. I'd reverted back to street fighting and trying to take my opponent out quickly with power. It didn't work like that at this level.

The pain of defeat was horrible. I was broken. I cried. I was close to setting a record for winning the national ABAs with the fewest number of fights in advance, but that dream was gone.

I knew I didn't want to fight in the amateurs any longer after these ABAs, so that defeat meant I'd also missed out on the opportunity to get on the radar of the pro promoters.

Hero to zero. Time to work my way back up again...

8

Jamaica

"Mark, you're not ready for the pro game yet, but I'll tell you this – if you stay dedicated and you listen to me, stay in the gym and work hard, I'll turn you into a pro boxing champion. How does that sound?" **Carly Carew, 1993**

The night of the Chris Okoh fight was the night I met my pro trainer. I just didn't know it then. I was in the changing room getting ready, when Cham Joof, another fighter who'd boxed alongside me in the ABAs, walked in with some guy and introduced him to me. His name was Carly Carew.

He spoke to me nice and relaxed as if he knew me, asking how I was feeling.

"I'm nervous, man," I told him. "Okoh is a good fighter."

"Nervous? You see these guys you're fighting, you weren't even known a few fights ago and they all know you now. They're all scared of you. This is a simple fight. Just let him commit himself and counter him with a big right hand and it's goodnight."

I'm thinking, 'Who the fuck is this guy?' Whatever he was

saying was making me feel good and I liked that. I went out, beat Chris then didn't see Carly again.

It took me a few weeks to soak in the misery of losing my last amateur fight after Okoh, but when I had, I took it positively. I realised that I needed to experience failure and that nothing in this world is plain sailing.

I knew that I'd become a better fighter, a stronger person and more determined individual. I needed to feel that taste of defeat before I got to the pros, just to prepare me and make me mentally stronger.

After that fight, I had to make a choice of who to turn pro with – Eric Seccombe or Carly Carew. I knew Eric was going to spring me into the limelight, because he knew the top managers, held some sway and he was training a good fighter in Michael Watson. This was the best route for me. This is what I figured.

But there was something about Carly. It was probably going to be a harder journey with him as he wasn't a big name in boxing training circles, but for some reason I felt a strong connection to him.

There was no big formal meeting or procedures with Carly. We met and he explained what he thought of me as a fighter and how he saw me moving forward in boxing.

"I like what I saw in the Okoh fight," he told me. "You worked well to instructions and had the right attitude. You could be a good fighter. You could be a champion.

"But boxing is a very technical sport. You have the brawn, power and attitude, but they're just tools. You need to realise that any movement you make can be countered. You must have an answer for that."

We gelled easily. I was keen and enthusiastic, asking lots of questions about trying new things. Carly just said: "Let's keep it simple. Simple things are easy to work with and easy to remember. Let's drill on that." And boy did he drill.

He knew what style he wanted me to adopt and had a vision for me as a boxer. He didn't like my freeness of head movement or the way I was using my feet. He told me: "You've still got a lot of the street in you, but when I've finished, you won't recognise yourself."

That's a promise he'd end up delivering on. And with that, he was now my trainer, manager and promoter.

★★★★★★★★★★★★★★★★★★

Carly had fighters in Jamaica and was always going on about how fit and tough they were, because of the training and conditions they had back home. In order to get me and Cham in the best condition for our pro debuts in early 1993, Carly decided to take us to Jamaica.

Cham was a good friend, but it was this trip that bonded us for life. When Carly said Jamaica, me and Cham looked at each other like 'holiday time' but we didn't have a clue what we'd be in for. Jamaica is seen as a paradise island where everyone is laidback, but this trip was the total opposite. We were going there for specifics. To train and get into shape.

At the time, there was some featherweight called Dave something or other and he worked at North West Airlines and helped us with flights getting out to Jamaica. I'd never flown before, so I was loving every minute of the experience.

When it was time to board the plane, we walked up to the point where you showed your ticket and you could hear the stewards saying: "Down there on the left, down there on the right," that sort of thing. We got our tickets out and the steward said in a totally different tone: "Good morning Mr Prince and Mr Joof. You are sitting upstairs. Have a pleasant journey."

It was at that point we realised Dave had proper sorted us out. Business class. What a top man.

When we sat down, they started coming round with a tray of champagne. It was all free. That was it. Every time they walked past with something we took it. If we weren't hungry or thirsty, the stuff went in our bag for later. It kept coming non-stop. There was one air hostess between two of us and they gave us whatever we wanted, whenever we wanted it. It was amazing. That was the beginning of the adventure.

★★★★★★★★★★★★★★★★★★

When we arrived in Jamaica, we stayed with a guy called Castro Brown at his house in Constant Springs. We had our own cook, a swimming pool, a basketball court, the works.

Castro was a well known and massively respected figure in Brixton at the time, as well as Jamaica. He had this cool and laidback personality, which drew you to him.

Every time we'd come back from our early morning run, he'd be out on the balcony, smoking a big Ital joint, which had nothing but weed in it. At the time, I wished I could have sat next to him and shared some of that spliff. It smelt so good.

But it was far from fun and games over here. When I boxed as an amateur, I used to make the 81 kilos weight limit with the usual struggles boxers have, but when I turned pro, I didn't realise it was only 79 kilos. That was even more of a push.

However, when it came to dropping weight, that wasn't even a consideration in Jamaica, as the training was brutal. We'd train three or four times a day and would get up at four in the morning to do our five-mile run, just to beat the sun.

We'd be out there running the streets and you'd see all these dead dogs on the road, but the backdrop was beautiful. However, the hills were anything but. I thought the training I was doing back in London was decent. When I was running the hills at Ally Pally I used to think "I'm fit!"

No mate. In Jamaica, I got my ass broken in training.

After the run, we'd come back, rest a bit, eat some food. Not every day was the same though. Sometimes Carly would have you doing nothing but stretching for an hour and a half.

I'd never stretched like this in my life. All these different positions. Carly wanted to prepare our bodies for all these things he was going to put us through.

He'd also do this deadly drill where you'd be going around the edges of the swimming pool, learning footwork. One of my habits was always losing my form when I tried to go around an opponent, opening up and allowing him to catch me square at some point, where I should have been side-on.

"This is how you deliver the jab and this is how your feet need to be," Carly would say. He was all about the hand and footwork. As we were going around a corner, you had to imagine you were on your opponent and you didn't open up your stance.

Carly had some age-old techniques lined up for us out there, which were like something out of the 1980s movie *Kickboxer*. He chose a coconut tree, taped a boxing pad around it, bandaged our hands, put them in a nice thick glove, then said: "Now hit the pad. If you hit the coconut tree in a certain way, it rattles at the top. I want to hear it rattle. I don't want to see you jabbing the tree, I want to see you stab it with that punch."

We all looked at each other like Carly had lost his mind.

It was a technique that took ages to develop on a daily basis. It was one of those things where you practised something that people thought was impossible. Similar to the Japanese breaking ice or bricks. You'd have to keep going until you rocked the tree.

As mad as it was, it definitely helped develop my punching power and I took that mindset with me into the pro game. I'd be hitting my opponents like I was hitting the tree. That's why most of the guys wouldn't last very long in my early fights.

Whether it was my left or right hand, I had that raw strength, but in Jamaica I needed to work my legs to get that extra power to make that shot stronger. So we worked up and down the side of the swimming pool, getting me to practise my balance and use precision footwork.

The hardest part wasn't doing the drills, it was looking at the water with the heat banging on us.

"How many times we gotta keep going around this pool?" me and Cham would ask.

"Just keep going," was always Carly's response. You never knew when it was going to be over. It was as if the more you suffered, the stronger you became, in his mind anyway.

We had the same issue with sparring. You get the brunt of the sun after midday in any tropical country. Sparring was around one in the afternoon. While we were working, the sun was getting hotter and hotter. The temperature went from the 80s into the 90s, then into the 100s. As much as you'd try and concentrate and blank it out, the rubber soles on our boxing boots were on fire as the rounds went on.

At one point, I started running on the spot and Carly said: "What you doing? We're not here to run on the spot, we're here to move around."

"It's not that Carly. Our feet are on fire," I replied.

"Stop being a pussy," would always be his response. "When you go to fight, these little things here in Jamaica will seem like nothing. I want you to do an extra two rounds now." Great.

When I went back to the corner at the end of each round, instead of pouring water in our mouths, he'd pour it on our feet and over our heads.

He did this on purpose, because if we could get through a session like this and still deliver, then having water on the night of a fight would feel like a massive luxury.

In terms of sparring partners; wow, what a shock. When we sparred back in the UK, the general atmosphere was very competitive. That's how Carly ran things. There were three Jamaicans who would come over, then there was me, Cham, Gary Logan and a heavyweight called Wayne Llewellyn.

When we sparred, it was full-on, but in Jamaica, it was up another level.

Half of it was to do with how brutal it was in the ring and the other half was to do with culture. One thing about Jamaicans, you can't show them no fear. They'll eat you alive, mate.

Me and Cham would be walking down the road minding our own business, stopping at the stalls and buying a bag juice or sky juice as they called it there, and people would start running their mouth off and trying to charge us more than the actual price or making threats.

We would give it to them back. If we kept quiet, they took that as us being scared. Remember, we were English, so to them we were already soft. 'No we ain't mate' was our attitude. It was the same in sparring. It was hammer and tongs, no holds barred.

Carly had lined up these hungry, big Jamaican guys who looked at us like, 'English pussies. You come on our patch. We're gonna beat the shit out of you.'

There was one guy called Currie, who I'm still good friends with to this day and he was a massive cruiserweight. Tall, experienced and just downright strong.

Then we had Big Man. He was around 18 stone. One day Carly told me to do some bodywork against him.

I took a deep breath and tried to act casual, but inside I was thinking, 'I got to go with this big bastard? Ain't he got anyone smaller for me?'

He was banging at my body so hard that I wanted to go down. Then Carly was shouting: "Are you gonna go down? Are you gonna quit?" which made it even worse.

I couldn't move as this guy was paralysing me with these shots, which meant I couldn't return anything.

I did manage to get him back a few weeks later though and almost sparked him out. He was swaying like a tree in the wind, so I went in to drop a right hand on him and he grabbed me. There was no way he was going to allow me to drop him in sparring with everyone watching.

Cham also had his battles in there. Carly put him in with this aggressive fighter called Guts, who was two weight divisions above him.

They absolutely went for it, with neither of them giving an inch. Unbeknown to us, Cham broke Guts' jaw, but being a proud fighter, he didn't let us know for about six months.

After you'd done your sparring, you'd think we'd be done for the night, right? Nope. Carly was at it again. He was the drill sergeant. A real nightmare. He never got tired of technique and getting us to perfect the simplest of things.

Then once the technique work was out of the way, he'd have us doing circuits around the pool and laps. That was generally how it went in Jamaica.

One day we decided enough was enough. We needed a break. "To hell with this. Six days is good enough. Day seven is for us," Cham said.

That first Sunday, we got up early while Carly was still asleep and crept out of the house. We were off exploring Jamaica. For the next few Sundays we went to Fort Clarence beach, Elsha beach, Dunn's River Falls, you name it.

When we came back, Carly would be like: "Where were you? I had some techniques I wanted to go through with you both."

He'd start about boxing and we'd be walking away laughing like a couple of kids.

Carly did see the funny side of our little day trips, but he always made sure he made us pay in sweat when we were back in training.

What an incredible experience though. What a trip.

After two months we headed back to London, which was a good thing as I was badly homesick by this stage. On the up side, I was really looking forward to the VIP treatment again on the plane.

We boarded the aircraft and as we handed over our passes, the steward looked up and pointed to the economy seats.

After taking off, the guy in front of me leant his chair back to the max. Remember, we had a full-length bed flying out, so I was thinking, 'You can't do that. There's no space. Where the hell am I supposed to put my legs and feet? And why is the menu so shit?'

Thankfully, with my pro debut round the corner, I had more than enough to occupy my mind for the 10-hour journey home.

9

Rising Up

*"It always seems impossible until
it's done."* **Nelson Mandela**

Fourth of April 1993, Crofton Leisure Centre in Brockley, London. That was the date and venue of my first fight as a professional boxer.

Unlike many fighters who love to have a nickname, I wanted to be a serious guy entering that ring. All that mimicky stuff wasn't for me. Cham was known as 'The Wild African', which came from a song one of his DJ mates used to play.

Over the next few years they tried Mark 'The Crown' Prince, because at the time they were looking to get me sponsorship and Crown Paints was an option. Then Mark 'The Dark' Prince, because of my attitude in the ring, but nothing really stuck and I was more than fine with that.

Back to Brockley. There were only four fights and I was headlining against Bobby Mack, who'd won two and lost two. Funnily enough, my old opponent Kenny Nevers was on the undercard, as was Cham – by now my closest friend in boxing. My nerves, as always, were terrible, but I had an added bit of drama. When I got to the changing room I realised I'd forgotten to pack my shorts, which I'd got made specially, because I wanted to impress on my debut. Thankfully, most fighters pack two pairs and I was able to borrow a pair from this other guy.

I soon conquered the nerves as I stepped into the ring and started to enjoy who I was. There I was throwing out my jab from a solid stance and everything was going well.

The problem was I still had that street mentality. The moment I saw I had my opponent hurt, even only a little bit, then I went in for the kill. But this was pro boxing now. Even if you see you've hurt someone, you've still got to be careful.

As I'm throwing my punches, I got over-excited, thinking I was on for an early night. Then Mack went and spoilt everything. He dipped underneath, caught me with a left hook which had me hurt and then hit me with a right hand.

As I was on the way down to the deck, he tried to hit with a swooping uppercut before I hit the canvas. Fair play to him, because I would have done the same.

I got up quickly and mad as hell, looked at Mack and thought, 'Are you nuts? All these people have come here and bought tickets to see me beat your ass up. You think you're going to win? No way.'

I actually felt like I was on the streets again. Everything Carly had taught me went out the window. I was back to being old Princey, the aggressive, bad-tempered guy that was looking to bang you out. When the ref came to check I was OK, all I kept thinking was, 'Move man. Let me get this guy.'

The thing is, I was actually hurt. My legs were wobbly and physically I wasn't quite there yet. My emotions were driving me. Thank God for the minute's recovery at the bell.

Second round, I went after him again, but this time hurt him enough for the ref to jump in. He was turning his back on me, so I started throwing punches round the side. I won the fight, but I had a lot to learn as a pro.

The moment the fight was stopped, my fans went absolutely nuts. The feeling of that victory was beautiful. If you see the fight, you can see me jumping around, over-excited with the victory and shouting out to the crowd.

When I had my arms in the air, Carly pulled them down, waved his finger in my face and said: "Keep your ass in the gym." That was his way of saying I didn't need to hit the deck if I learned my defence and boxed instead of brawled.

★★★★★★★★★★★★★★★★★

Back in the gym, the sparring was brutal as Carly wanted me to understand the importance of a good defence.

I was sparring this cruiserweight who could really hit and I was only allowed to use my defence. Then bang, he hit me smack on the hooter. It was the first time I'd experienced a nose bleed in boxing and when it started, it didn't stop. I couldn't breath as the blood was going in my mouth and spraying everywhere.

The ring apron was new, but by the time we'd finished that session it looked like an old one. From that point onwards, my nose became vulnerable to bleeding. It took about three years to fully repair.

A month after the Mack fight, I fought John Kaighin. I respected him a lot. I kept knocking him down and he was getting back up and wanting to fight on. Even when the ref stopped it in the third round, he still wanted to carry on.

There's not a lot of fighters like John anymore. A lot of them get dropped, stay down and get paid. John wasn't like that.

When I got home, I watched the fight on VHS and I remember hearing the commentator say: "Prince's defence seems to be improving." You're damn right! No way I was getting my nose smashed up again.

Next up was Art Stacey. He'd sent me some message that he was going to bang me up. I didn't have time for all that trash talk as I was too busy dealing with my own flipping nerves. As it goes, I stopped him in the second round and he didn't message me after. Funny that.

By April 1994, I was 12 months into my pro career, had racked up six wins, no losses, with only one fight going the distance. I'd even had one fight live on Sky television, which started getting the attention of the big promoters.

My seventh fight was without a doubt a good learning curve. I was in with Tony Booth, who was a prolific journeyman with genuine talent. The only issue I had coming into this fight was that there was a bug going around our camp and I had the flu. I was supposed to pull out, but I didn't as I needed the money.

Back to Booth. He'd had 41 fights and won 15, but I had no knowledge about his fighting style. We didn't live in the age of YouTube to check out someone's form.

The problem with journeymen is that you don't have time to find out how they fight because they come in at the last minute. It's not like the title fights later on where I'd get six to eight weeks' notice and you could go away and do your homework.

For the first couple of rounds, I felt he was getting the better of me. He was beating me to the jab, countering more and basically making me look silly.

The flu in the meantime was getting messy. I was blowing out my snot from the corner of my nose and at one point I realised I was a bit too close to ringside, as I looked down at some of the officials on their tables as I unloaded.

When I came out for the third round, I decided to hurt him to the body. Bang. It didn't put him down, but made him angry and he came after me. That's what I wanted, because he was boxing me up to that point. I went back against the ropes as I knew he was going to throw a right hand. As soon as he threw it, I pushed a right uppercut straight through the middle.

The second it connected, there was no leaning to the left or right, it was like somebody cut his legs off. He went down on the spot.

After that, I didn't fight then for seven months while Anthony G [my then promoter] was trying to get me my next bout. The struggle was staying on target for training without a date in the diary for my next fight. Thankfully I stayed on the right path, although my mouth almost got me in trouble one day.

We were in this office Carly had, with Anthony G, Carly, a few fighters, the writer Ron Shillingford and a couple of guys I hadn't met before.

Somehow, Lennox Lewis' name came up in conversation and I started spouting off about his brother Dennis and said: "I hear he's living off his brother's name and fame."

From everyone being really chatty and laughing, it went deadly silent and there was this tumbleweed moment. You could cut the air.

The second we came out, Cham said: "The guy who was sitting to your left that you didn't know, that was Dennis Lewis."

I felt like such a knob. Fair play to Dennis, he didn't say a thing.

Years later I met Lennox and I never mentioned that episode. A good thing as he had the biggest hands I'd ever shaken.

When I did step back in the ring on 25 February 1995, it was against Kofi Quaye and I was now being promoted by Frank Warren. Being with Frank was a new experience on a number of fronts, especially when he put me through an MRI scan when I came on board. I've always suffered from claustrophobia and when I was told to wear this gown and go into some full body scanning tube, I panicked big time.

When I came out, it was so embarrassing. My gown was soaking wet and it looked like I'd pissed myself.

Back to Quaye. It was all about image with me now. Nose pierced, gold teeth, tramlines through my eyebrows, big bracelets, brand labelled clothes and let's not forget my velvet green Fila trainers.

Inside the ring, I had this little genie shaved onto the top of my head and walked in looking like this mean monster who came to do damage.

The fight was at the London Arena and there were some big names on the bill, including the likes of Colin McMillan, Crawford Ashley and Lloyd Honeyghan. The two headline fights were between Mike McCallum and Carl Jones for the WBC light heavyweight title and Nigel Benn against Gerald McClellan for the WBC super middleweight crown.

I was told when I got to the arena that I'd be fighting around six that night. The whip walked in: "Get ready Prince, you're on." So there I was shadow boxing getting a real sweat on, all mentally focused, nerves kicking in.

Suddenly the whip popped his head back in: "No, no. Prince, hold it. You're not next, we've moved things around a bit."

Me and Carly took it down a level to keep warm, but not blow myself out. About an hour later, same thing. "You're up Prince." I started doing some flurries to get the sweat going again, then a minute later: "Errrrr. Listen. Change of plans. You're coming on after Nigel Benn's fight."

That basically meant I was fighting late. Really late.

By the time someone finally said: "Nigel's on, you'll be on next Prince," it was near midnight. I was tired. I was lying down on the bench in the changing room and had given up, to be honest.

Then it got delayed because of what happened to McClellan, which everyone knows about. Ambulances and doctors were rushing in and it was obviously serious.

By the time I walked into the ring, I was like Dopey from *The Seven Dwarfs*. There was no fight in me. That fight was left in the changing room when I'd been told two or three times ago to warm up. When the first bell went, Quaye was all over me. He had a good record of 11 wins with only one loss and could fight.

I was trying, but I knew he was doing better than me and hurting me. But by the sixth round I started waking up, realising I was about to lose my first fight under Frank Warren. If I was looking to impress, this was not the way to go about it. Seventh round, I went out there and stopped him.

Four months later I fought Steve Osbourne. I did my ring walk wearing a pair of shades and one of the commentators said: "His career is so bright he has to wear sunglasses."

But the fight was shit. The ref spoilt it because he stopped it early. Osbourne was cut, so I didn't get to display my skills.

A month later I was up against Tony Booth again, almost a year to the day since we first fought. I was in great condition for this one, unlike when I had the flu the last time.

The fight was at the London Arena in Millwall and I knew I had to show how much I'd improved since I last fought him.

Thankfully I did and stopped him in the second. I stalked him, my punches were on point, I hurt him badly to the body and did everything I wanted to do. When I watched the fight back a few days later, I enjoyed seeing those improvements.

Just to say about Tony – he was a good fighter and beat some tough opponents after our contest. There was a lot of fight still in him and he upset the apple cart for a lot of good fighters along the way. He wasn't some journeyman who you could walk in and think, 'Look how many losses he's got.' You did that with Tony and you'd come undone.

Next up on 9 September 1995 was Scott Lindecker in Cork. We were fighting on the undercard of the Steve Collins versus Chris Eubank rematch. It was my first fight outside of London and we'd been put in some scrubs, a banged out cockroach hotel.

When we walked in I turned to Carly and said: "Fuck this man. I ain't staying in here. No way. Where's Frank staying? Let's go back into town and find out where his hotel is."

We go into town and found it. Glenn McCrory and all of them were in there. We went to the reception and booked a room. Job done.

The next day I smashed Lindecker in two rounds and as the away fighter I thought I might be in for a rough response from the crowd. Far from it. When I stepped out of the ring, people were shouting my name and coming up to me wanting my autograph and photos.

One fan shouted: "Give us your hat."

I had this really nice Timberland hat and threw it to him. He was over the moon. *Boxing News* even had the headline 'Prince of Cork!'

We left the hotel without paying because we thought Frank would sort it out, even though he'd already set the other hotel up to be paid.

There was some palaver after and I can't remember if he did pick up the tab or if it got deducted from my purse, but either way, it was a nice hotel.

A month later I fought a big 6ft 3in American next called Lenzie Morgan, which was a good learning curve as I had to go the distance with him.

A couple of hours before the fight, I went to the toilet. It was a long lonely walk to get there. When I came out, he was there about to walk in. He stood in front of me with a mean look and said: "Yeeeaaah. You ready?"

Inside I was thinking, 'Errrr yeah' but on the outside I looked at him and growled: "Yeah. That's right. I'm ready."

But when I walked off I knew he meant business. We were in for a fight.

I was sensible with my boxing skills and even dropped him with my jab at the end of the first round. The commentators couldn't believe I dropped him with a jab and were talking about it being a slip, until they watched the replay.

By the end of the third round, I could see that jab was busting his face up and I thought I had him. I started mixing it to the body, but this guy was really difficult because he had that Yankee side-on, take-away-the-punch-at-the-last-second style of defence. It made it difficult to land clean.

Even though Morgan hit me and hurt me during the fight, I didn't let him take control and won it easily on points.

My strongest memory was actually not of Morgan, but this annoying woman in the crowd. She was constantly screaming: "Come on. Hit him. Hit him. Hit him."

I was thinking, 'Someone please gag this woman.' I don't think she was a boxing fan, just someone who had some drinks and wanted two guys to pummel the life out of each other. I would have preferred to have got the knockout, but overall I think I did well. So did *Boxing News*, who had the headline 'Hopeful Prince makes mighty big impression against Lenzie.'

After the fight, Morgan came to me and said: "Where did you get that jab? I couldn't read it."

That put a massive smile on my face. I'd been working on that jab for months. Sometimes, that was all that I was doing in the gym with Carly and he named it the cobra jab.

He'd set you in the stance, then say: "You've gotta sit there and then you've gotta strike without him seeing it coming. Do it correctly and you'll knock someone off their feet."

With the cobra jab, you strike from A to B, in a straight line, using your back leg to push onto the jab. So you got a little distance between the guy and he thinks you're not going to hit him, then you use a strike pushing from the back leg, pushing onto the front, like when you're pushing a car.

It's an old-school technique which the likes of Pernell Whitaker, Meldrick Taylor, Donald Curry used.

The jab is the most important weapon. When you get hit by surprise like that, it takes you off your feet. I worked on that jab so much that I had a cobra shaved into my hair for the fight.

I'd just like to pay tribute to Morgan, because in September 2014, he was shot in the head by some guy over what was apparently a stupid argument. What a waste of a life. He was a true warrior and lost his battle against a coward with a weapon, something I'd unfortunately be affected by many years later. RIP mate.

My next outing was in Glasgow, on 16 March 1996, against journeyman, John Pierre. I could have done without the five-month wait, but the plus side was that I got to spend more time with my kids.

Tannisa was eight by now, Kiyan was five and I now had another daughter, Jodeci, who was one. I had a routine of picking them up on a Sunday, spending the whole day with them and then I'd take Tannisa and Kiyan back to Tracy's later that night. They'd always be knackered and would crash out in the back of the car, so I used to carry them to Tracy's front door in Edgware, still asleep.

Then with more time on my hands in between fights, the days became weekends and then in the summertime, I'd have them for a couple of weeks. Thankfully they got on really well. As all brothers and sisters do, they had their arguments, but they loved each other to bits.

You'd often see Kiyan and Tannisa watching a movie, then they'd re-enact the scenes. They loved that film *The Mask* with Jim Carrey and they'd do the dance after. Hilarious.

Kiyan still absolutely loved football. The only problem was, he'd be playing indoors. Tracy would be in the kitchen cooking and you'd hear a crash as the ball smashed something. Like father, like son. Thank God Tracy didn't have a paraffin heater in the house.

Another time, he was about six, playing outside. He liked to throw stones over into the railway, which was at the back of Tracy's garden.

He decided to go up the top of the road to get a better aim. This time it hit something and ricocheted off the neighbour's car sunroof, smashing it to bits. The owner came over in a right rage and Tracy now had to pay for the new sunroof. Kiyan got grounded for ages.

He wasn't allowed out of the house, so he ended up sticking his head out of the window to have conversations with his friends on the street.

But that was about as bad as it got really. He was never malicious or nasty, just cheeky.

★★★★★★★★★★★★★★★★★

Back to John Pierre in Glasgow. This was a stacked card on a 15-fight bill, with Naseem Hamed topping against Said Lawal. Pierre didn't cause me any problems, but I do remember hitting him and thinking his head was quite hard.

Frank Warren's matchmaker, Ernie Fossey, always used to say about my opponents, "Look at this guy. Even I can knock him out." Not on this occasion mate!

He took me the distance, which I wasn't happy about. I wanted to stop him too much and I forgot what I did in the Morgan fight, which was staying behind the jab.

By now I was 13-0, with only three fights going the distance. I was ready for my next big challenge and thankfully Frank Warren was happy to oblige. As a boxer, everything was going as well as I could hope. It's just a shame that I was about to walk into a power punch outside the ring.

10

O.K. Corral

*"A gunslinger knows pride, that
invisible bone that keeps the neck stiff."*
Stephen King

A few weeks after John Pierre, I was offered a fight against
either Dean Francis or Maurice Core. Both really good fighters.
At the time, I didn't care about who was who, I just wanted to
move up the rankings.

I was enjoying looking at *Boxing News* and slowly seeing my
name moving up the list, so when Frank offered them to me, I
asked him who was higher up in the rankings. Maurice Core
was ranked the number one light heavyweight at the time, so I
replied: "That's the fight I'll take then."

The other bonus was that we would be fighting for the WBO
Intercontinental light heavyweight title. I was really excited, but
really nervous, because now it got real. This was my seventh
fight with Frank and he'd delivered quickly on his promise to
get me a championship bout.

The training camp went well, but Carly was the first to point
out Core was a step above any other fighter I'd been in with.

He said: "Maurice is well schooled, whereas you're not yet. However, you have something to equalise that. Your punch. You need to get at him. Don't let him sit too long or get into his rhythm and if you get hurt, handle it."

I did a lot of work with British and European cruiserweight champion Terry Dunstan, who had also been a sparring partner to Frank Bruno for a while. Terry had good height, which is what we needed because Maurice was 6ft 5in.

But Terry also made me think. There was no way you could go in there and bang him up. We got on well and had really competitive sparring. Without a doubt he got me on point.

It was a packed bill at the NYNEX Arena [now the Manchester Arena] and we were on the Nigel Benn v Steve Collins undercard. If you watch the fight, you won't recognise me as I started off like a pussy cat. Maybe I showed Maurice a bit too much respect, but I just wasn't going for it like I should.

Then I got cut in the sixth round over my left eye. Maurice had dipped his head, came up and bang. A nasty cut. Carly had been screaming at the ref about Maurice's use of his head throughout the fight, but I told him to shut up.

This was the first time I'd been cut in a boxing ring and I went mad. I dabbed the cut with my glove and saw the blood, which reminded me of how I used to react in my street fighting days. Before I had the chance to go after him, the bell went.

The second I got to the corner the cut man went to work, so I knew it wasn't good. The ref came over, stepped in between me and Carly, had a look and said: "That's a bad cut. I'm going to give you one more round then I'm pulling you out."

A lot of fighters get quite nervous and panic. My fighting instinct kicked in. I knew I had three minutes to stop Maurice.

Carly told me to finish this guy and that's exactly what I did. I came out not even thinking about the eye, with no defence, no side-on stance. The boxing textbook was thrown out of the window. Here's the target Maurice. Hit me.

I knew that if I showed enough of me, he'd try and go for it. Yeah, I'd take some shots, but if I could catch him on the way in, he was gone. And that's what happened.

I clipped him with a long overhand right which we'd been practising in training. It made him wobble, then I ran in, maybe a bit too much as I was missing with hooks.

I could hear his coach Jimmy Tibbs shouting "roll, roll, roll" so I started to throw low hooks. But he was just getting under. Then I threw an uppercut and bang, he was outside of the ring.

I was watching him thinking surely he wouldn't get back in the ring on time. The ref was getting towards the end of the count, about to reach 10. Incredibly Maurice just made it and the ref let him carry on.

The second he said "fight" I sprinted across, but over-ran. I went in with a right hand and he slipped underneath it. I just kept throwing punches and this time the ref stopped it.

I leapt up in the air and Carly grabbed me – it was an ecstatic feeling. It was without a doubt one of the most exciting moments in my boxing career. From being told the fight was going to get stopped, to holding a championship belt.

Jimmy Tibbs later said: "Maurice was British champion and a good boxer. It was a great fight, but I have to say, Mark was just too good that night."

We now went back to the changing room to wait for the doctor as this eye needed stitches. I kid you not, for many doctors back then, going to the fights was a night out and this guy was no different. As he walked in, you could smell the alcohol on him. He took a look and said: "You'll need five stitches."

To make it worse, he added: "Do you have a belt to bite down on? I've got no anaesthetic. You'll need to bite into something."

"What? Do you know how much that hurts?" I replied.

As the doctor started stitching, Carly said with a disgusted look: "What's this guy doing? I can do a better job," and you could see the doc thinking, 'Yeah. You probably could, mate.'

I sweated more getting those stitches than I did for the whole fight. It was pissing out of me. Whoever's hand I had a hold of, I felt sorry for them. I nearly broke the chair handle too.

Each stitch was long and he did a crap job. Half of it was still gaping open once he'd gone and he left me with a nasty scar.

Thankfully the feeling of victory was stronger than the pain. The next day, I put the WBO belt on the dashboard and drove through Tottenham. People on the street were waving, shouting praise and other cars were beeping their horns. What a feeling.

★★★★★★★★★★★★★★★★★★

After the Core fight, things started to crumble around me.

At the time, I was still living in my flat in Tottenham. The council had even knocked out an old laundry room next to my place, to give me another bedroom. If I had my head together, with the money I got from the Core fight, that flat could have been my first investment, especially as it was council property.

They would have given it to me at some ridiculous cheap rate. It wouldn't have cost more than 20 grand. The problem was, I didn't have my head together at the time. It was all about boxing and training, not business sense.

I owed the council five grand in rent and ended up in court. I spoke with my sponsor and he said: "Tell the judge I'll pay it."

So there I was in court speaking to the judge and I told him: "My sponsor will pay for it."

The judge gave me a look as if to say, 'You dickhead. Who do you think you are? Your sponsor will pay for it!'

I lost my flat. I was told to move out by the morning or they were going to lock it up with all my stuff in there.

When I first moved into that flat, it looked like a shithole and smelt like someone had died. I'd just put a new carpet down, new wallpaper and new electric blue settees. I'd proper done it up. I was furious that they were going to kick me out after all this work and money I'd put into the place, so I wrecked the joint. I got some big pots of paint and threw them everywhere.

I didn't have a penny to my name. The only roof I had over my head was my Beamer. I'd bought that car through boxing and was proud of my wheels.

It was a two-door BMW 520i in Calypso red, with leather cream seats and red piping on it to match the outside. Everyone used to know me by the car in the area.

The night I got kicked out I drove round the back of some estate in Tottenham Hale and went to sleep there. I started asking myself some serious questions.

One night when I was trying to fall asleep, after about a week roughing it, I started thinking, 'You're boxing well and you're supposed to be this great up and coming prospect. You need to get some balance back in your life again.'

That's when I decided to call Mum.

"Can I stay back in my room? I've lost my flat."

"Just drive over, son," she replied.

Mum answered the door and made no fuss. She said I could stay until I got sorted, then added: "Tell your father." Everything still had to run past him.

So here I was at home again. Some things changed, others didn't, like Dad's rules. Be in by 10pm or the door's locked Seriously. I was a grown-ass man. There were times I'd end up sleeping in my car, because the front door was locked.

I'd either end up back in the Beamer or I'd go and stay with my sister. It took a while, but Dad removed the curfew and I was finally allowed to come and go as I wished.

Going back home was also difficult for another reason. I still had issues with Dad from when I was last in that house with him as a kid. I wasn't worried about him beating me anymore, but I knew that I'd have to tackle those issues I had in my heart.

As it goes, moving back allowed me to deal with the mental and physical pain of what had gone on in that house, which then helped me move forward. I managed to get things resolved with Dad and I settled back at home for two years.

Mum had a profound effect on me at this point. She said: "Mark. You've got all these things going on in your life, debt, whatever. Sort yourself out. Bit by bit. Pay people off and get your credit good. Save your money. Don't squander it. Do something good with it so you don't end up with nothing."

I bought into that. It helped me to think about buying a house. I wanted to win fights, save money. Simple as that. Over the next couple of years, I took out PEPs, ISAs and stuff like that, so I could save. I started putting money away – seven bags here, five bags there and not touching it. I even bought a house in South London as an investment. I was trying to be sensible.

Dad changed a bit around this time. There were two reasons

for this. By now, he was kind of sucking up to me, because I was a boxer and was to an extent living the life that he wanted. But the other change was forced on him.

Dad was 50, but he'd still go running with Junior early every morning. One day, they went for this run and Junior could hear Dad puffing really loud. Then he stopped and said: "Let's walk." That was not like him at all. When they'd finished, Dad said: "Everything seems to be going purple. Just one colour."

Dad being Dad, he wanted nothing more said about the matter. Over the next few weeks, people were making comments that Dad was walking down the road like he was drunk. He wasn't. Mum told him he had to go to hospital. He never admitted to anything. He was very proud. He just kept quiet.

Then came a defining day. Junior had gone out running by himself and he caught Dad just coming back from his run out by Alexandra Palace. "You just finished?" Junior asked.

"Yeah, yeah," Dad replied. Then he collapsed on Junior.

It turned out Dad had something called Multiple System Atrophy [MSA]. It's a really rare degenerative disorder that's very similar to Parkinson's and starts affecting your body's functions. Breathing, your bladder, your muscles.

Now we knew what was wrong, I worried about him attending my boxing, because people at fights don't give a shit. They want to get to their seats, there's big crowds and it's a bit rough.

I was getting on to bigger shows now and there was one time Junior said someone had started something with Dad, but obviously he couldn't defend it like he used to, because he didn't have that ability no more.

Now we had the MSA diagnosis, I said: "That's it. Don't come to the fights, because I can't do nothing to help you if anything kicks off. I might be in the ring or something." Dad started watching all of my fights on telly instead and we'd even watch them back together and analyse them.

Unfortunately, over the coming years, being a full-time carer for Dad would almost kill Mum.

★★★★★★★★★★★★★★★★★

Around this time I started talking to God again. I told him, 'I want to get to know you properly, I want to build a relationship with you.' It didn't mean going to church necessarily, it just meant reading my Bible, learning and getting to know him.

I'd built up a reputation and career over the years and thought all of that was going to make me happy. But I wasn't.

Carly started to notice I was praying before training and afterwards I'd meditate. It was a really powerful time of my life.

By 1997 you could see the change in me. I think some people thought I was turning soft, because they knew me as this dark, cold-hearted individual who intimidated people in the ring. They had nothing to worry about, as my next fight would show.

About five months after Core, I was told I'd be up against Michael Gale on 3 February 1997, with only a few weeks to prepare. It was a British title eliminator with the winner to fight Crawford Ashley for the title, which I desperately wanted.

I was earning about 15 grand for these fights. Fifteen bags sounds like a lot and I was grateful, but after you take away taxes and the trainer's cuts, I was left with a few hundred pounds each month to spread out over that five to six month gap.

I'll be honest, after a fight, I'd normally celebrate by having a fat blunt. You'd empty the insides of a cigar and fill up the inside with weed and stick it back together. We used to call them Phillies, because the brand of cigar we used was called Philly Blunts – they were big out in America.

So you couldn't leave me without a fight date for any length of time, because, without that structure and discipline, I was finding it difficult to say no. I started having the odd joint here and there, because I had no focus on the boxing. When I got the call to fight Gale, I should have said no, because I didn't have my full eight weeks to get ready. But I needed the money.

Sparring was tough. Apart from Terry Dunstan, I also sparred with three-time WBC light heavyweight world champion Dennis Andries, which was a real learning curve.

As it goes, Carly trained Dennis for about 15 fights and I ended up being his chief sparring partner for the next two years and became a better fighter as a result.

Dennis was teak-tough but what made him so good was his experience. Here was someone who had fought Thomas 'The Hitman' Hearns, Gerald McClellan and been in the ring with so many great fighters from Detroit's Kronk gym, under the master coach, Emanuel Steward.

It was known that if you stepped in with a Kronk fighter, they'd put a banging on you and Dennis was no different. One time, we were sparring and he gave me a busted lip and a bloodshot red eye, but I always went back the next day.

On the third day I knocked him down with a beautiful punch and was thinking 'Yes!' because it had been two days of merciless sparring and he'd been trying to pummel me non-stop.

Over time, I started knocking Dennis down and Carly could see that neither one of us were backing up. Four rounds of sparring went to six and then to eight. Neither wanted to be the first to hang up the gloves, so Carly said we might as well do four-minute rounds instead.

After people saw those spars, Carly had difficulty getting me sparring with anyone else.

Despite the Andries sparring, the rest of the camp wasn't perfect. I'd been struggling with weight. I'd been walking around at about 13 stone, but with very little body fat.

Two weeks before the fight I was racing off weight trying to get down to 12 and a half stone. On certain days during this camp I was just having one meal even though I was training at least three times a day.

Back then, I didn't have the nutritional knowledge. I was sucking on about five to six lemons a day, thinking it would cut weight. Dad also used to make me Irish Moss, which was a West Indian drink with seaweed in it. If it was now, I'd go on to Google and 10 minutes later I'd be sorted.

Last week of training I was at the top of Ally Pally hill on a run and said, 'God, I need your help. I'm not ready for this fight. I need the victory though. Whatever happens, please let me come out with the win.'

★★★★★★★★★★★★★★★★★★

Come fight night, as we're getting ready to walk out of the changing room into the arena in Sunderland, Carly said: "This is an experienced guy. He's 21-1-2. He's a step up."

I tried motivating myself, but I was weight drained and felt weak. When the bell rang, I was doing the things I'd learnt, but there was no explosiveness. Early on I felt my legs wobble. I knew that if Gale clipped me on the chin, I'd be in trouble.

I came out next round and I hurt and cut him. My head then came up and butted him accidentally and I followed through with a right hand. He now had two cut eyes and his team were saying they'd both come from heads, but they didn't.

The ref told me off and his corner were wiping off his cuts and shouting at him to come and get me. I was in my corner thinking that was a good round and I could now finish him.

I came out for round six and he was going for it. He wanted a dogfight now and I'm always really confident in dogfights. We were both swinging and he caught me on the chin. The second it landed, my legs went.

The crowd in Sunderland went crazy as Gale went for the stoppage. I was throwing looping punches which were all missing, but Gale also couldn't find that finishing punch.

Out of frustration, he pulled me to the floor from a clinch and I got up, telling the ref that it wasn't a knockdown. He agreed.

Gale came straight back over strong, which I liked, because that was a good time to nail him. As I was staggering back, I was waiting to throw this banger of a right hand and after missing a few, he walked straight into it and hit the canvas.

Slowly I started to feel stronger. Gale's face was covered in blood, but the ref allowed it to continue. We both kept swinging.

I ended up knocking him down, he received an eight count, then I threw this jab and missed, but almost like in slow motion, while it was still extended, I turned it and threw the left hook. Bang. I followed up with a right hand and he went down again.

We went at it one more time, but now I'd found my legs and after about 10 seconds I landed a left hook that put him down for the last time. The ref didn't even start the count.

A number of TV channels and publications later picked it as

their 'Round Of The Year,' and I even got an award presented to me at some big Sky boxing dinner a few weeks later. Straight after, I said a prayer in the ring on my knees.

That was the first time I'd done that. It was a real prayer of thanks. I was in trouble and needed some help to win and God provided me with that help.

After that, I never got a chance to fight for the British title. It never happened and I have no idea why. Every British boxer wants the coveted Lonsdale belt and to win it outright, but it just wasn't to be.

★★★★★★★★★★★★★★★★★

With time on our hands, Carly organised a two-month trip to the US for some quality sparring. First stop, New York, which I was in awe of. We were staying in Brooklyn, so you can imagine how made up I was when we got to meet a number of people who showed us Mike Tyson's hangouts from back in the day.

Carly used to train fighters in Cleveland and New York back in the 1980s and knew some great gyms, with great fighters, including the world famous Gleason's in Brooklyn.

He wanted to expose us to different fighting environments and levels of sparring I couldn't get in England. Every region was different and would come with its own unique vibe. As Carly said: "Once you've done the circuit and sparred from Cleveland down to New York, you're a more rounded fighter."

But what made Gleason's special was the people. I trained alongside some great fighters such as Junior Jones and William Joppy. Mitch Green was also there and he used to bring the most noise with him, running off at his mouth about something.

Carly had worked with some great trainers in Gleason's, including Hector Roca and also the late, great Victor Valle, who came with real presence and brilliant stories.

Victor was born in 1917, had over 40 pro fights in the 1930s and had trained some great fighters over six decades, including Esteban De Jesus, Doug DeWitt and Jose Torres. However, it was his heavyweights that he loved. He was always known for having guided the career of Gerry Cooney, who went on to knock out Ken Norton in the first round.

When I started training with some of his cruisers and heavys like Jeff Lampkin, Victor could not only see that I was good at attacking, but that I was developing my defensive skills.

He was so impressed that he asked Carly if I could stay out longer on a regular basis. He basically wanted to train me full-time. It was a big compliment, but I knew where my loyalty was and there was no way I was going to be away from my children longer than I needed to.

Gleason's was like a melting pot. Very cosmopolitan. You had some real characters from South America, the Caribbean, then you had the New Yorkers from places like the Bronx and Brooklyn. But in the ring, the place was like a war zone. Everybody wanted to kill you.

Cham was also with us, but he didn't enjoy training as he had bad toothache and needed root canal surgery. Getting punched in the mouth probably wasn't the best thing for him, so he stayed around for the ride and that turned out to be pretty colourful.

After a few weeks, we drove down to Cleveland in this big people carrier. The intention was to do more sparring down there in a few gyms and rack up some more experience with different fighters.

It was about a 10-hour journey and we took it in turns to drive. I took over from Carly around 2am and drove for about five hours, while everyone was snoring their heads off.

It was one of the deadliest drives, because every time I looked over the cliff edge, there was nothing there. I was also really tired. Having a 40 [oz bottle of beer] and a spliff before we headed off probably didn't help.

I was suffering, but somehow, by the time it hit daylight, I was still driving. I was straying all over the place, getting stupidly close to these cliff edges and at one point Cham woke up.

"You alright Prince?"

"I'm cool," I replied, but he looked at me and said: "Let me take over." Thank goodness for that.

A few days into the trip, I went to this jeweller's and decided to buy a watch. Two days later, it stopped working. I told Cham that we were going to get my money back.

We went over there and the Russian owner, who was built like the world's strongest man, was standing behind the counter. I casually walked over and said: "You know that watch you sold me the other day, look, it's not working bruv."

His wife had a look, and everything was calm at this point. Then all of a sudden, the owner started shouting: "You guys think you can come here and make trouble? Eh? You think you can do that to me?"

Me and Cham look at each other, baffled.

"What you talking about? I said. "The watch doesn't work. I just want you to change it or give me my money back."

He didn't want to reason. He was raising his voice and getting really aggressive while I kept thinking, 'Be cool. You're getting your damn watch sorted today.'

Next minute, he dropped his arm under the counter and pulled out a handgun. "Get out of the shop," he shouted. He then started to go on about how another jeweller's down the road had been robbed by a couple of black guys, added two and two together and came up with .22.

You'd think me and Cham would be shitting it and doing a runner, but we didn't move. I told the jeweller: "Mate. I'm getting my watch changed. I ain't moving until that happens."

The wife freaked out after the husband pulled out the gun and began screaming. The owner started having a go at his missus and they were now having an argument in Russian.

Halfway through the row she handed me over this new watch and basically wanted us to fuck off. But we didn't. I examined that watch to make sure it was working then put it on, checked it out again and said: "OK. I'll take this one." We walked out.

As we stepped out and the door closed behind us, me and Cham looked at each other and I said: "Did he just put a gun in our face? Oh my gosh! This guy pulled a strap out on us. We could have got blasted in there."

As you do after having a gun in your face, we stood there laughing – which is more than can be said for another episode soon after. A couple of days later, me and Cham were in the back of this Cadillac. In the front was a guy and a girl who we'd met recently.

We were driving down the road and a car coming the other way passed us. Cleveland was a new place to me, so I was looking at everything and as this car went past, I looked at the guys in the car for a split second. I wasn't staring, I was just looking at a car as it was passing. That was that. Or so I thought.

For some reason, in that split second I caught the eyes of the driver and my intuition told me that was not a good look. I turned around and could see this car was now following us. My gut instinct was right.

I didn't say nothing to the driver, but I kept turning around and after looking about five times, I could see this car was definitely on our tails. I started to get worried and said to the driver: "Listen bruv. I think that car's following us."

He went: "You sure man?"

"Yeah. I've been watching him."

"Aight," he said, as he reached down and pulled this gun out from the side of his seat. My eyes almost came out of my head.

I was now thinking he was going to drive us to some busy area, to discourage the people from following, as they wouldn't want to start any nonsense with witnesses and all that.

But no. We started taking lefts and rights and ended up in some dusty old neighbourhood, with quiet dark roads and only a few street lamps.

My heart jumped out of my chest when he turned to the girl next to him and said: "You got the nine?"

The nine? Nine what?

She went: "Yeah. I got it," as she pulled out a handgun.

We drove down and parked up in between two houses in the pitch black and all you could hear was the sound of our engine. Next thing, the other car pulled up slowly behind us and you could now hear two engines purring.

They were looking at us and we were looking at them in the mirrors. It was like a proper stand-off from the movie *Boyz n the Hood*. I was thinking: 'Any minute now they're gonna get out of the car and spray us with bullets.'

They only stayed there for about a minute, but it seemed like an hour. Sweat was pouring down my face and I was starting to wonder if my time on this planet would end on a dark road in an old American car, somewhere in downtown Cleveland.

Then the engine noise increased slowly as they started to drive off, very slowly. Maybe they thought about what guns we might have and whose house we were parked in front of and just thought it would be better to move on.

Whatever their reasons, I've never felt so relieved in my life. Very little gets me rattled, but I'll be honest, I was scared. I couldn't wait to get back to the UK and fight the old-fashioned way, with fists. This whole gun-slinging thing was not for me.

11

End Of The Road

"I could have been a contender."
**Marlon Brando in 'On The
Waterfront'**

Eleventh of September 1997, I was up against Bruce Rumbolz.
He had a good record of 18 fights with only one loss and had
recently won the USA Illinois super middleweight title.

In all honesty though, it didn't matter who you put me in
with that night. I felt so strong. I had nice Reyes gloves, which I
loved, because they were puncher's gloves.

I loosened them up in the changing room before going out
by punching them against the wall, because they were new and
cushiony. I wanted Rumbolz to feel my hand hitting his face.

As predicted, I totally dominated that fight and Rumbolz
felt my presence and power. His boxing technique and style
was never going to cut it in a million years with me. He was a
blown-up super middleweight and I walked straight through
him and broke him down in three rounds.

I was defending my WBO belt, but as we were waiting for the ring announcer to give the official decision, some guy from the IBF walked in with another belt.

When the announcer said: "And still the WBO Intercontinental champion and now the new IBF Intercontinental champion..." I had no idea. When they presented it to me, with a big grin on my face, I thought, 'Alright. I'll have it!'

I really liked the IBF belt, not because of what it stood for, but because it had two big metal birds on the front of it.

Straight after the Rumbolz fight, Frank Warren put a brilliant opportunity our way. I'd be defending my WBO light heavyweight Intercontinental title against Chris Eubank.

This is the moment all boxers dream of, being in the ring with that big name. I knew that beating Eubank could change everything for me. My bank balance would change, my kids' lives would be better and I'd be able to plan for the future.

I knew I could beat this guy. Whenever he fought, he took a lot of breaks, standing around a lot. I knew that with my punch power, nobody would be able to stand around in front of me.

I was going to do what Michael Watson did to him. I was going to stay on him from the opening bell and not give him any breaks.

All excited, me and Carly spoke with Frank Warren, expecting to hear some big money being offered, especially as I was the one bringing the belt to the table. There were rumours Eubank was getting a six-figure sum, so I was expecting something similar. That wasn't the case. I was offered 25 grand. Frank said taking the fight, win, lose or draw, would lead to bigger purses, more publicity and would show the market what I was made of.

What he said made sense, but instead I had a chat with Carly and he advised me to not accept any Mickey Mouse money. I then made a stupid decision. I refused the offer, just based on the cash. I wanted at least 50 bags. As soon as the offer was there, it had gone. No fight. To this day I regret that.

Instead, on the night we were supposed to fight, Eubank dropped another seven pounds and fought Joe Calzaghe for the vacant WBO world super middleweight title.

Reading the likes of the BBC say: "Eubank, meanwhile, had been training to fight Mark Prince at light heavyweight, but with just two weeks to get down to 168lbs the 31-year-old chose to accept the title bout..." drove me insane.

That night I sat by my telly with my head in my hands as Calzaghe did a number on Eubank. It was a lost opportunity.

Not the way I wanted to finish 1997, but three months later I fought Wayne Hankins, another Yank, who was the USA Illinois light heavyweight champion. Basically, he was the next step up from Rumbolz.

I sparred some big strong guys for this one down at Miguel's gym in Brixton, like heavyweight Keith Long. However, the most memorable was against former WBO heavyweight world champion Henry Akinwande, who was 6ft 7in and had fought some great fighters.

When Akinwande looked at me, because I didn't have a reputation as a boxer and maybe because of my short CV at that point, he probably thought, 'Who's this guy? Please. I've won the ABAs twice, went to the Olympics and was heavyweight champion of the world.'

But Carly had already given me a talk to overcome all that. He told me: "I want you in with the guys who've done great things for England as amateurs and pros. I want you in with all the dogs. You've gone straight from the street to the amateurs, had nine fights and turned pro. Show them who you are now. Show them what time it is."

Akinwande liked banging out guys in sparring and he tried to do the same with me. We weren't having it. When I came back to the corner after the first round, Carly said: "Listen. Get in your shelter, use your jab, cross the right, come back to the body, come back to the head, then push him back."

And that's exactly what I did. At the end of the second round, Carly said: "I don't think he wants to stay in here much longer," then with a smile, told me to get him in the next round.

It turned into a proper ruck. We really went for it and Akinwande didn't like the pressure. He leant back on the ropes as I swung at him. After that round, Akinwande's trainer said: "That will do. We need heavier guys to spar with than Mark."

Riiiiiiight. That's why you pulled him out. As a heavyweight your ego starts to go when lighter guys start putting it on you. He wasn't very warm with me after that spar.

The training camp for this fight was memorable, mainly for the unexpected guests who turned up. Some PR guy phoned and asked me to come down with my belts because he had some people who wanted to have some photos taken with them for a promo. They'd booked out the whole gym for the session, so I started to wonder who was coming over.

When I walked up to the gym, there were hundreds of people trying to get inside for a photo or an autograph. I got escorted to the entrance by some bouncers and when I walked inside, there were Dr Dre and Eminem, with this big entourage and media team. Wasn't expecting that.

Once they'd taken a few shots with the belts I managed to

have a little chat with them in the office. Really nice, down-to-earth guys. It turned out they were big boxing fans and talked to me about my career so far, who I'd fought and what the belts represented. Before you knew it, they were out of the door and I was hitting the heavy bag. All very random.

Despite boxing better than Rumbolz, on 13 December 1997, Hankins' lack of experience let him down. I stayed calm with him, waited for my moment, then bang!

I stopped him in the third and that was a straight KO. He went to sleep in the air. When I say he crumbled, he landed in a foetus position on the floor, back where he began life.

★★★★★★★★★★★★★★★★★

Six months later I was fighting Kenny Whack, on 30 May 1998. This was the fourth time I was defending my WBO Intercontinental title and was now rated in the top 10 by most of the world sanctioning bodies. That was a tough line-up to be part of, with the likes of Roy Jones Junior, Dariusz Michalczewski, Montell Griffin, Virgil Hill and Michael Nunn.

For this one I sparred with some good fighters, including Spencer Fearon, Howard Eastman and James Cook. They were all boxers who stretched me to my limits, which was what I needed. I was about to be pushed to the full 12 rounds by a notoriously tough fighter who had never been stopped before.

In all honesty, if I had to go 12 rounds in my previous fights, I would have struggled. For this one, I added swimming to my training routines and that helped my cardio.

Fight night. Whack started off well and swelled my eye in the third round. It was his movement I remember. He had nice feet.

At one point I was thinking, 'I like the guy's moves.' It was no surprise that he'd been Sugar Ray Leonard's sparring partner.

About midway I realised this fight was going the distance, so I needed to box clever.

By round eight, Carly told me: "You've got to win every round now. This guy is being crafty, hitting and holding, and stopping you from doing your work. He's not as fit as you. This is not a fight about him trying to knock you out, it's about trying to nick the rounds. Push him off and start first. Be first every time."

That's what won me the fight. Even though the score cards were wide, if I hadn't gone into those last rounds with the mentality that I was behind, it would have been much closer, making me look ordinary. As it goes, I looked far from ordinary and what I was about to be offered confirmed that.

★★★★★★★★★★★★★★★★★★

Shortly afterwards, I got a call from Frank Warren. "I've got you a shot at the WBO world light heavyweight title," he said. "You'll be fighting Dariusz Michalczewski on 19 September in Germany.

This will sound silly, but I wasn't overly excited for this one, even though it was for a world title. I was more excited when I'd heard I was fighting Eubank because everyone knew Eubank.

Even though Dariusz was a great fighter, he always fought in Germany, which meant he wasn't that well-known in the UK. The media wouldn't be swarming around like when the Eubank date hit the newspapers.

At the time, Dariusz was a 37-0 fighter and had defended his world title 13 times on the bounce. He was also a serious puncher and only about five of his opponents had gone the distance with him. But I didn't give a shit.

When I heard I would be getting 125 thousand, I was over the moon. I thought it was pounds though. Turns out it was US dollars, which almost halved the amount. I found out later that Dariusz's pay cheque was seven figures. Either way, I wanted to get paid and have some money in my pocket as opposed to carrying Mickey Mouse change. I accepted the fight.

For this one, me and Carly had a serious disagreement. In fact, it was the first and last time we ever had a full-on argument. Carly had gone to Gambia for a four-week holiday and when he came back, I said: "I've signed for the world title."

He was shocked and angry. "How could you do something like that? You're two years away from a fight like this. You are knocking everyone out, but you can't do the same with this guy. You've got a fantastic record, but you don't have no world level experience yet. Look at the amount of rounds you've done as a pro. It's nothing. I would walk out on this fight right now."

Carly was really pissed off. Once he'd cooled down, he said: "Listen. I've been here from the beginning and whether you win, lose or draw, I'm still gonna be here. But after this fight, let's work a strategy for how to move forward."

We decided to train in America again, because it worked last time. It turned out to be the worst training camp of my life. This time we trained at the Wildcard gym in Los Angeles, which was run by the Professor [Freddie Roach].

I'd met Freddie a few months before, because he was in Kenny Whack's corner. In fact, Whack ended up being one of my sparring partners, because he was a clever boxer, but he came forward and that's exactly what Dariusz did. He was a plodder.

What an absolutely lovely bloke Freddie was. When we walked in, he gave us a big hug and made us genuinely feel at home. The facilities at Wildcard were quality. I remember their speedballs especially, which were much better than anything in England at the time, because they had some special swivel.

Running was done in the hills in California, accommodation was awesome, but there was one issue – we were skint. We were eating two-dollar Chinese meals once a day and about a month before the fight, I only weighed 174lbs, which was below the light heavyweight limit.

At this stage I would usually be at least 190lbs and would then cook down. I looked ripped to bits on the outside, but inside my engine was missing a couple of cylinders, which meant my heart and mind just couldn't get into the right place.

There was also something outside of boxing which wasn't helping me. I'd met a lady called Laurel, who I'd eventually end up marrying. On a number of occasions, Carly would come to my room at 5am to wake me up for the early run and I'd been up all night on the phone chatting to her.

Carly went mad and told me it was messing me up. Then, as a result of being tired, after doing the cardio at the gym, I'd tell him I didn't want to spar. It was a weird situation, because, for the first time, me and Carly weren't in sync.

He said: "Bro. This fight needs more attention than you're giving it. You haven't sparred, your fitness is not there, you're not ready. You're not a 12-round fighter yet. You're naturally a 10-round fighter. Going 12 with Michalczewski is a totally different proposition."

My head was in a different place and I didn't listen.

After a six-week camp, 10 days before the fight we went

straight from LA to Germany, which was a long flight. I came off in such a bad mood, looking like shit, feeling like shit and just wanting to go to my hotel, have a decent meal and sleep.

As we started walking through the airport, the German press jumped in front of my face wanting to do interviews and snapping away loads with cameras, with flashes going and all that. I just wanted to tell them to piss off.

My training over there was also crap. Going running in the morning in Oberhausen was like running in the Twilight Zone. It was just a weird place. Maybe it's because I'd just come from LA where gyms smelt and looked like gyms, but in Germany, everything was spotless.

I walked in thinking, 'Has this gym ever been used before?' They must have had a cleaner walking around every minute looking for dirt. Even the streets were clean and tidy. It was just very different to what I'd been used to.

It's easy to say now, but my camp would have been much better at home. I would have eaten Mum's food, slept better and flown over to Germany the night before. How could I think I could come away with the light heavyweight world title, when I hadn't paid the price for the belt in training?

Two hundred rounds sparring was needed for that fight and I'd done nowhere near that. It was closer to 50. Even for the likes of Bruce Rumbolz I sparred 180 rounds, so when I was doing the ring walk, I knew I could win.

For this I was flat. My belief walking into the ring for this fight was about me as a person, not how I'd prepared for it. Even though I wasn't in great condition, mentally, I never once felt like I wasn't up for the task of beating Dariusz. I just wasn't enthusiastic, which meant I was walking into trouble.

The atmosphere in the Arena Oberhausen was huge, although it was all about Dariusz, as he was the darling of Germany. We were headlining in front of 12,000 people and the eight fights on the undercard included the likes of future world champions, Wladimir Klitschko and Ricky Hatton.

One thing I did notice about the crowds in Germany was how well behaved they were. Fight night was a big thing for them over there. Everyone was dressed up and it was all very civilised.

The other thing I noticed was the size of the ring. I could almost jump from one side to the other. It was phone-booth tiny. That was made for Dariusz, because he was a tracking down fighter and they would have known that I might box.

When the referee brought us together to give us our instructions, I gave Dariusz the serious stare-down. It wasn't something I'd normally do, but because of who it was and what was at stake, I felt I needed to look at him and let him know I wasn't scared. Even when I was walking around the ring waiting for the bell to go, I was scowling.

From the opening bell, you could tell Dariusz was class. The way he moved made me feel like he was always going to punch. But when he didn't, I did, and that's how I started to punch myself out and get caught.

Carly started trying to get me to punch what I saw instead of throwing four and five punch combos in anticipation, landing maybe one punch, just to show I was in the fight.

The other problem was that my punches didn't have the power in them. My heart was there, but I was too tired to land anything that would hurt him. I didn't have the legs to stick and move and nick rounds either. By the sixth, I was gassing and had no bounce. My conditioning was letting me down.

Round eight, I knew there was absolutely nothing left in the tank. It was like picking up an empty bottle and shaking it upside down to get the last dregs out of it. That was me.

As he started to throw bombs I shouted at him: "Come on," because I knew I was done and knew what was coming. I wanted to go out on my shield.

I went to throw a punch and next thing I remembered was opening my eyes as I was lying on the canvas with the referee and doctor looking over me and wondering what had happened.

I'd been knocked out cold. When I got back to the changing room, my family were there, Cham and a few others. I started crying and apologised to everyone for letting them down.

Later at the press conference, Dariusz said he didn't think he'd stop me, because in the early part of the fight I wasn't allowing him to get his punches off. The only thing was, I hadn't prepared to keep that going for 12 rounds.

In my interview, I told the Sky guys I had no excuses and had been beaten by the better fighter. Dariusz had a rematch clause in the contract in case he lost, but I didn't. That said, Carly wouldn't have wanted me fighting him again so soon anyway.

Back home, I went to see my parents. The moment Mum saw me she said: "Praise the Lord. You OK? Not hurt?"

"I'm fine," I replied.

Then she said: "For this fight, I was kneeling down and praying. When I hear you knocked out, I stop watching it."

Mum had never watched a single one of mine or Dad's fights, so I asked: "Before this fight I'd stopped 15 out of 18 guys and you had to go and watch this one as your only fight!"

We both started laughing, which was nice, as the immediate future wasn't going to smell of roses.

12

Jack Of All Trades

"Having a normal knee would make life a lot easier." **Andy Murray**

Believe it or not, I didn't go into a slump in the weeks after that fight. In fact, losing my first fight as a professional relaxed me as I no longer had to defend an unbeaten record.

I'd also learnt a lot by being in with a fighter of Dariusz's calibre. I took on a couple of things that he did really well in that fight and added them to my own routine. For example, his jab style. I practised it and added it to my tool box of jabs. I had the flick jab, the cobra and now the Dariusz jab.

I still wanted to fight again before the year ended. Not so much for the money, but to keep my name up in the rankings and keep me active. I kept training and sparring. One of the most memorable sessions of early 1999 was when Cham and I went down to Miguel's gym in Brixton and light middleweight Spencer Fearon was there.

At the time, Spencer was 6-0 and an up and coming prospect,

whereas Cham had been retired for a couple of years and was a lightweight. Cham had just come out of a tough spar, when Spencer jumped in and gave him a technical beating.

Cham was there getting angry saying: "Come on. Knock me out." Spencer put it on him and controlled that spar without a doubt. I was up next and wanted to give him a bit back.

He threw a jab and I caught it with my left glove, then threw a right hand over the top. It didn't knock him over, but you could see Spencer's eyes open wide. For the rest of that spar he danced around the ring as I threw some weighted shots, but not heavy to the point that would hurt him. I started mixing it to the head and the body and systematically broke him down.

I kept him on his feet for the rounds, didn't knock him out. As the heavier fighter, I never took liberties like that. Just to say, Spencer is a good mate, now one of Sky's best boxing pundits and even came to my first wedding. But in the ring, back then, sparring was sparring.

Despite wanting to bounce back quickly, I didn't get a fight for 13 months and when I did, it was against Kevin Mitchell, who'd had 14 fights and lost nine. How do I go from headlining in a world title contest to fighting this kind of opponent at the Kingsway Leisure Centre in Widnes?

That's a very good question.

The fight was at cruiserweight and I dispatched Kevin within 43 seconds of the first round. Soon after I was offered a fight with Johnny Nelson for 40 bags.

Johnny could still punch, was a good defensive fighter and a good mover, but I knew he was going to run in the ring as that was the Brendan Ingle style. However, I also knew there's no way he could run from me for the distance.

I still needed a proper fight before I faced him. Johnny had been fighting every two to three months, whereas I'd had 43 seconds of ringwork in 13 months, which wouldn't cut it. I needed to see where I stood fitness, technique and stamina-wise.

Unfortunately, I wasn't able to get that tune-up fight and decided to pass. I didn't stress though, because I knew I was not far from another title shot and that I'd get the chance to climb the ranks again quickly. Or so I thought.

★★★★★★★★★★★★★★★★★★★

My brother Colin used to do outside security and he'd get me and Junior to help him. Randomly, around this time, Colin was also about to appear in the movie *Kiss of the Dragon* with Jet Li.

Back to the security. There would be a few other guys as well as us three. The Princes had a reputation for being good at their work and being able to do it with no problems. Issues were swiftly dealt with. We'd cover concerts at Wembley. Tina Turner, Bruce Springsteen, that sort of thing.

This one time, the organisers called Colin and asked if he could bring his team down to Wembley Stadium, as there would be lots of dodgy fake merchandise being sold at this concert. Our job was to move them on, as these guys kept popping up everywhere. In a matter of seconds they'd put a plastic sheet down on the ground, take out their t-shirts and start shouting: "Get your t-shirts here. Five pound."

By now, everybody knew us, as it was the same guys that used to come over from Manchester, Bristol, Liverpool, wherever. When they clocked us, they'd pack up and move on without us even needing to say a word. This particular day, there was a new guy that none of us had seen before. It's crazy, because about half an hour before, I was saying to Junior: "We do this job and we must thank God that we come in, do this work and are able to go home safe." I spoke too soon.

When we did these events, we each had a certain area we'd look after. On this night, I was on this corner and I spotted this stocky, well-built guy. I told him he needed to move on, pointing away from the venue. This guy looked angry and said: "Who do you think you are? You can't tell me where to sell my gear."

I said: "Let's not make it difficult."

"I ain't going nowhere mate," he replied. "I'm selling my stuff right here." He then went for me. I was thinking, 'Don't hurt this guy. You're a professional fighter at the top of your game and doing this little side thing to put a bit of change in your pocket.'

I could tell he wasn't going to let up though, so I grabbed him by his Adam's apple so hard he sounded like he was choking. He was now trying to wriggle free and I could see he was going to throw both his fists the second he was loose. Now I knew I needed to take him to the floor. I adjusted my stance and twisted. Although my body turned, my right knee didn't.

The second it happened, I could hear my knee crunching in its socket. The pain was unbelievable, but I couldn't take my eye off this guy, otherwise he would have been all over me.

I was on top of him UFC-style, but I didn't want to damage the guy, so I punched him once in the face and said: "Listen. I could really hurt you badly out here, but I don't want to. Get up and leave."

By now, Colin had turned up, but I told him everything was cool. One of my other mates had also appeared, who was more of a weapons guys, so I definitely didn't want him getting involved. Thankfully, the seller got up and ran out of there. As we walked away, my leg was shaking like a leaf. I told Colin: "My knee don't feel right. I think I've done some damage."

I was angry with myself and also this guy, because if he'd have moved on, I wouldn't have hurt myself in the first place.

A few minutes later, who do we see? The same guy again. He'd gone to another spot and tried to sell his t-shirts again. I walked up to him and said: "What you still doing here bruv?"

He was loading up to punch me and in a split second I knew I didn't want to hurt my hands, so I threw one of the first moves I'd learnt in karate, the elbow. Bang. As he was going down I went to throw the next elbow, but that one went over his head. Then I decided to kick him.

Being right-footed, I instinctively kicked him with my right leg, despite my brain telling me not to because of what had happened to my knee a few minutes before. The second I made contact with him, I was on the floor. Then I looked down and saw my foot was about 90 degrees to the right of my knee. It was obvious that the knee joint had come clean out of its socket.

I was screaming: "My leg, my leg." Everyone looked over and it was like a freeze shot. I remember looking at Junior's eyes and the second he looked down, he said "Shiiiiit" and turned away.

I was screaming at Colin, telling him to put my knee back in. He didn't know what to do, but I shouted: "Just put it back in!" Colin grabbed my leg and went crack, like something you'd see in a *Rambo* film. It was horrible, but he got it back in.

As I was screaming with pain, the police came round the corner. The guy who was selling the t-shirts seized the opportunity, got up and shot off. As I got up, it felt like my leg was loose from the knee down, just hanging.

The arena started to empty and there was no way we were getting through these crowds to a hospital. The police got me in their van, put on the sirens and took us to an ambulance. We blasted it to the hospital, where they loaded me up with morphine and put the whole leg in a brace.

About six weeks later, I had an appointment with a consultant. When he walked in with this set of notes and a grim look on his face, I knew I wouldn't be boxing any time soon. When the injury happened at Wembley, I knew I was in trouble, but it's different hearing it from a professional. It kind of makes it final.

There was no way I was ever going to officially retire as a boxer. Never. Instead, I had the depressing task of watching myself going down the rankings every week, because I was inactive. I went from not being ranked in the top 10 in the world, to not being ranked in the top 20 in Britain, to disappearing from any boxing media. That was my pro boxing career over.

★★★★★★★★★★★★★★★★★★

I now had to think about how to pay the bills. The problem was, for a number of weeks, I was very limited because of my knee. Thankfully, my friends and family helped do the basics.

Kevin used to pick me up in his convertible Peugeot and he'd take the top down as I sat in the back with my leg out of the car. I used to look forward to him coming round, because he'd make me smile at a time when things weren't great.

I'd also started to question my faith in God, because I'd asked him to help me with my life path and then this happened. My faith started to fade and when that happens, the quality of your life also starts to deteriorate.

Life had to go on though. I was back on my feet much sooner than I should've been, limping around getting on buses and trains looking for jobs and going for interviews.

After applying for about 50 jobs with no success, I saw an advert looking for a computer salesman for a firm in Walthamstow. I knew absolutely nothing about computers, I just needed a job.

All I wanted to do was go, blag the interview, get in and start earning some cash. My application got accepted, I blagged the interview and everything looked good. They asked me to come back for another interview and some tests.

After the tests this guy looked at me and said: "I recognise you. I know who you are."

I wondered if that was a good or a bad thing.

"You're that boxer. What are you doing here?" he asked.

"I'm not boxing anymore. I'm looking to start a new career."

I got the feeling he was saying, 'You might have been a boxer before, but now you're under my power.'

Even though this guy really drilled me in the interview, I passed all the tests and they took me on.

The plan now was for me to do a couple of months' trial and sit some more exams, but once I'd passed those I was good to go. I'd always been confident and knew that if money depended on it, I'd study for those exams and get that job.

So there I was, a few weeks into this job, taking exams and passing everything. My knee was still massively swollen and hurting, and I was still wearing a brace from my groin to ankle. I didn't take my painkillers, because they were making me high and messing up my head.

The best I could do to help with the pain was raise my leg up, to help reduce the swelling. And that fighter's mentality never

ove my little brutha Colin,
ut still can't get him to
mile as much as me

One of my favourite pics of Mum and Dad

vas always copying Dad. Here we are on a
re family outing with sister Tannisa. Check out
ose flares and shirt!

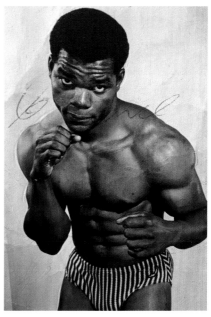

Dad during his pro boxing days

own the wrong road.
etting 'red' on high grade

Amateur ring action.
In full flow against
Kenny Nevers

Belting up: Proudly popping round to Mum and Dad's (above) after winning my WBO light heavyweight Intercontinental belt and (left) also with my IBF Intercontinental belt

(Top) A rare escape to the beach, while preparing to turn pro in Jamaica and (above) Carly giving last minute instructions before I defend my title against Bruce Rumbolz

Man in the mirror: In Los Angeles, under weight in advance of my world title shot

All smiles. Full of fun and enjoying life.
An early family picture of Kiyan

London Academy photo of Kiyan, aged 15,
at a sports day in 2005

Hanging out with Kiyan on his ninth
birthday at the arcade

Kiyan in action for Queens Park Rangers
where he was on the books

Dark day: The Mirror (above) breaks the devastating news and everyone comes together to remember Kiyan's life

Mourners console each other outside the church after the funeral

Police photo of Hannad Hasan after he was convicted of murder at the Old Bailey in July, 2007

(Left) The look says it all. (Below) Kiyan's old QPR shirts hung outside Loftus Road in tribute

Foundation activities. (Far left) Meeting Gordon Brown (Centre) Chris Eubank lending his support to a KPF event and (above) a fundraising skydive

Sending the message out loud and clear to QPR fans

(Right) from boxer to doctor with my beautiful wife Daz and Mum. (Above, right) receiving a Pride of Britain award from Ross Kemp. (Right) Another fundraiser in 2014

(Top) Ready to rumble, with my brother Colin (left) and friend Jonan

(Above) Driving the jab home against opponent Jiri Svacina in February, 2014

(Below) The proud moment of victory. Wearing the QPR colours in the name of my son

oing it for Kiyan. Fired up for my comeback…

elebrating against Oleg Lopajevs, so in February, 2014

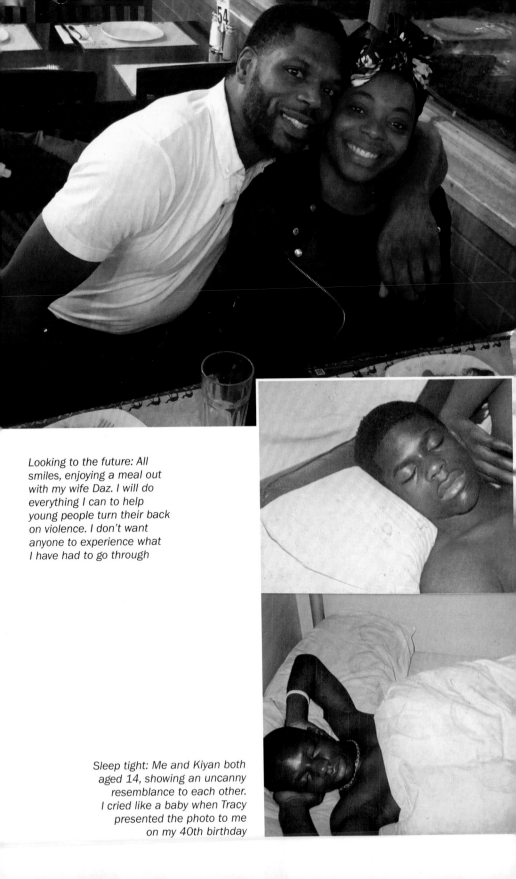

Looking to the future: All smiles, enjoying a meal out with my wife Daz. I will do everything I can to help young people turn their back on violence. I don't want anyone to experience what I have had to go through

Sleep tight: Me and Kiyan both aged 14, showing an uncanny resemblance to each other. I cried like a baby when Tracy presented the photo to me on my 40th birthday

left me. I was always competing and testing myself. If I was coming off the train, I'd see the stairs going up to the Tube and say to myself, 'Come on. You can do this.' I hated people coming over and offering to help me, so I used to put a swag into the way I was walking with my crutches, as if to say, 'I'm fine. Back away', even though by the time I'd done those stairs, I was finished.

Then one day, I went into work and this guy, the same one from the interview, called me into his office.

"Listen. I don't think it's really working out."

"What do you mean?" I said. "I've passed the tests."

"No, no. It's not that," he told me. "You're still in your trial period and we're going to let you go. Security is going to escort you out of the building. Now."

No reason, nothing. I felt so angry. I was walking down the street like a madman. I thought about waiting for him to leave the office and fronting him outside. I hadn't done anything wrong and he had me walked out of this building like a criminal. He made me feel so small. I tried to do everything right, but everything went wrong. That hurt.

A few months later, I got a job for a private ambulance service based in Hackney. I did the basic training that an ambulance guy needed to have, but what the job was really about was picking up patients many with different illnesses and disabilities.

When I say picking them up, I mean physically. I'm talking lifting them out of bed, putting them onto a bed with wheels, then lifting that on to the ambulance. This was a tough job.

We went to some flats and the lifts weren't working That's when you had to climb the stairs. When we used to arrive, I'd be praying, 'Please, be able to walk with a stick at least.' Nope.

Nine times out of 10 it would be this massive, obese patient and we'd have to carry them in one of those metal chairs.

Sometimes I'd get spotted on the job. This geezer once said with a smirk on his face: "Oi. Are you Mark Prince? You were a top fighter. Why you doing this job?"

It was a massive fall from grace. A few years before I was headlining a world title fight and now I was lifting some 35-stone sweaty arse onto a bed and having to listen to his bullshit along the way. In general, I really liked the patients I met during this job. Seeing these people always made me think, 'You have no idea how you'll end up when you're older. It's important to look after these guys. You never know if one day that could be you.'

Give good into life and it will always come back to you.

After a 12-hour shift, I'd get in, sit down and before dinner was ready, I'd be snoring. My back was gone, my shoulders were gone, even driving the van the day after, my body was in so much pain, more than I'd experienced in boxing. That job was insane and I was only getting £800 a month.

Unfortunately, around that time, I had to experience another kind of pain. The kind I'd hope I'd never be exposed to. My wife was about six months' pregnant and I got a call to say she'd been taken to hospital. The doctors called me into this room.

"Mr Prince. Your wife's had some pains. We're very sorry."

I don't remember the rest of the conversation clearly, because I was dazed now, but the bottom line was that our son, Mark Prince Jr, was dead before his life had even started.

Because the pregnancy was so far gone, my wife had to continue with a normal birth. I remember sitting there, holding my baby boy and him not moving. Even though I knew he was dead, there was still a part of me that was hoping he'd open his eyes and start crying. The moment your child is born is a moment you tend to attach joy to, but not this time. It was grief and devastation. I didn't know how to deal with it.

We had a burial and it was only me holding this tiny little coffin. It was an experience I never wanted to go through again. No parent should ever have to bury their child.

★★★★★★★★★★★★★★★★★★★

Even though the hours were bad with the ambulance job, I decided to start doing youth work as a volunteer at the same time. It was actually my sister who came up with the idea.

I didn't get paid until a year later, as opposed to the three months they'd promised, but I loved it. The kids were responding well and I could see I was genuinely making a difference. By 2003, I'd managed to get qualified in NVQ levels 1 and 2 as a youth worker, then I did a counselling course.

The council asked me to be a support teacher at White Lion Youth Centre Islington, off Upper Street. I still get kind messages from some of the students to this very day.

One student who certainly did alright was Alexandra Burke. I used to mentor her and it makes me smile to see how far she's gone with her music. The flip side was that I'd recently got married and the youth work wasn't bringing in the money, so I was getting it in the ear, understandably.

Loving a job doesn't necessarily mean it pays well. In fact, the weight of money problems from the start of that marriage were so heavy that the bailiffs ended up coming to my house in Roedean Avenue, Enfield to repossess the place.

After receiving letters from the solicitors of the mortgage

lender, going to courts and losing the case, they said they were coming to repossess the house. Shortly after, the bailiffs turned up with a load of people including locksmiths. I went on my knees at the window and prayed to God to help me.

They came in the house and introduced themselves. They then asked me if I'd packed all my things and I said I hadn't, which was the truth, because I had no intention of moving.

They basically said they didn't want to lock all my stuff inside and asked me again to take all my stuff out. They also said that the people who'd sent them really wanted that property today.

But without no money, I knew I was screwed. I had nothing else to lean on apart from my faith in God, so I leant hard. I got on my knees by my settee and started praying.

While the bailiffs were waiting for me and I was walking around like a headless chicken, I saw a couple of them talking between themselves. Then they walked over all nonchalant and said: "Listen. We're gonna go now. Nobody else can take possession of this place apart from us. We're the only ones with the authority. But we're gonna go now. Good luck Mr Prince."

Before I could say a word, they drove off. I was left standing there wondering whether they were coming back with a lorry to take all my gear and lock it all up. Nothing. They just left.

I lost count of how many times I was in court over the next few years as they tried to take my house, but it never happened. I ended up selling the property in 2013!

★★★★★★★★★★★★★★★★★

I had to get a number of jobs on the side to make ends meet. One of them came via Junior, through a guy called Les Quinn.

Little did I know that Les would become a very close friend. Junior asked Les if there was anything going, he made a few phone calls and got me a job at the Youth Offending Service. I was mentoring young offenders, taking them out to do activities like canoeing and climbing. Kiyan used to come with me and we had some good laughs.

I also worked with an old mate and family friend called Laban Roomes. Now and then you meet people you know are always going to be a success, whatever they turn their hands to and Laban was one of them.

At the time he was building a gold-plating business, working out of a tent in his back garden. A few years later he ended up getting a deal on the programme *Dragons' Den*. He taught me how to gold plate phones, and within a few months I was getting pretty good at it, although I almost wrecked his house once. I was doing some work at his place, and had my younger sons Kishon, Malik and Micaiah, with me. Malik went to the toilet, washed his hands in the sink, but left the tap running with the plug in.

So there I was on the ground floor when suddenly I heard this dripping noise and looked up and saw this bulge in the ceiling. I ran up and saw the bathroom was totally flooded. I was worried the floor and ceiling below had been damaged, but thankfully everything was OK and Laban never even made a fuss.

One thing me and Laban always made sure of though; no matter how busy we were in work, we always made time for our kids.

Kiyan and his son Kain had joined the same football academy and their future and happiness meant everything to us. That's where the real wealth was.

13

Kiyan

"We were trying to get new players into the academy team, when one of the scouts gave me a recommendation about a kid called Kiyan. He said he was strong, fast and athletic. I thought, 'Sounds good.' I called his parents to check he was OK to come to the trial and they said yes.

On the night of the trials, I was walking across one of the pitches to get to where the Under-13s team were and I remember seeing quite a big guy and thinking, 'Who's that? Whoever it is, he's much bigger than anyone else. He should be with the Under-16s. Maybe he's on the wrong pitch.'

Then someone told me: "That's Kiyan Prince."

There was something about that name that was distinctive. Even before meeting him, the name had presence. It sounded like it would be connected to someone special.

Without a doubt, just based on that trial, I knew we needed to sign him up. It was a good decision, because it soon became apparent he was one of the best players in that team and nothing changed over the next three years.

I used to watch the games on a Sunday and he was always pretty much a standout for the Under-16s. He was big, rugged, fast, strong – bit of an old-fashioned English No. 9 really. He needed to brush up technically a bit, but that wasn't an issue, because he was scoring goals and running through everyone. He had something else which equally as positive – his personality.

It was huge. He had this energising effect on the team in training and in games, with his raw commitment. No matter how hard training was, he'd always have a smile on his face.

Everyone loved him and the kids all looked up to him in that team. He was the main man. He was intelligent, a leader, confident, but nice with it.

Out of all the lads in the academy, less than five percent will get football careers. Would he have gone on and played for the QPR first team? I can't see any reasons to the contrary. Technically, after four or five years of training, he would have continued to get better and better.

But based on his pace, power, athleticism, confidence, personality and most importantly, goalscoring ability at the time, teams would have been crying out for him. I wasn't privy to that kind of information, but I'm almost certain a number of top teams had their eyes on him."

Joe Gallen, 2017, (QPR Head of Youth Development/Youth team coach 2006)

I started seeing Tracy when I was 17 and I'll be the first to admit that my head wasn't screwed on properly at the time. Within a year of Kiyan being born in 1990, we split up, but looking back, we probably didn't even need to. Maybe if we had a break, that could have been helpful and we might have got back together, but we didn't.

Tracy decided to move to Edgware, but we made a strong pact that no matter what outside influences were happening in our lives, we would always bring up Tannisa and Kiyan together.

Tracy especially wanted them to have a father figure and wanted them to talk about their dad and experience good things with him, because she never had a father in her life.

Making sure the family dynamic still exists, even if there's issues with the parents, has always been very important to me.

I've got six children and even though they don't all share the same mum, one thing I've done is keep them together. I've always had this outlook. I'd say to them: "You're all brothers and sisters and this is how we are going to be as a family."

I wanted to give to them what I had growing up with my brothers and sister, that unity. Thankfully, Tracy was a very good partner in terms of making that happen. She would always call me and talk to me about Tannisa and Kiyan, and make me feel like I was a part of what was going on.

When Tannisa was born, I was so proud I was a father and loved that little girl to bits. What a cute, little beautiful thing. Then when Kiyan was born a couple of years later, I was over the moon that I now had a son. Kiyan was one of the cheekiest little chappies – he was naughty, but fun naughty.

That playfulness about him as a little kid was the best thing to see. I used to go around to my mate Slider's with Kiyan, as he had kids, and we used to sit there and laugh as young dads. There was this adventure playground near his house and Slider would say: "You know that's you innit. He's fearless. Look at the way Kiyan's scaling that wall. He's just like you!"

Then when it came to the PlayStation – oh my days. The kids were really competitive, but me and Slider were even worse. There was no mercy. We even made them cry on occasions. Those tables soon turned as they got older and they'd beat us all the time!

The other thing Kiyan adopted from me was the colour pink – my favourite colour. As Kiyan started to grow up, he asked his mum about the first time she saw me. Tracy told him: "When I first met your dad by the bus, he had a pink jumper on."

From then, that was his favourite colour, because in his mind it was like, 'Dad wore pink and Dad met Mum when he was wearing that.'

★★★★★★★★★★★★★★★★★

By the time he was seven, it became obvious Kiyan had serious talent. Despite having bad asthma, he was selected to run against all the other schools in the 100m at Barnet Copthall stadium. Well, he only bloody won it. That's when we really noticed he could run – fast. He was in the papers and everything.

A couple of years later, one of the mums of Kiyan's friends asked Tracy if he could play in a football match as they were short of a striker.

This lady's son played for a local team called Watling Boys. He was so excited when he heard, while Tracy was hoping it would help get rid of some of his energy.

Kiyan loved the match and Watling loved him as a player. He stayed with them for two seasons and they even gave him the nickname 'The Bullet', because he was so fast.

Then when he went to secondary school, he played for the school team and was top goalscorer. One day, when he was 11, one of his mates said: "They're doing trials at West Ham and I'm going along. Shall I put your name forward?"

"Sounds good, but let me ask my mum first," Kiyan said. The boy came round and Tracy asked him about how it all worked. She then called me and we were happy to let him attend.

The first couple of sessions, Tracy took him, so she could see how long the journey was and what the people were like. West Ham liked him straight away. We agreed that I'd take him to the away games and Tracy would take him to the home games.

The Prince of Peace

But then he got something called Osgood-Schlatter disease in his knee, which is quite common with teenage boys who run a lot. They basically said he needed to totally rest the knee for about five months otherwise he could damage all his ligaments.

He wasn't happy about it, because he was an active kid and missed football, but between me and Tracy, we both made sure he rested whenever he was around us.

Thankfully, his brothers and sisters always kept him busy and I have great memories of having them all over at my house for weekends and holidays. I'd pick them up and there would be me, Kiyan, Tannisa, Jodeci, Malik and Kishon, all crammed into my car.

Kiyan, being the joker he was, once dropped this fart and it was so bad we had to pull the car over to air it. Then back at the house, they all stayed in one room, but we always fitted everyone in. We'd even make up beds on the floor. We had a lot of fun together as a tight family. I really enjoyed those times.

When he did return to football, he came back with a vengeance. Months later, this same friend asked if Kiyan wanted to train in the park with him and the West Ham players. Kiyan went along. The guy taking the session was a scout for Arsenal, West Ham, QPR and a few others. He said: "Your son is really good. I'd like to put him forward for trials at QPR."

In the meantime, Arsenal had shown an interest and West Ham wanted him to come back. Tracy asked me: "What shall we do? West Ham is a real trek, whereas QPR is much, much closer. That's a better journey. And what about Arsenal?"

"All I can do is tell you how I feel," I replied. "West Ham had a really great youth team. But if he goes to Arsenal, he might be overlooked, because they've got some really good players

170

there already and I don't want him to have that pressure on his shoulders from day one. I want him to still enjoy his football while learning. I think his talent will shine through with QPR and if one day Arsenal want him in their team, or Chelsea, or whoever, they'll be able to judge him from his talent on the field. I don't want him getting lost in a big team's system and politics at a young age.

"For some reason, even though I don't know much about QPR and their youth system, that's the one I'd go with. I just feel they will appreciate Kiyan's talent more."

It just so happened that QPR's youth system is one of the best in the country. Tracy took him for his trials at QPR but the final decision rested with Kiyan. If he was going to do his best, he'd do his best where he felt most comfortable.

★★★★★★★★★★★★★★★★★

With QPR, West Ham and Arsenal on the table, another option then appeared. His school, the London Academy, wanted him to travel around the world and represent England at table tennis. Again, we left that decision to him. In the end, Kiyan decided to choose football over table tennis and QPR over West Ham. A week after the trials at QPR, Kiyan was getting ready to sign for the Under-13s.

For many kids, being signed up by a professional football club can be the worst thing to happen to them, because they can get dazzled by the falsehood of fame.

However, for Kiyan, it was the best thing that happened to him. When QPR signed him, he was on report at school, for being naughty. Nothing too serious, just chatting in lessons and acting the class clown. Tracy spoke to this lovely woman at QPR called Terry, who took care of the boys' welfare. She called Tracy and said: "They want to sign Kiyan. We want you to come in."

Tracy said: "Terry. Can you do me a favour? Kiyan's on report at the moment at school. Could you tell him, if you do sign him, that he needs to sharpen his act up at school?"

"Leave it with me!" she replied.

We went over to sign the paperwork and Terry turned to Kiyan and said: "We also want to know how your progress is at school. If you're not doing well at school, then we'll have to reconsider letting you play games on a Sunday."

That was it. I knew he would hate anything that would affect his football and within one conversation, he matured by about five years. I was so happy. Without a doubt, signing at QPR changed him. He now did his homework, didn't get into any more trouble at school and became a model student.

By now, he was so strong and talented that he even played for the Under 16s when he was only 14. Laban's son Kain had also joined QPR, but because he was a year younger, Kiyan acted as a bit of a mentor for him, due to how mature he already was, both physically and mentally. Kind of took him under his wing.

Even before he'd signed for QPR, he was already getting himself a name for breaking up fights on the football pitches at the park all the time.

I had no problems with Kiyan helping his mates out, but I also wanted him to have the right head on his shoulders and not do like I did at his age and scrap all the time. I used to tell him: "Whatever your passion or anger is, let your feet do the talking," and that's exactly what he did moving forward.

Kiyan

Tracy would always be worried about Kiyan, to the point she was paranoid. She used to worry the police were going to knock on her door one day and say: "Miss Cumberbatch. Kiyan's been found dead." But from an asthma attack.

I'd always be like: "Relax! He's fine. Ain't no harm coming to Kiyan." But one time her gut instinct was good and it had nothing to do with asthma.

Towards the end of 2005, Kiyan went to this party round the corner from the house. As it goes, his first and only party. It was around the time of his 15th birthday and Tracy didn't even want him to go.

Anyway; he went off and came back not long after midnight. The morning after, Tracy went into his bedroom and saw his clothes which he'd left on the floor from the night before. They were covered in blood.

She woke him up in a panic. "Why have you got blood splattered all over your clothes? What happened at this party last night?"

"Mum – calm down," he replied. Apparently some boy was standing right next to Kiyan, when some guys walked in and glassed this kid in the face and the blood went all over Kiyan's clothes. Me and Tracy agreed it was a really close call.

★★★★★★★★★★★★★★★★★

Second week of May, I was driving past Tracy's house. Normally every week or every other week Kiyan would stay at my house from Friday to Sunday, but sometimes, if I was passing, I'd drop in. This was one of those days. The weather was lovely, I had my hand weights in my car and thought I'd go and do some training with him. We did a nice session for conditioning and endurance in the garden, then after we just talked.

We had a good chat about life, training, football and how that was going. Just the usual banter between father and son. Hours would often pass without either of us noticing. We were close man, close.

The bond between Kiyan and his brothers and sisters was also tight, especially with Tannisa, because by now they'd reached an age where they'd do more together.

With Tannisa having a lot of male friends, they started enjoying being around Kiyan and started knocking on the door for him to come and play on his PlayStation. Tannisa used to joke that Kiyan was stealing her friends.

The truth is, it made Tannisa really glad to see her younger brother getting attention and being happy. Although he did wind her up to her limits on occasions.

By now, she'd started college and was studying childcare. She had to take this baby doll home that cried, pooped, needed to be changed and everything.

So there was Tannisa in the kitchen chatting with Tracy, while Kiyan was chatting and laughing with three of Tannisa's friends, when the doll started crying. All of a sudden it stopped and Tannisa walked into the living room, only to find the doll flung across the room, with the head pulled off.

Tannisa shouted: "Who's done this?" and Kiyan's pointed left to one of his mates. The other three pointed back to Kiyan and said: "It was him!"

Tannisa wanted to be angry, but couldn't and they all burst out laughing. They even managed to put the doll back together.

As tight as we were, I was first and foremost a father with

Kiyan and was always concerned about his safety, especially in the area we lived in. He might have been strong as a man, but as a 15-year-old, he still had a lot to learn.

I could start to see signs of myself shining through in him, so I wanted him to replicate the goodness I'd done in my life, but steer clear of the madness.

Around this time, there was on a knock on our front door and Kiyan went to answer. It was our neighbour, Jack, who was the same age as him. I was listening and Jack was complaining about a group of guys who were scaring him, picking on him, threatening and stuff. Kiyan calmed him and said: "Don't worry Jack. Everything will be alright."

Kiyan finished chatting with him and came back in the house. I told him: "Kiyan. Be careful. You're popular and you're the go-to guy. I used to be that guy and people would look to me to back them up, because they knew I could. Don't make that mistake and start doing that. Please. People on the street carry weapons now. Don't get involved in other people's stuff. I don't know how I'd survive if anything happened to you."

"Don't worry Dad. I'll be good," he replied.

Do you know what he did to make Jack feel better? He got up next morning and followed him on his paper round, just to make him feel confident that he had someone with him. He wasn't trying to play the tough guy, he was just trying to make Jack feel better – and it worked.

Little did I know, this was something Kiyan had been doing for years. He hated bullies and he hated seeing people left out in any way. The only problem is, most bullies are big cowards and when a coward realises they are out of their depth, they often resort to any means to win. Any means.

14

18 May, 2006

"*I dropped Kiyan off to school in the morning and that was the last I saw of him.*

In the afternoon I went to Carpetright in Colindale as me and Kiyan had talked about decorating the house and had picked out colour schemes. I'd wanted chocolate-coloured carpet for the passageway and he said "alright then mum," kind of like "whatever mum". So there I am in Colindale when my neighbour calls.

"Tracy. Have you heard?"

"Heard what?" I said.

"Kiyan's been stabbed. I just got a call from my daughter [who was at the same school as Kiyan]. You need to get up to the school now. I'll meet you there."

When I got the call that Kiyan had been stabbed, I knew he wasn't going to survive. Just a mother's instinct.

My heart was racing like mad. It's a 10-minute drive from Colindale to Edgware, but it felt like forever. When I got to the school, the area was cordoned off and loads of people were standing around. I can't remember who I went up to, but I said: "I'm Kiyan's mum." One of the teachers from the school said: "They're working on him in the ambulance." I hated that word 'working', because in my mind that meant they were basically trying to get somebody back to life. A police officer told me to wait in the car, which I did.

All these thoughts were going through my head. I couldn't fully understand what was going on. An air ambulance had been and gone, but there was a van still there. I didn't know what that meant. They were debating which hospital to take him to and I was thinking, 'Why are they taking so long? Why don't they just get him there already?'

I was waiting around the school for what felt like an hour. Maybe it was, maybe it wasn't, but that's what it felt like. During that time, I was told that they had to cut open Kiyan's stomach and massage his heart by hand. That must have been in the ambulance.

We followed the ambulance to the hospital in a police car. I had a horrible memory of standing in the hospital and Kiyan being wheeled past on a trolley in front of me, with blood dripping like mad from this trolley. I kept thinking, 'Where's this blood coming from?' The rest is just a blur."

Tracy Cumberbatch, 2017
(Kiyan Prince's mother)

Monday 15 May 2006, my wife picked up Tannisa from Tracy's, as she was spending the next four days with us, helping to look after my youngest son Micaiah, her 18-month-old brother. When my wife went to get her, Kiyan wasn't home from school yet, so Tannisa phoned him and got through to voicemail.

For absolutely no reason, she felt weirdly emotional when she left the message, like she was really going to miss being at home with her brother and Tracy. "I'm going to Dad's now. I'll see you when I get back on Thursday," she said.

Thursday 18 May was a lovely, warm, sunny day. I got up, then headed to Laban's around 9am to gold plate some phones.

I'd been working for Laban for about a year by this point and was pretty quick at plating, which was handy as there was an explosion of orders for the Nokia 8800 and we were doing literally hundreds per week.

Later that afternoon, about half three, my phone rang. It was Tannisa. She was at my house with Micaiah, which was only five minutes from where I was.

I assumed she was calling to say he was acting up or something, but what she said and how she said it is something that would stay with me for the rest of my life.

"Kiyan's been stabbed. Kiyan's been stabbed," she screamed hysterically. I didn't want to jump to conclusions. As I picked up my car keys I said: "What else do you know?"

"Nobody can give a clear picture of what had happened apart from that he's collapsed outside school after being stabbed," she replied.

"OK. Calm down. Find out what's happened. I'm coming home right now," I said.

The second I got off the phone, Tannisa started calling her friends to keep an eye on Tracy, because she was up at the school by then and would have been in a bad way.

I was working on an emergency order for Laban, but now I had my own emergency to attend to.

"I've got to go. Kiyan's been stabbed..."

Laban interrupted me: "Get over there straight away. I'll check up on you later."

I headed to my house as quickly as I could, picked up Tannisa and Micaiah, because whatever we were going to be around next, I didn't want him to be around it. I called Mum: "Can you look after Micaiah? I'll tell you what's going on later."

I didn't tell her what had happened to Kiyan because I didn't want to stress her out, but I had a feeling she might find out the story from someone else before I got the chance. She knew something was up though.

Tannisa and Micaiah got in the back seats and as we closed the doors, I said a prayer out loud to God. "Save my son. Don't let him die."

There was more to the prayer, but I said it in my head, because I didn't want Tannisa to hear.

'If he doesn't survive, help me to accept it.'

I don't know where that last bit came from. I then turned the keys in the ignition and then headed off to Mum's.

Mum had only just come home after having spent a year in hospital, due to a severe stroke. At the time of it happening, she'd been given a 30 per cent chance of survival and couldn't walk. Here I was now asking her if she could look after my baby. I didn't want to ask her, but I had no choice.

Micaiah and Kiyan had a really close bond. Whenever a group of people would come into the room, it was always Kiyan's smiley face that would cause Micaiah to laugh and go towards him.

So there we were in the car now, Tannisa was in the back with Micaiah and she was getting a lot of phone calls. Although Micaiah was just a baby, there was a look on his face like he kind of knew something wasn't right. Every time Kiyan's name was mentioned he'd looked bemused as opposed to happy.

It was very difficult for me to stay focused on driving with Tannisa sounding so frantic, talking to all these people about what was going on. I was taking in pieces of the conversations.

One moment she was speaking to one of her friends who

said: "Trust me, he's alright, he's alright," which comforted us, because these friends were at Kiyan's school.

But then seconds later we started to get all sorts of new information. "There's an air ambulance there... A tent is now over the area as it's a crime scene... He's being taken in for surgery... It's bad." That's when it went quiet in the car.

We dropped Micaiah off at Mum's, then me and Tannisa jumped back in the car. The phone calls were still non-stop. One second Tannisa would be saying: "He's at the school" so I'd floor the accelerator and head over that way.

Two seconds later she got another call saying he was being moved by ambulance. But to where? Which hospital? The destination changed a couple of times, but once it was confirmed as the Royal London Hospital, on the Whitechapel Road, we then had to work out the best route, as we didn't have a sat-nav.

My phone was also ringing continuously but I had to ignore it. After a while, I put it on silent.

Kiyan's stabbing was now all over the national news. Television and radio were all talking about it, while newspapers were getting the story ready for front-page coverage. The sickening part was that Tannisa was getting calls from Kiyan's friends saying that the press were offering them money to tell their story of what they'd seen. What sort of human beings do that?

We finally got to the hospital. I don't remember where we parked, how we got out of the car, I just remember us being in there. We went to a waiting room, where my sister was with Tracy and a load of others, crying and hugging. Tracy ran over to Tannisa in hysterics, then turned to me and said: "He's gone to theatre. The surgeon is trying to keep him alive."

I tried to keep positive and just said: "OK."

It was quiet in that room. Nobody spoke. The only sound was us pacing up and down, breathing heavily and worrying about what news we'd be getting.

Tannisa found it really difficult to see Tracy in that broken state and struggled to find anything to say. In the end, she went outside and kept answering calls from friends and family.

Soon after she walked out, the surgeon walked in.

"How's Kiyan?" I asked. I can still picture his face as he replied and the feeling that ran through my belly.

"I'm sorry. I tried to keep him alive. I opened his chest, massaged his heart with my hand to try and keep it going..."

Me and Tracy both started screaming in a way I'd never heard and will never forget.

★★★★★★★★★★★★★★★★★★

A policeman had now gone outside to see Tannisa. The second he appeared, she started to well up. He looked at her and just shook his head. Tannisa started screaming uncontrollably.

I didn't know how to take the news, so rage took over. I began punching the wall. I mean really punching it, like I wanted to break something. I was pacing up and down, and didn't realise there was blood trailing behind me from my hands. I just carried on kicking and punching stuff.

The police soon turned up and tried to restrain me. As they came in, I remember thinking, 'I've never seen a policeman that big before. He's done a serious amount of weights.'

But it didn't matter how big and strong they were, they weren't restraining me. They tried but could see the state I was in, so they let me go until I calmed myself down.

After about five minutes, they asked us to go in to a room and identify Kiyan's body.

It was surreal as this copper stood there silent in the corner. I was there to identify my dead son. It was happening, I was there doing it, but in my head it wasn't totally registering.

He was still warm. Still warm. Still warm. He looked like he was just sleeping on this inclined bed.

He had a white sheet covering him up to his shoulders and there were spots of blood coming through around the chest area. His arms were flat by his sides, with the palms of his hands facing upwards.

They didn't let you see where he got stabbed, but I could see his arm, which was cut up and looked like he'd probably been trying to block the knife from going into his chest a number of times. One blow obviously got through. There was also a cut on his head where he'd fallen over after being stabbed.

I started talking to him and kissing him, telling him how much I loved him. Tracy just said to him calmly: "Don't worry darling. Mum will be with you one day."

Tannisa was saying: "Wake up Kiyan, wake up. Get up. You're alright. Get up. Come on. Wake up."

Soon, Tracy's brother Dean had to take Tannisa outside.

I went from being at Kiyan's side to wanting to kill the kid that had stabbed him. As the night went on, more and more people turned up who were friends of the family or school friends of Kiyan. I was now trying to get any information off anyone. Where's this guy live? Who knows this guy? Nobody knew anything. Or so I thought.

The truth is, moments after Kiyan had been stabbed, Tannisa had been told that the guy who'd stabbed him was called

Hannad Hasan. He was a year older than Kiyan and was a mate of Tannisa's. Well, a former mate.

Tannisa was trying to contact him to ask what had happened but he wasn't answering his phone.

Nobody had told me because they knew I'd go ballistic.

Nobody had told the police because a number of people on the street wanted to deal with this their own way.

As far as I knew at this point, the killer was still unknown.

Back at the hospital, the police were still trying to calm me down. I didn't care about them and what they wanted to do. Procedures and all that.

I said: "If you don't get him before me, I'll get him. I'm going to kill this guy myself."

They kept saying: "Mr Prince, we don't want that to happen. Please stay calm. Let us do our job. We can do this. We have information and he won't escape for too long. We're going to catch up with him."

I said: "Whatever, man. I'm going to do it. It's not a problem."

I was now starting to plan my revenge and was almost having an imaginary conversation with the murderer.

I was thinking, 'If I can't find you, I'll go to your house. The first person that comes to your door, doesn't matter if it's your mum, your dad, whoever – they're gonna get it. They're gonna get to feel some of this. What I've got. What I'm going through.'

Kiyan was now going cold. I didn't like that. I didn't want to see him not real, actually dead dead. That sounds the stupidest thing to say, but that's how I felt.

When he was warm, there was still a little bit of life, but now his colour was leaving him and his lips were going blue. I didn't want to be talking to that empty figure. It was like Kiyan had officially gone from that room. I was now getting ready to leave. A father abandoning his 15-year-old son, forever.

That image haunted me and still does to this very day. I knew at that moment that I'd never see him again. There wasn't going to be an open coffin or nothing like that. I had to remember what I had of him. The day Kiyan died, I felt like I died. It was worse because we looked so alike.

We left and everyone was offering me a lift and telling me I couldn't drive, but I did. What a drive over to Tracy's that was. I don't think I went over 20 miles an hour all the way.

Cars beeping, pulling their windows down and shouting at me. I was in my own little world, numb, in shock and in a world of grief.

Tracy's house was packed. My brothers and sister were there, Tracy's brothers, all their kids, all the cousins and loads of friends. Throughout the night, more people kept appearing.

Phones were going even more now. "What's happened? Is it true? Who did it?"

We all had the same answer.

"He's dead. He's dead. He's dead."

I don't know how many times we all said that and it didn't get any easier each time.

Some phone calls I remember distinctly. My barber Eddie for example. He'd been cutting my hair since I was 21 and I don't let anyone else cut it apart from him to this very day. He's like a star barber. Everyone for miles would get their hair cut by Dennis and Eddie. Their shop is always full up. He'd watched my kids grow up and Kiyan had been getting crisp haircuts from Eddie since day one.

When he called, he had this cagey sound in his voice. "Errrr

Prince. Ummm. I just saw something on the telly yeah. Ummm. I just phoned to hear you tell me that it's not true."

Then there was a silence, before I managed to say: "It's true."

Eddie screamed out: "Noooooooooooo. No. No."

Then a noise came out of me. That's all I can call it, a noise, because a noise like that had never come out of me before. It was like a slow built-up wail that got louder and louder. It was insane.

★★★★★★★★★★★★★★★★★★

19 May 2006. I woke up in the early hours and started wailing again. Darren came down and tried to console me, but nobody could help me at that point. A full house can sometimes be a good thing when you're feeling down, but it had the reverse effect on me, because all I could hear were people upstairs with Tracy in tears. I was worried about her.

Tracy carried that boy for nine months and gave birth to him. There's always that special extra dimension, that bond which a mother has with their child. She loved that boy so, so much.

Whenever she'd drop Kiyan off at mine, she'd kiss him about 20 times. I'd be laughing and Kiyan would be laughing, embarrassed like teenagers do. "Alright Mum!"

I always used to say: "Your mum loves you. Embrace that."

Kiyan was the apple of her eye and the last thing he said was now plastered all over the media: "If these are my last words, tell my mum I love her," which was tearing us both up inside.

By about 8am, the road in front of the house looked like a crowd emptying from a stadium. These were people just wanting to pay their respects. People who might have only met

Kiyan a few times, but had been touched by his warm heart. One lady knocked at the door and really politely said to Tracy: "I hope you don't mind me knocking. My daughter used to see your son at the bus station all the time and they would chat. She begged me to find out where you lived, just so I could tell you what a lovely boy he was."

It carried on like that for the rest of the day.

Tannisa had decided to put on Kiyan's clothes and was asking if anybody could take her to his school, because it was a Friday and she wanted to be where he would be on a normal Friday.

When she arrived at the school, assembly had just finished and all Kiyan's friends and teachers were all coming out with flowers and notes to place on the spot where he'd been stabbed. The playground was full of stuff from all kind of students. Black, white, boy, girl, they all loved him and that made us very proud.

When they saw Tannisa, they all came running over, crying and hugged her. Apart from the sound of sobbing, the school was silent. The teachers let her come in and do as she pleased, because they were sharing in the same grief.

She then asked his friends to take her to where he would've been right now. They walked her to his art class and she sat there on this chair and had a breakdown, while the teacher and students sat there either quiet or crying.

The tributes by now were coming in hard and fast. The teachers and pupils at Kiyan's school had said some lovely things and the then-caretaker manager at QPR, Gary Waddock, said to *The Mirror*: "The whole club is mourning the loss of one of our own. We are all devastated. Kiyan was certainly one for the future, a talented lad who wanted to forge a career in football."

The article also compared Kiyan's ability to Theo Walcott

in terms of his speed and ball control, which was lovely to read, but sad to know that he'd never enjoy that limelight or opportunity now.

Frank Warren sent a lovely letter of condolence, while the Arsenal manager Arsène Wenger also wrote a really nice letter to me, Tracy and our children, offering his and the club's deepest sympathies, as Kiyan was an Arsenal fan.

With all this happening, the search for Kiyan's murderer was still on. The BBC website had a headline of 'Boy hunted in Kiyan murder probe,' but because the suspect [Hannad] was only 16, the media weren't allowed to mention his name.

The police were out looking for him, but they weren't the only ones. My 'boys' on the street phoned me. These were people who had watched Kiyan grow up and were hurting at this news.

"Prince. We're going to handle this. We're going to take care of this for you."

I told them: "No you're not. He's my son and that's my choice. That's down to me."

The phone went quiet. "Aight Prince. Cool."

It would have been an easy option to say: "Thanks. I'll leave that with you," but whether I was going to retaliate or make peace, that could only come from me. Thankfully, the police took that decision out of our hands.

They'd told us that if they hadn't found the suspect by midnight on the Friday, they would release his details to the press. Literally a few minutes before midnight that Friday, we got a phone call to say his mum had given him up. Although it didn't bring Kiyan back, it was the first step to getting justice served. The first step of many, unfortunately.

15

Aftermath

"Am I sleeping? Have I slept at all? This is insomnia."
Chuck Palahniuk, 'Fight Club'

Although I didn't know at the time, Tracy's house would be my home for the next four months and I wasn't alone. Tracy's three-bed house was stacked. If people weren't on the settee, they were in Kiyan's room or on the floor. Tannisa's room alone had eight people in there at one point.

I started staying in Kiyan's room all the time. His bedroom became my bedroom. I just needed to be near him. I used to get up and want to see him, hear him, but I knew that wasn't going to happen.

I could smell him though. I'd go to his clothes and inhale hard every last ounce of his smell that each fibre had to offer. Again and again. If I wasn't smelling his clothes, I'd be wearing them.

Even when we went to his school a few days later to see where he'd been killed, I was wearing an Ecko basketball top that I'd bought him, which he loved. It was one of his favourite jackets. I've still got that top.

When I saw the newspaper a few days later with me wearing

his clothes, I broke down in tears and at the same time thought, 'Kiyan would have been laughing at his dad wearing some clothes that weren't even fitting him properly.'

But I didn't care. It was his stuff and I had it on.

And when it came to sleep, that was a luxury I'd taken for granted before. I had so many things and thoughts running through my head, there was no way I could rest.

'What actually happened on the day? I know Kiyan can defend it,' as we say on the roads. 'So how did this guy just stab my son like this?'

As the days went on, it got worse. The shock was starting to set in and I hadn't even begun to tap into the reservoir of water to be released out of my eyeballs. Tears just poured out of me.

When I did manage to close my eyes, all I had were vivid dreams of Kiyan. Then when I woke up from a couple of hours of delirious napping, I'd often be crying because Kiyan was so alive in those dreams.

Every time I woke up, it was a reminder he was dead.

Tracy was going through the same and we'd be telling each other our dreams. She always dreamt of when he was young. It was always when he was about three or four, but he never spoke.

She'd wake up in the middle of the night crying, as if he was still here, thinking, 'Why am I dreaming about him at his cutest?' That was just playing with her heartstrings.

Unfortunately, that wailing noise I'd let out previously would be heard several more times in the coming months along with some worrying behaviour.

There was a coffee table at Tracy's house and I was shuffling around it like a patient on a mental ward on heavy medication.

Every now and then I'd start that wailing sound, then I'd stop, but I never stopped moving round this table. Even if I got interrupted by a phone call, I'd take it, then come back and go round the coffee table again. I must have looked a right state.

During those months, the only place I found refuge was in my car. I was able to spend time on my own and speak with God, but it was also somewhere I could get away from everything that was going on at the house.

I'd only allow certain people in the car with me, like say Laban or Darren and most of the time it was silent. It was inspiring for them to hear me speaking more positively when I was in there. It was like God was starting to answer my prayer I'd said on the way to the hospital when I'd asked him for the strength to deal with Kiyan's death.

My brother Colin was like a shadow to me at the time and wanted to ensure I had my privacy, as he could obviously see I needed some space.

The thing with Colin, he's quite a figure of meanness when he wants to be and on this particular day, I'd gone for a walk down this road I used to take Kiyan when he was a little kid, on the swings. When I got into the house, Colin was there with this big expensive camera.

"Where did you get that?" I said. "Flipping press out there bothering you all the time. I just took his camera," he replied.

"No bruv. No. Give me it," I said.

I took the camera and walked out to see this cowering guy parked outside the house.

"Here. Take the camera. I apologise for everything," I said.

The photographer was panicking, saying sorry, so I interrupted him: "You've got nothing to be sorry for. You're doing your job. Do what you need to do, as long as it doesn't bother my family. Nobody's going to trouble you anymore, so don't feel threatened. My brother's just emotional. He's looking out for me. Don't be fearful. Just give us some space."

Another time, I was at the school as I wanted to see where my son died and ended up having another episode with the press. I was chatting to a lot of his close friends who were also hurting from losing their mate and we shared some special moments.

They took me round to the spot, when suddenly one of the kids said something to this press guy and he responded, giving it the large. Next thing, a fight's about to kick off between them. A grown man and a kid. I went over and put him in check.

"Are you serious? My son's just been killed and you're going to kick off with this kid, who's just lost his mate. Don't you understand his emotions? Are you not old enough to control yourself in this situation? Don't blame a single thing on these kids. Squash that anger you have, not their grief."

★★★★★★★★★★★★★★★★★★

The closest I came to getting into trouble during this time was not with any media people, but randomly, with the dustbin men outside Tracy's house.

They came round weekly and because the house had been full with tons of people, we had a lot of rubbish. They knew who we were and all about Kiyan, but decided to be funny about the rubbish. Some real jobsworths.

When they went past the house on this day, they left the rubbish outside Tracy's. Her brother Dean, who's not an aggressive guy at all, went out to sort it. Next thing, all I could hear was someone shouting: "The dustbin man has got Dean. They're beating him up. Help him.'

I flew outside and saw that this dustbin man had Dean in a headlock and was trying to choke him. I ran straight over to them and bang, I hit him with an elbow and knocked him flat out on the floor.

Then the other two dustbin men decided to have a go at me and that didn't go well for them either. Next thing, Colin ran out and they all backed up.

The guy down still hadn't moved, so the dustbin men now called the police. In the meantime, everyone was trying to get me back inside. As I walked in, I could tell the guy on the floor was not knocked out, he was playing clever.

The police arrived and soon after an ambulance, which took this guy's ass away. I was thinking, 'He's trying to make a case to get some money'.

The police were understanding, but at the same time, they had to do their job. They told me that they needed to arrest me, even though everyone explained I'd been defending Dean.

We had some good family liaison officers, but it was one particular policeman I'll always remember. The police booked a day for me to come in and this officer said: "Look. Because of what's going on, we don't want to arrest you."

They also said that they thought the dustbin man was trying to milk the situation, but more than anything, they expressed their concern for what I'd been going through.

So they didn't want to aggravate things by charging me, which would have ended up in the papers. The press would have had a field day.

You can imagine the headline: 'Former boxer and father of

murdered footballer beats up dustman.' The police were cool and I'll always remember their support at that time.

Everyone was worried for me. I wasn't eating, I wasn't sleeping, I was drinking a lot of alcohol and my friends were bringing me weed so I wouldn't feel the pain.

There were no comedowns from the drugs and alcohol, because there were no go-ups. I was so deep in grief that I wasn't getting buzzed by anything I took. It just put me in a zone and kept me there.

The thing with grief though is if you don't tackle it, it's gonna creep up on you and crush you later. If you deal with it, the pain will lessen.

It's like an infection that gets worse and then one day you take off the bandage and reveal what's really going on underneath. And by then it's a mess. You've got to deal with it while it's fresh.

Thankfully, we were blessed with a lot of good people around us, especially Mum and my sister. "Mark. Have you eaten? You've got to eat." They kept me going. No doubt.

My mum came round at a time when I really needed her. It was like I was a kid again. She hated seeing her boy going through so much pain and whenever she saw me suffering, she had to leave the room.

She had enough to deal with, between her stroke and Dad, who was really ill by this stage, but she just kept on motoring forward, which I was struggling with.

Something else was causing me a lot of pain and if it wasn't for Tracy's intervention, the suffering would have continued a lot longer.

When Kiyan died, I took a picture of him on that hospital bed, when he was dead, but still warm. I kept it on my phone and would look at it occasionally. That's when I started to develop panic attacks for the first time in my life. My heart was going like mad, my breathing was all over the place and it was like I was losing control of my whole body.

It used to upset me because I wanted to look at his picture, but when I did, I'd panic.

In the end, Tracy said: "Mark, you need to get rid of that picture. If you don't, it will keep taking you back to that place, that sadness."

This went on for a while, but in the end I deleted it. She was right. I needed to move on. We all did.

★★★★★★★★★★★★★★★★★★

The layers and levels of stress were unbelievable. One of the things that people forget when a loved one dies is that you're not just coping with everything that's going on, but the financial struggles that death brings.

You've got people round your house all the time offering their condolences and you need to cater for them. On top of that, we had the funeral costs hanging over us, which was money we just didn't have.

It's at this point I need to give a very special mention to QPR. They didn't know about our financial situation and never asked, they just approached us and said: "We want to pay for the funeral," and I mean all the costs.

Tracy said: "You really don't have to."

"No, we really want to do it," they said.

Apart from the catering, which we insisted on, they paid for the plot, the cars and everything else. They were absolutely amazing. As a football team and club, even though our son wasn't there a long time, they were so supportive. The Gallen brothers [Joe and Kevin] even went to visit Tracy at home and brought a priest with them.

I couldn't have wished for a better club for my son to have represented. If they looked after Kiyan like that, I'm sure they look after every young person at QPR, in the same way.

But it was more than just that. The QPR supporters were unbelievable. In the immediate hours after Kiyan was stabbed, there were flowers being left at the stadium, scarves, messages, cards, photos, football tops, you name it.

Throughout the day and the weeks that followed, the collection of tributes and messages of condolences grew and grew and grew. Although Kiyan wasn't in the first team, he was a QPR player and that made him part of the family.

The next game after the funeral, a minute's silence was observed at Loftus Road before the match against Southend. Again, it just showed the true backbone of that club.

We can never thank everyone, but we'd just like to say from the bottom of our hearts – the players, the supporters, the QPR family – thank you.

★★★★★★★★★★★★★★★★★★

Soon it was time for the funeral. I've already talked about it in detail at the start of this book, and it's very painful to keep going back into it again.

The day itself, the burial and everything that went with it, was all soul-destroying.

Sometimes when you lose a loved one, you have the space

and time to move on. With Kiyan being the centre of a murder investigation, we didn't have that luxury. We were about to enter the Central Criminal Court of England and Wales, otherwise known as the Old Bailey. There we would relive some of the worst memories in graphic detail, over and over again.

16

Trials and Tribulations

"Court hears of stabbed schoolboy
*Kiyan's last moments." **The Guardian***
website – 17 October 2006

The truth is, I'll never know exactly what happened on 18 May 2006 between Kiyan's best mate and Hannad, and how serious it was. Were they mucking about and testing each other's strength out, or was it a real fight?

All I do know is that Kiyan rocked up and saw a mate of his in a tussle, then the guy pulled a knife out. I'd gone through it all a million times in my head, but now was the time to get a lot of my questions answered.

Kiyan got stabbed in May, was buried in June and by October we were in the courthouse. It took ages to get to this stage because the barristers were preparing their cases. Mind you, for a murder trial like this it could have been a lot longer. So from that side, we were lucky to have had the trial in five months.

Arriving at the Old Bailey on 16 October was a form of closure for us, because the sooner we went into the courtroom and saw Hannad get convicted, the sooner we could all walk out of there and get on with our lives.

If only it were that simple.

Trial one, day one, court number one. We were in the main room at the Old Bailey and both mine and Tracy's families turned out in droves, along with loads of ours and Kiyan's friends. There were only a handful of people there for Hannad.

Our lawyer Nick Hilliard was not only good, but was a nice guy. He briefed us about what was going on then we went inside.

It wasn't the first time I'd been in the Old Bailey. In 2004, I was working for BT as handyman in Holborn and used to walk over in my lunch breaks and sit in the gallery to see the cases.

Whatever went on there was always high profile and I found it really interesting listening to see how the proceedings worked. But I would have never thought in a million years I would have been in there under these circumstances, sitting there wearing our pink shirts in support of Kiyan.

When I looked up at the gallery, which was packed, loads of other people were also wearing something pink. That was nice to see. We were limited to the numbers we could have in the court on the ground level, but thankfully, I had Tracy and my brothers and sister with me, which was a massive support.

Hannad walked in wearing a grey suit, white shirt and no tie. He had a very hard face on him and it was difficult to tell if he was acting arrogant, was angry or scared. He didn't have that 'I'm so sorry' look about him.

He almost looked bored, like he was sitting in a maths class, or maybe he was playing the part like an actor who knew they were going down. Either way, the second he walked in, rage started to build up inside me.

That first day was all about giving an overview of the case. Hannad's brief admitted his client killed Kiyan, but was only going to plead to the charge of manslaughter, which made me even more mad.

Nick had told us to be calm and not do or say anything stupid, but it was hard knowing they would be trying to defend this guy when he was obviously guilty.

He kept us well informed throughout the trial and kept it real with us. He told us when Hannad's brief was going to try and get away with things, that he'd press him hard. He was basically asking us to have faith in him, which we did.

Tuesday 17 October. Nick refused Hannad's plea for manslaughter and he was now on trial for murder. Because Hannad was 16, his name had been kept from the press, but trust me when I say, a lot of people knew that he was the killer.

He might have been sitting there in the court with his little lawyer friends, but we wanted his name to be aired publicly, so that he'd have to take the full brunt and shame for his actions. But patience was what we needed at this stage. Patience.

Nick now started to run through the events from 18 May.

Kiyan saw his mate in a play fight with Hannad, walked over and told them to "stop playing around," then Hannad turned to Kiyan, asked what was going on then pushed him.

Kiyan pushed him back. Hannad then put his hand in his pocket and said: "If you push me one more time, see what I'll do to you."

Kiyan pushed him, Hannad pulled out the knife, got Kiyan in a headlock and then stabbed him. Kiyan's mate then jumped at him and wrestled him over to a car, which resulted in the wing mirror coming off.

One witness remembered: "He went for his leg and chest. He was stabbing everywhere. Kiyan made a painful noise. It was pretty fast."

Another said that he'd been stabbed in the stomach and arm, then Kiyan collapsed to the floor. That was horrible to hear.

If that wasn't bad enough, one witness said he saw Hannad stab Kiyan in the arm as he lay on the ground and another said that if it wasn't for another one of the students jumping in, Hannad would have most likely carried on stabbing.

At that moment, it sounds like Hannad's red mist had cleared and he suddenly realised the implications of what he'd done. Being the coward he was, he turned to all the students in a panic and said: "You can't grass me up, I was just playing."

Then he did a runner, before passing the knife to one of his mates to hide. Didn't matter though, because they found the knife soon after arresting Hannad's sorry ass.

There was a teacher, Miss Hernandez, who had seen Kiyan's mate and Hannad 'playfighting', but when it looked like it was getting out of control, she walked over. When she got there, Kiyan was already on the floor, but she didn't know how serious it was. She immediately called for help.

Miss Hernandez was badly traumatised by the experience and when she took the stand, she broke down in tears.

I'd just like to say that we're grateful for everything she did on that day and there's nothing more she could have done for our son. She should always remember that.

The police arrived within minutes and very soon after an ambulance van and an air ambulance turned up. On the day, we couldn't understand why they weren't just taking him to a hospital, any hospital, but it turned out that his wound was so bad that putting him in the helicopter would have been too much of a risk. Although by that stage, it wouldn't have mattered anyway, as he was already having a major heart attack from the wound.

When the surgeon stepped up to give evidence, he said that the knife had punctured Kiyan's left ventricle and his heart filled up with blood. I hated listening to all the details. It was horrible.

Hannad's defence counsel had made out that Kiyan had punched [not pushed] him and then he pulled out the knife.

When he apparently punched him the second time, that's when he got Kiyan in the headlock. He said he didn't intend to stab Kiyan in the heart, but wanted to cut him on the arm to scare him. His exact words were: "Just a little scratch there, but it went deep in ... cos I never used a knife before."

He said he'd been carrying this blade for ages, but thought it was like a toy and had never used it on anyone before.

The worst bit was that he referred to Kiyan as a friend and said he would never hurt a friend like that. The fact that he made out they were mates made my blood boil.

Listening to the defence incensed me. You start learning about the justice system, which you soon start to believe should be called the injustice system, because it's hard to find justice in a system that seems to protect a murderer more than the victim.

I was looking at the brief for Hannad and thinking, 'Are you for real? How do you even do this job? You're not stupid. You know that's such a dickhead excuse. I didn't mean for the knife to hurt him? Just a little scratch? Are you serious?'

He even said he didn't realise the knife could penetrate human skin. Now that's taking the piss. Think about it; if you scratch something, you run something over the surface. When you stab, it requires a motion that goes forward, not sideways. Then to make sure that stab is effective, it needs force.

I saw Kiyan's arm at the hospital and there was enough evidence there to show he'd tried to stab him a number of times. There was no scratching going on. You can play fight, but you don't play stab and friends certainly don't stab each other.

★★★★★★★★★★★★★★★★★★

I won't lie; from the moment Hannad was caught, I wanted to kill him. When I went home that evening after the second day in court, I called my mate Kevin and started to cry.

"I'm going to break this guy's fucking neck," I screamed.

Kevin sobbed as he listened to me. The power from the anger was electrifying me. I wanted to release it on his neck.

Third day, I woke up and thought, 'Do it today.' The day before, he'd walked past me and I couldn't believe how close he was. A foot or so in front of me. So this day I'd worked when he walked past me again, I was breaking that neck. I turned to my brother Colin and said: "Today's the day. I'm gonna get him."

When Hannad walked out, the security was sloppy and let him walk out about three feet in front of them, as if they were trying to bait me. Darren looked over and saw the look in my face and you could see his 'oh shit' expression.

I tried to position myself ready for him, but suddenly these three policemen stood in front of me, asking how I was. Maybe they saw something in my body language or they just knew from day one that I had this mad look on my face, but either way, of all the days they decided to have a chat with me and block my chance to kill this guy, this was the one.

You sometimes hear about how the friends and family of the accused are very hostile towards a victim's family, but that was not the case here. No way. Hannad's lot were absolutely terrified to look over. I used to stare at them like, 'Please give me an excuse to come over to you. Look at me wrong, say something, do something, because I want to get you.'

The Wednesday and Thursday more witnesses came forward. One of those was Kiyan's mate, who Hannad had been play fighting with. The thing with Kiyan's mate was, he had this stammer and his self-esteem wasn't the best.

The defence sensed his insecurity and tried to take him apart. He wasn't like one them boys in the hood who would respond with: "What you talking about? Why you trying to twist my words?" It weren't like that. This brief kept at him and tried to confuse him, tried to fill his head and the jurors with doubt.

"I thought you said..." the brief kept saying, as he tried to get him to admit something that would work in Hannad's favour. Then he'd go quiet. I was dying to shout out: "Just tell this twat what time it is mate!"

However, when it came down to it and the going got tough, Kiyan's mate didn't budge. At the point we thought he would crumble, he never changed his story or backed down. We knew how tough it was for him to do that and we'll never forget what he did for Kiyan in that court.

Another witness mentioned Hannad had said to Kiyan's mate: "Who the fuck do you think you are? You think you are big so you can come and stand up against me?" Then when Kiyan came over, he said: "What – you think you're big as well?"

The same witness also mentioned that the silver knife had a red handle and was a Swiss Army knife. Before it was just a knife, but now they were helping us to visualise the tool that killed our son, which was horrible.

They also made it clear that this was not a flick knife. A Swiss Army knife needs to have the person intentionally select the blade they want and then use it. Without a doubt this was deliberate.

Then, when he pulled out the knife, Kiyan tried to grab his hand. That's when he got Kiyan in the headlock.

The same witness said that Hannad had taunted Kiyan by saying: "Who's laughing, who's laughing?" just before stabbing him. Knowing how Kiyan was, he wouldn't have given off any signals of fear, although inside he was probably nervous.

From Hannad's perspective, that probably made him scared and angry for looking the weaker person and then decided the only way he could be in a position of power was to use the knife.

He also had about half a dozen mates with him, so if he was seen to be beaten by a younger kid, he'd have been the laughing stock. The only way he could look like the big man was to beat Kiyan with a knife.

More information and colour started to come from each new witness. One said that once Kiyan had been stabbed, he lifted his t-shirt, touched where he'd been stabbed, saw the blood, then said to Hannad: "Why are you doing this to me?"

Then he collapsed on the ground as everyone around was screaming and running over to try and help. Hannad then stabbed him in the arm as he was on the ground.

The witness then mentioned that while Kiyan was on the floor, almost passed out, he said: "Mum," which made me and

Tracy break down big time. He then dropped to the ground and hit his head on the pavement.

The stress in that first week was unreal and not only affected me mentally, but physically too. A couple of days into the trial, after the proceedings had finished, I went to Slider's house. I'd hardly slept in three days and was there having some weed, when next thing he caught me as I started to pass out.

A couple of days later, I was at a coffee shop with Darren and a girl he was seeing at the time. She said: "You don't look great. I really think you need to get checked out at the hospital. You're not eating, you're not sleeping, you're passing out."

She took me to the hospital. They put all the wires on me, did an ECG [electrocardiogram] and all that, then basically said it was a manifestation of the grief I was going through, which had now surfaced by way of exhaustion and stress.

They were basically saying my body was at its limits of being able to tackle everything.

The second week of the trial, we were all waiting for Hannad to walk in and defend his case, but nope. Nothing. He refused to give any evidence. Instead, there were a load of tapes for the defence to listen to of Hannad's interviews with the police.

For the next three days, the jury chewed over the evidence from the conversations, but were struggling to reach a decision. What was so difficult to see here? He stuck to his manslaughter plea, but not murder. Me and Tracy were going mad.

Unfortunately, something else happened during those three days which took our attention away from the trial. This was inevitable, but nonetheless very hard to deal with.

★★★★★★★★★★★★★★★★★★

There's never a good time for a loved one to pass away, but getting dealt a double blow was tough.

The year before Kiyan was stabbed, Dad's health started going downhill pretty quickly. He couldn't sleep at night, because he couldn't keep his water. Every five minutes he'd be saying to Mum: "I want to go again."

At one point, she never knew what sleep was. Then when she did get out of bed, she'd be flat out caring for him. She got burnt out and the doctors reckon her stroke was a result of the stress of looking after him.

It took the next year for her to start walking again, and during that time Dad was moved to a care home. I used to take him to see Mum at the hospital a lot, because I knew they must have been missing each other.

Whatever they'd been through, they were soulmates and loved each other dearly. I used to go to the home and read the Bible to Dad and just chat with him.

I also asked him about why he beat us growing up. I'd see tears running down his cheeks. He'd never give an answer. I didn't ask to torment him, I just wanted to understand why.

When Kiyan died, I didn't go and visit Dad as much over the next five months. I never really got to speak to him about how Kiyan's death affected him because I was in the middle of it.

Then the week before the trial, I had this thing in the back of my head saying, 'Go and see Dad. Go and see Dad.' I went down to his care home late one night. It was out of visiting hours, but they let me in. I walked into Dad's room and he didn't even know I was there. If the Grim Reaper actually exists, then I knew he was in that room. That haunted me.

I used to bring Dad stuff he liked to eat, like pears, but he couldn't eat now and was on stuff with straws. I didn't know whether to give him some water or do something. I felt helpless and just stood there and cried.

I drove home in the early morning and was that upset and tired that I couldn't even see properly. I ended up banging into the back of this car in front of me.

When the guy came out, he could see the grief in my face and didn't make anything of it. He checked if I was OK and then drove off. A week later, Dad had deteriorated pretty badly. We got a phone call from the doctors saying they wanted us to come down to the hospital where he'd now been moved to. By this stage we were halfway through the trial and I was emotionally and physically drained. I felt like I couldn't manage it, but something inside me said, 'You better manage it. Go down there and see your dad, because you might not have a chance to see him again.'

It was the right choice. The moment I walked into the room, I knew he was going to die very soon. He was sitting up in the bed and I was talking to him, even though I was getting no answers back.

I whispered in his ear: "It's alright Dad. You've done really good. You put up a good fight. Just let go. Let go Dad.'

I didn't want to see him suffering. I kissed him, hugged him and sat with my brothers and sister for a bit, then I left.

He died the following morning, on 25 October 2006.

The thing about trials is they don't stop for nothing and later that morning we were back at the Old Bailey. I do remember what a class act the judge was though.

When we walked into the court, one of the first things he did was look over to us and say that he'd heard about Dad passing away and wanted to offer his condolences. That meant a lot to all of us.

I'd also like to say something about my sister Chris. She was a solid rock during this time, supporting Tracy during the trial and helping to sort out Dad's funeral arrangements. Dad's passing affected us all in different ways. Junior especially was devastated, but Chris took responsibility, took care of everything, without being asked or ever wanting recognition for herself.

She never complained or moaned to anyone else – she just motored forward and did the best she could to get things sorted out. I don't know if I've ever said thank you, but I'd like it to be known what an unbelievable job she did.

RIP Dad.

★★★★★★★★★★★★★★★★★

As the old expression goes, 'The show must go on.'

On Thursday 26 October, after three days considering their verdict, the jury was sent home. The day after, the judge asked for their decision. The seven men and five women couldn't reach a conclusion. Seriously?

They'd been sucked in by the whole bullshit that it was all an accident and he only intended to scratch Kiyan. They'd also bought into the knife being of a legal size.

That really vexed me. Just because it's legal, does that mean its ability to cut and stab is taken away? Why would you carry it on you? For what purpose? How can there be a law allowing any knives to be carried?

You only need a sharp blade edge to cut an artery, it doesn't have to be inserted deep into someone's flesh. It's ridiculous. If it's more than three inches, then it's illegal? So he was carrying a knife of a legal size. There shouldn't even be such a thing.

Somehow Hannad's defence had done a good job of convincing them.

The second the judge announced it was a hung jury, I looked over at the jurors and was like, 'How dumb are you? Seriously? Don't you know what's going on out here? Didn't you listen to what was being said? What are you hung up about?'

Obviously I didn't say any of that, but that was coming out loud in my head. That meant we'd have to do it all over again.

We were totally gutted. Going to court is horrible, because until a decision is made, nobody can get on with their lives. Police liaison officers coming to your house, driving to the Old Bailey, going into court and sitting there all day. It takes your life energy out of you and churns it up.

Our brief was trying to be positive, telling us to look forward and not to worry about this decision, because we'd have another opportunity. We'd learned more from the case and what we could do better next time round. It all sounded good in theory, but after what had just gone down, I now had a serious lack of faith in the justice system.

On 3 November, we were told the date of the new trial would be 11 December. Round two.

17

Strike Two

*"Every strike brings me closer to the next home run." **Babe Ruth***

The thing about trials, whether you have one or 20 trials of the same case, it's still the same case. That basically meant, with the odd new angle or piece of evidence from either side, we had to listen to the same horror story again and again.

For the first trial, evidence had been found about Hannad's violent past, but was presented too late so it was thrown out of court. Guess what, same thing happened for this one.

To this day, I still have no idea why. All I know is that if that evidence had been introduced at the beginning, we wouldn't have gone beyond the first trial.

For the second trial only, I decided to keep a small pocket diary. I called it *Issues and Thoughts in Court*. I'm going to take you through the detail in the way I wrote it.

Day 1 – Monday 11 December 2006
I was still struggling with not killing him, because, in my head, killing was the easy option.

Hannad made some little changes to his plea, but he was sticking to this story about how murder wasn't what he intended to do. They still wanted to show it wasn't a premeditated action and he wasn't the sort of person who would do such a thing. Please.

The second bunch of jurors were six men and six women of mixed nationalities.

Day 2 – Tuesday 12 December 2006
Case is about to start – my eyes well up as I got to hear about all this again. I really feel for my family and Tracy's. As soon as the prosecution start to open the case, tears start to flow from mine and Tracy's eyes. We begin our difficult and painful journey to get through all the evidence and when my son's name is being mentioned, the hurt from both of us cannot be hidden. I thought it might be a bit easier, but no, I was shaking with grief as I listened again with Tracy to the evidence that led to Kiyan's death. Seven months later and I still can't believe my son's gone. The grief and crying is deep.

I ain't slept much in two days. About three hours, so I know I'm going to be physically exhausted after all this crying in court. I feel that Nick, our prosecution, is more detailed, more precise, clearer, for this trial. The teacher's evidence is emotional and she's evidently traumatised.

I've decided to give the defence team a name – Rumpole of the Bastards [R.O.B.]. I've taken it from the telly series Rumpole of the Bailey that was on in the 1980s, which featured this defence lawyer called Rumpole who hardly ever lost a case.

In the cross examination, R.O.B. didn't have much to say. He spoke about the teacher not seeing blood and not hearing noise when she'd turned her back to make her phone call at the time Kiyan had been stabbed.

Next is Kiyan's mate who was having the so-called playfight with Hannad. All the evidence from everyone else was good, but it's his evidence that sinks Hannad. Like before, because of his stammer, his evidence is very difficult for the jury and the court to hear and understand. I know he will be OK, but the defence are going to try and capitalise on his speech impediment, so I'm still nervous about him as a witness again.

R.O.B. was being a real bastard to him. You could see how frustrated he is by the way he's being attacked. Verbally Kiyan's mate is getting a bit more forceful with his answers and is standing his ground. I'm able to sit through without being terribly angry and frustrated at the proceedings because I understand how this worked out by the last trial. The defence have nothing to go on, so they tried to intimidate and try to confuse the teenage witness, but he's now warmed up and is raising his voice and giving it to R.O.B.! He's had enough and it's added spice to the whole proceedings. I'm so glad I never walked out! He's classic!

R.O.B has to move on. He's wrapping up after Kiyan's mate has been in the dock for over two hours!

The judge is fabulous so far. When R.O.B was asking him silly questions, the judge stepped in and asked him to be realistic or shut up.

Day 3 – Wednesday 13 December 2006
I turned up late because of traffic and came in to see the second witness already in the stand.

Jury listening to interview tapes of her testimony. It's more graphic than Kiyan's mate's and really gives us a feel of what

Kiyan suffered and went through. It's very difficult for me and Tracy to listen to Kiyan's last moments on this earth. Only God knows the thoughts that went through his head.

In no time at all, the court think I'm intimidating the accused, so they have moved me back another seat. In the first trial, if you could have got imprisoned for that, I would have got life, because I wanted to hurt him so bad. I looked at him like he's not a 16-year-old. I looked at him like a murderer that is getting a man's sentence for a man's crime. I want to hand him some Mark Prince Justice.

There's a different feel about this trial, almost like the other trial was not meant to be and this was the real one.

Another witness gets in the stand. He didn't see much, but he thought he saw enough to give evidence about the stabbing. Why he decided to testify, I don't know. He was absolutely useless. He was weak and the defence led him along and he followed them. He said that my son was smiling with Hannad and play fighting. NOT TRUE!!! He then had amnesia and kept saying he forgot. I'm pissed with him, but not too bothered because you could see the expression on the judge's face, like a GP would say in a surgery. "Next."

Day 4 – Thursday 14 December 2006
Day four was possibly the hardest day of this trial as statements were read from the paramedics as they tried to save my son. Same thing each time. Didn't become any easier to listen to. It was like a raw wound and someone kept pushing their finger into it each time they talked about it.

My mind's racing with pictures of Kiyan and thoughts of what he must have been going through before he stopped breathing. My heart's beating fast. I feel a panic attack coming. It's horrible.

They bring the knife that plunged into my son's heart. It came out in a little bag as 'Exhibit' whatever. I'm thinking that the penalties for knives need to be treated the same as someone who carries a gun. No tears from me, but I see Tracy crying.

Now we are going to listen to the murderer's statement on cassettes again, taken after he was arrested. Listening to his story of events is so vexing. His lies, his cowardly behaviour, his acting to pretend he's upset about what he done, when we know he planned to stab my son. He was jealous of him.

Just anger from myself and Tracy now. Horrible listening to his voice and the shit that comes out of this cold-blooded killer's mouth, acting like a snivelling, stabbing, mummy's boy. This same little BITCH couldn't hold a candle to my boy. [That means he's not as good as my son.]

I'm getting so mad listening to this son of a bitch talking about how he saw Kiyan at parties. My son only ever went to one party and it wasn't with him.

He just mashed up his statement. How could he say he was mucking around after he got pushed on to the red car by Kiyan's mate? Then he says it wasn't his intention to hurt him and he contradicted himself by saying he just wanted to scratch him. His lies are trapping him.

Then he contradicted himself again, by claiming to pull out the knife slowly, so Kiyan could see it shining in his eye, then it was down by his side where he couldn't see it. That makes no sense; show it, then hide it. What was he trying to do? A magic trick? Then he said after Kiyan 'punched' him twice, he used the knife, because the second punch hurt him. Then he said the knife went into the arm. So he knew it went in! Then he stuck to his theory that he didn't know it could penetrate. All contradictions.

He then called Kiyan a friend, yet again. Said he was always trying to compete with him and he was surprised that a young boy could be so good. This just showed his jealousy of my son. It was lies after lies getting him in deeper and deeper. Then he said he stabbed him three times. Said he would have cried, collapsed and panicked if he knew he had stabbed Kiyan through the heart?! If he saw Kiyan drop and he says he never saw anyone drop like that, and he suspected he was hurt, why didn't he go back if he considered himself a friend?

Then more lies. He said he lost his phone, then he said he gave it to a friend. But how could he receive a call if he gave his phone away?

He didn't want to see the blood he says, so why stab him? Any fool knows what happens when you stab someone. You don't have to experience a car crash to know what will happen when a car hits you at speed. Then he said he didn't want to hurt him. I'm soooo mad after listening to his fucking shit about how he knows how Tracy feels, because he knows how his mum feels?!?

Tears flow freely as I hear Tracy and Tannisa's statement read out, that the murderer was no friend of Kiyan's. It hits me hard how Tannisa's brother, who she lived with, is no longer here and how distressed she's getting talking about it.

I felt like I needed to hold her as she was talking, but the thought makes me cry even more. This trial is so much clearer than the last one. I'm amazed how clear it is that the murderer is a living cold-blooded killer and he needs to be put away for a very long time. If only hanging were still available.

Now the pathologist is up, but his statement doesn't make much difference because I don't think the jury care how much force was used. If the defence try and say it was all an accident, it will fall through.

Our team is arguing about the size and depth of the wound. Before, Hannad, in his statement, said he used minimum force, then changes his mind to moderate.

This judge is amazing. It's almost as if what I would say to R.O.B, the judge is saying it.

R.O.B wants the judge to take into consideration the murderer's age in terms of giving evidence. The judge is not swaying to any stupid requests.

Day 5 – Monday 18 December 2006
Closing speeches.

Came in late on train because I woke up late after a terrible night's sleep. Our team closed up first. Nick did this in more detail than before. I walked in at the point where he was talking about why the murderer was at the school in the first place when he had been excluded. Nick goes down the road of it being a play fight and the murderer getting serious.

Then the murderer describes Kiyan's mate's actions as playing about, when he tried to disarm him! More lies. Nick shows by his anger that the murderer and all his evasive actions after the murder, that he never intended to be honest or own up.

The defence have got nothing to go on, but to try and be very clever and fool the jury into believing this idiot isn't responsible for murder. The defence is total bullshit and talking about how the heart was only nicked by the knife. Then he said the witnesses never saw what they saw. Seriously? Then he went over the [non-existent] friendship and tried to use Tannisa's statement to back up his point, because Tannisa said he was in the same group of people she hung around with.

He's no friend of anyone in our family. After he stabbed Kiyan, he ran from the school to McDonald's and the first thing he said to his mates was: "I've just killed Tannisa's brother." You're on your own now.

No point in me getting any more fired up from the defence's smoke screen.

Day 6 – Tuesday 19 December 2006
Arrived at 10.30am on train.

The jury's already come and gone. They haven't reached a decision yet. We go for lunch and I receive a call from Paul [detective]. My heart's beating as he tells me the jury are coming back in. But then my mood switches when he tells me: "They can't come to a decision." I went quiet, then a rage came over me and in my heart I knew that if they didn't come to a decision, I would.

I go back to the entrance of the court room and pace around like a hungry lion waiting for the word to come in. When I hear the word, I go in and to my shock and amazement, the jury requested to have the meaning of 'murder' and 'manslaughter' explained to them [again].

It was bad enough having to listen to 12 people at the last trial proving how incompetent they were, but this lot had now proved that they weren't any better. There was one lady in particular that gave us the impression that everything was just a joke.

She was whispering and smiling all the time, cracking jokes.

This was not a place to crack jokes and there was nothing that was being said at that trial that should have made anyone smile. That was really getting to me.

Next minute, you see a piece of paper, a request, from the jury, asking if they could hear two of the witnesses' statements again. Guess who requested that? That same dickhead woman. The only job she had to do was listen.

It was horrible having to hear all this stuff about my son being stabbed as it was, so she could have done me a favour by listening properly the first time. Even the judge told the jury off and explained this was a sensitive thing we were going through here and that they needed to be taking down notes first time round and listening carefully. The judge tells them they can't have it.

After some arguments about the issue, the judge decides to read out the witnesses' statements again. I'm getting angry as we begin to endure the details of Kiyan's murder again.

I walked out in disgust as I didn't believe the jury are doing their job properly. This was extremely stressful and emotionally draining and I started to feel that we were about to get another hung jury.

When we came out of the Old Bailey, I walked to St Paul's tube station and I'm chatting with someone along the way. When I got to the station I was chatting about how tough the day was and all that, but hadn't gone through the turnstiles yet. Then, who do I see? That same woman from the court. I didn't think about things like court rulings and went straight over. I needed to let her know what she was doing to us as a family and that she needed to fix up and do her job right. I went up to her, very calm and said: "Excuse me. Do you know how much what you do in court directly affects and hurts our family? Having to listen to the same witness again. Please do your job so we only need to listen to this once."

She looked at me in shock, like 'oh shit,' then walked off quickly without saying a word. What I didn't realise was, she'd gone back to the court and reported what had happened.

Day 7 Wednesday 20 December
They had to throw that trial out. The Recorder of London, Judge Peter Beaumont, ordered a retrial. He said: "The jury was discharged as a result of an incident having taken place away from court and during an adjournment during the course of the jury's deliberations." [www.independent.co.uk]
    [MY DIARY ENDS]

When I came out of the court, I was crying like a baby. Really sobbing. Everyone was really upset, but it was me that felt the guilt more than anyone. It was the process that upset me.

Knowing that I might have messed up the trial and pushed it in favour of Hannad in some way. It made me feel really alone, because it was only me that had done this.

Everyone had different emotions but apart from my brother Junior, nobody tried to support me by saying, 'It wasn't the right thing to do, but I can see why you're acting like this, because it's getting to you. It will work itself out. Don't worry.'

Tracy stopped speaking to me for a couple of weeks, which hurt me simply because the last thing I wanted to do was upset her. My sister and Tracy are like sisters, so I was really happy that she had that support from her, as I knew she'd help smooth this out.

The last thing we needed was an argument at a time when we needed to be closer than ever.

Junior walked me to my house. When we got there, he jumped onto the sofa and crashed out immediately, whereas I sat there at the table with a picture of Kiyan on my lap.

The experience I had next helped to give me the direction I needed to come to terms with the grief, anger and frustration that was running through me.

As I was sat on this chair with my head bowed down, I started crying like a tap. I couldn't stop. I was just stooped over limp, with my arm hanging down. I looked at the wooden floor at one point and a small puddle had formed.

I then started talking to God.

'I'm done. I give up. I can't deal with this. Show me what you need me to do and what my part is to play in this. Help me. Help me.'

By now, this murderous feeling was eating away at me and I felt alone. But then, as I was crying out, it felt like this heavy, suffocating weight was being physically lifted from me.

I felt like God had taken the burden and grief from me. I wiped my tears and could physically feel that something had changed. I felt lighter. I knew that I'd be entering the courtroom for the third trial with a different head on.

18

Familiar Place

*"Familiarity breeds contempt, while rarity
wins admiration." **Apuleius***

Tracy had mentioned after the first trial that she wanted to set up a charity in Kiyan's name, but didn't have the time. I'd also had a similar idea. The plan was to create an organisation that could realistically make an impact against knife and gang crime. I didn't know how to do it back then, but I had a feeling in my stomach that this is where my future was. The day I had that almighty sob was the day that the concept of the Kiyan Prince Foundation [KPF], was officially born.

The date for the third trial had been set for 18 June 2007, so I now had six months to start making some moves for KPF. Even before Kiyan had been stabbed, I had aspirations of starting my own practice as a counsellor, or at least putting into practice what I would learn at an effective level.

I'd already done youth worker and mentoring courses, so not long before the second trial, I started a 10-week counselling course.

I was very anxious going into the course. I didn't want

sympathy from my classmates, but I knew it was going to be inevitable, because I knew I would have to talk about Kiyan.

Counselling is a lot to do with self-awareness, your reactions to hearing people's stories and listening skills. I had thought my listening skills were good, but it wasn't until I started this course that I realised how difficult it was to do properly.

Listening is about clearing your mind of your own thoughts. I improved by not only listening to what people were saying, but what they were not saying.

I thought that being a counsellor was being the expert, or trying to rescue the client with some clever words. Now I understood that's exactly what you don't want to do. As a counsellor you enter into a professional relationship where they can feel safe while you enable your client to connect their thoughts and feelings. It was all positive stuff.

I think now is a good time to introduce Chris Rogers. I'd got in touch with him the day Kiyan died. Chris was the only reporter who seemed to understand the grief Tracy and I were going through, instead of looking for an angle to sell newspapers.

About a week after the stabbing, I met him and he told me about the idea of the film called *Put The Knives and Guns Down*, which I was humbled about. The fact that someone was willing to put in so much time to help raise awareness of my son's death and highlight the problem with knife crime was very special.

Me and Chris developed a real bond. I used to go up to his house, met his wife and ended up spending a lot of time with him for the film. If it wasn't for Chris, Kiyan's case wouldn't have received anywhere near the publicity it did.

Yeah, you've got the newspapers and television who were covering things, but they put their own spin on it. Chris kept it real. Because of his publicity, my phone started to ring about me doing talks on what had happened to Kiyan and how it could be stopped for kids in the future.

Not long after I'd finished the counselling course, in February 2007, I was having a conversation with Chris about how I wanted to move KPF forward.

He helped me get the charity registered, but also suggested we needed more publicity to help get money. That's when I suggested we made a music track. I didn't have a clue where to start, but Chris did.

He looked at me like I was crazy at first, but within a few days, he'd sorted us out to meet with a lady called Anne Barrett who'd worked with some big names.

Mind you, I'm surprised he stuck it out, because I wasn't a model student when it came to timekeeping. In the film, as I rock up to the studio with a big smile on my face, Chris says, with a sympathetic voice: "He's two hours late. I've learnt that behind his positivity, he's still struggling to cope with daily life."

It wasn't like that! Chris, if you're reading this, I just want to say, I'm really sorry, but being late was just me, nothing to do with any struggles. Standard.

It used to drive Cham Joof mad when we were boxing. We'd have a photoshoot and I'd keep everyone waiting for two to three hours. That was normal. And when I used to meet with Cham on the social, it got to a point where after about 20 minutes he wouldn't even wait around. He'd text me the address and say: "Meet me there." Nine times out of ten I was in the barbers getting my hair done.

The two people Anne had chosen for the track were Maresa Macbeth and Tinie Tempah. Maresa had the most unbelievable voice and Tinie at the time was relatively unknown. It was another three years until he released the track *Pass Out*, so at that time, he wasn't what you'd call a mainstream musician. Either way, the two of them were brilliant.

Even the *The Guardian* shared our faith, writing: "*Put The Knives And Guns Down* is, simultaneously, a call to end street violence and a celebration of the life of schoolboy and aspiring footballer Kiyan Prince... The contrast between Maresa's soaring soprano and Tinie's gritty rap makes the message of the single powerfully clear... A grime symphony that – if there is any justice – will go top ten on its release."

Unfortunately, it didn't work out like that. The radio stations turned their backs on us. Publicity wise and financially, it hardly even got off the mark. It was circulated online a bit, but it was like the track was made and then dropped like a hot potato.

It was only QPR that gave it a big push at one of their matches. Around that time, they also had me and Tracy presenting the first ever Kiyan Prince Trophy, with QPR's academy. It felt so good that they did a trophy in Kiyan's name It showed recognition for him and highlighted knife crime, which is more than can be said of the radio industry with the music track.

★★★★★★★★★★★★★★★★★★

The counselling course and the Tinie Tempah track were great, but unfortunately, there was a lot of shit going on outside of that which I was doing my best to deal with. My marriage with Laurel was falling apart and money was really tight.

Colin would always find me a few days here and there doing some security work, but my monthly income wasn't great. I was keeping a diary at the time and on 13 March 2007, I wrote: "Deep money troubles. Like, no food sometimes!"

I had weeks where I would only eat once every couple of days and would be drinking tap water. I had to approach my mum to help me out with some shopping. These were low times.

With the third trial rapidly approaching, on 11 June I wrote a new, more positive diary entry:

"Here are some things that are not going to happen anymore:

1] Having no food in the house
2] Having no set regular income that covers bills
3] Being at the bottom of the food chain.

"I feel totally ashamed, I feel this is all on my head and the realisation of that is all on my soul. I haven't made the right decisions. That's the hard truth and that's the driving force pushing me every time."

It wasn't going to get fixed overnight, but writing it down and creating that mentality was going to change my world. I'd created a negative state of mind and now I had to act positively. Without the mindset, nothing in my life would change.

★★★★★★★★★★★★★★★★★

18 June 2007. By the third trial, we just wanted it over. We were used to the format, the surroundings and everything that came with the trial, but this wasn't something any of us wanted to become familiar with.

When we went back to court, that same feeling of lightness

stayed with me after I'd spoken to God. In the first two trials, I could never look at Hannad's family without feeling a fight was going to break out. Tracy had even said: "Don't say nothing to the jurors. Don't even look at them." But this time I was actually telling everyone that it was all going to be alright, instead of the other way round.

The same witnesses went over the same stuff again, but there were also some new angles that surfaced to help with our case. The jealousy thing in particular was insane when I look back.

On the day Hannad had gone to the school, he'd gone in to speak with a girl. One of the witnesses had said that Hannad had once referred to Kiyan and his mate as "the biggest boys in Year Ten," at school, so maybe when Kiyan appeared, he decided to prove how tough he was by fighting them.

Hannad thought of himself as a sportsman, especially his ability with basketball and admitted in a statement: "I was always trying to compete with him [Kiyan]. I was actually surprised that a kid younger than me was better than me."

The problem was, it wasn't just basketball. Football, throwing the javelin, Kiyan was better than him. He also had a better physique and that's where he probably really felt resentment, because all the girls fancied Kiyan.

Apparently Hannad was seeing some girl and she liked Kiyan. She even had pictures of him in her bedroom. It was like everything Hannad did, Kiyan was doing better in his eyes.

Towards the end of the second week, one thing happened that Tracy believed was a turning point. Our family liaison officers decided to re-enact what had happened between Kiyan and Hannad. It allowed the jury to see it couldn't have happened the way Hannad was telling it.

After they'd finished, Tracy said: "We're going to win." I kept an open mind. I was positive, but I'd been positive in the first trial and that didn't have a happy ending.

★★★★★★★★★★★★★★★★★★

On 2 July 2007, two weeks after the third trial had started, the jury had come to a decision. Half of me was prepared for the verdict to be manslaughter or another hung jury.

If he got away with something like a six-year sentence, coming out after three years with good behaviour, I honestly can't say how I would have reacted.

I wanted the justice system to restore my faith this time. It was the head juror's turn to speak now.

What was probably a second seemed like an hour as we waited to hear the decision. Then finally it was read out, 11 to one votes in favour of Hannad being guilty of murder.

The moment the verdict was read out as "guilty" I just remember thinking, 'Wow, we got what we wanted.'

It was elation, but of a different sort. There were people, screaming, shouting and crying with joy in the public gallery, but we didn't feel like that. We got the result we wanted, but we still had to deal with the loss.

I have no memories of Hannad's reaction and couldn't care less. I was holding Tracy's hand the whole time and when she heard the good news, she collapsed. It was like a release for her.

When Tannisa heard the verdict, she had a panic attack and had to run outside. The emotion got to her. While she was outside, one of Hannad's relatives came over and said: "I'm sorry." Tannisa didn't respond.

The moment the judge announced the verdict, Hannad's identification was also brought out. Now everyone would know the person who'd killed my son. I was thinking, 'Now let's move on to the next bit, the sentence.'

Once the verdict of guilty had been passed, the court was adjourned and a date of 26 July 2007 was set for sentencing.

Jaswant Narwal of the CPS said: "As well as the deep loss felt by Kiyan's parents this senseless knife killing has shaken an entire school and community. Knives, including penknives, are not toys and we prosecuted for murder as we would if a gun had been used.

"No child should live with the risk of seeing their friends frightened, wounded, or killed and certainly not outside their own school.

"We thank the Prince family for their determination to follow us through these trials and also the pupils and teacher from the London Academy who bravely gave evidence a third time."

When we walked out of the court, we were mobbed by the press. We were wearing our *Put The Knives And Guns Down* t-shirts, which Tinie Tempah had sorted for us, and I made a speech live on ITV.

I said: "We're gonna focus on trying to make changes. We're gonna focus on trying to educate the children, we're gonna focus on projects and see what the young people need, so other parents don't suffer the way we've suffered."

The time had come to put all my energy and soul into KPF. I knew I was about to embark on a new journey, the only problem was, I wasn't one hundred percent sure where to go and how to get there.

But before that, there was still the sentence to go.

Twenty four days of wondering if Hannad was going to get the full brunt of the law, or just some petty sentence.

★★★★★★★★★★★★★★★★★★

Thursday 26 July 2007 – Judgement day.

A trial can make you lose hair, get sick, all kinds of stuff, but to have three of them was horrible. I just wanted to get through this last day. I couldn't face hearing it all again.

Thankfully, the judge in his closing speech wasn't having any of Hannad's sloppy excuses. His defence tried all sorts of different angles to reduce the sentence, but the judge wasn't giving into the pleas of mercy.

When the judge sentenced Hannad to 13 years, me and Tracy instantly broke down crying. There was a massive roar from our friends and family up in the gallery and I wanted to shout something out to recognise their support, but the best I could do was hold up my thumbs, as I was sobbing heavily.

The judge said he wanted to give Hannad the maximum time he could give, with no reprieve. No getting off early for good behaviour. Tracy had put in a request to the judge for Hannad to be deported back to Somalia after his sentence and he agreed to it, without batting an eyelid.

When the judge passed the sentence, Hannad showed no emotion, he just dropped his head slightly. Exactly the same as when he walked into the court room on the first day, first trial. I knew, or hoped, that inside he was rotting.

Now that the sentencing was done, the judge was able to spill the beans on all the evidence that had been kicked out from the previous trials, due to late admission.

He criticised the prosecution for failing to give the defence enough notice of the evidence and called it a "catastrophic failure."

From our side, you're just hoping whatever evidence they bring in is going to be enough to make the jurors listen. We're not having a go at Nick, because we always knew he did his best for us.

For whatever reasons the evidence didn't get submitted on time. We're not holding any blame on anyone, especially as we got the result we wanted. It's all water under the bridge now.

However, it was still worth listening to this new evidence. You could see Hannad's friends and family bowing their head in shame as they'd defended this piece of shit and probably had no idea of the full extent of his previous behaviour.

It turns out Hannad had been a very naughty boy and for each and every one of those jurors over the three trials who were undecided about whether this kid was a bit misguided, whether this was a one-off accident, what the judge was about to say certainly cleared that up.

Hannad was obsessed with Somalian gang culture. I hate using the word 'gang,' so I'm going to limit it from here on. I'll explain more later.

It turns out he had a nickname on the streets and was known as 'The Killer.' He'd come over from Somalia in 2001 and within no time started hanging out with a notorious bunch of guys called 'Thug Fam,' who were based near Edgware. They'd been responsible for murdering a policewoman the year before, in 2005. That was only the tip of Hannad's rap sheet.

Remember that statement from Hannad in the first trial about having never used a knife before and that it was a toy? Well, that got completely melted down. Six days before Kiyan was stabbed, Hannad had been suspended from school for pissing in the passageway in front of a teacher, then threatening to kick her in if she said anything.

A few days later, he pulled out that same knife on some girl on a bus, threatening to stab her if she didn't give up her seat.

He'd also hit some kid at school and burst his eardrum. In the previous three years, Hannad had been caught in over a dozen incidents for bad behaviour at school. He'd even been getting help for anger management, which obviously hadn't worked.

So by the time he'd stabbed Kiyan, this was no pupil who'd accidentally hurt my son.

Or tried to scratch him. This was a cold-blooded killer who was going to carry on doing this kind of thing until he was brought to justice.

Even though Hannad wasn't making eye contact, the judge laid it on thick to him: "This is yet another case of a wholly unprovoked stabbing, by a person who produced a knife and plunged it into the heart of their unarmed victim."

He added: "Taking the life of another is always a terrible thing, taking the life of a talented, popular 15-year-old schoolboy who had done you no wrong and had everything to live for defies description. You have deprived his family and schoolfriends of a role model."

The judge commended us for showing great courage and respect in the courthouse and for everyone who took the time and courage to take the stand. It was good to hear that, especially as it felt like it came from his heart.

We then had to listen to someone reading Hannad's statement, because he was too chicken to read it himself. It talked again about how Tracy must be feeling, because of what his mum was going through. What? Your mum can talk to you, you twat, because you're still alive. Nothing he said took any responsibility for what he did.

Never once did he say sorry for stabbing Kiyan.

That needed to be said. OK, he got 13 years, but he walked out of the court alive and would be free at the age of 30, doing his thing. He'd got a life sentence, but 13 years is not life. That was not even the length of Kiyan's life.

After Hannad's people had finished reading his bullshit piece, me and Tracy read our impact statements. It was a time for us to air some of our feelings and get a bit of closure.

I talked about how much of a role model and natural leader he was and how everyone that knew him was shattered by his death. Everyone he crossed paths with he impressed, not just with his talents, but with his warmth of character.

I finished off by saying: "This world cannot afford to lose promising young people like Kiyan to knife crime."

Tracy bravely read out a heartbreaking statement. She'd been having dreams very soon after Kiyan was killed, but that was him as a silent little kid. As the trials went on, her dreams started to change and he was now 15 years old again.

In the dreams he'd walk in after school, kiss Tracy and then ask her how her day had been. The vividness was overwhelming for her and she explained how she would never fully be able to come to terms with Kiyan's death.

She went on to thank everyone for their support, and said, fighting back the tears: "Kiyan was a devoted son and brother and there is not a day goes by where his family do not think about him and miss him."

Walking out of the court that day was closure on the case, but we all knew we'd never be the same again. The deep scars left by Hannad would haunt us for the rest of our lives.

I knew I had to turn my negative energy into something quickly. There's no way Kiyan's name was disappearing off the planet. His death had to mean something more than a stabbing. I wanted it to be a strong message for future generations.

Rest in peace Kiyan.

Justice was served.

19

KPF

"I'm very proud of Mark from the bottom of my heart for what he's done with KPF, but I don't want him to feel obliged. I've always said to him, 'If you ever feel you've done enough, you have nothing to feel bad about. You should feel very proud for everything you've done in our son's name.'"
Tracy Cumberbatch, 2017

"How many people have to die before somebody takes this seriously?" Those were the words of Phil Hearne, Kiyan's head teacher, speaking at the funeral. It's a good question. Will it ever be solved? Probably not. But can something be done to work out why young people are dying like this in the first place and try and remedy that? Yes.

A couple of years before Kiyan got stabbed, I was doing youth work. I was tuned in to what young people were doing out there and was seriously clued up about all the crime stats. Then when my son got killed, my outlook on life changed and it was all about looking to positively influence young people.

I started to see the public's perception of me change. Before, people would come up to me on the street and ask me if I was Mark Prince, the boxer. Now I was Mark Prince, the dad of the footballer who got stabbed. That's who I'm largely known as.

People thought I started KPF to help with the grieving process, but that wasn't it. You see people setting up charities every day, then next year they've disappeared. It's almost like they get caught up in the moment and then lose the motivation. With Kiyan's death, I had a strong lifelong inspiration and felt empowered that I had a pathway. Sounds cheesy, but I knew it was the right thing to do.

In early 2007, I received a call from Joe Gallen at QPR, asking if I could act as a mentor for up-and-coming footballer Ray Jones. He was a great talent and was going to become an incredible striker. He was only 18 at the time and they wanted me to help him develop some mental strength to deal with the pressures that would come his way on the pitch.

I was really excited about working with Ray, but because of everything that was happening with Kiyan's trial, I was slow off the mark to do it. That's something I regretted, because on 25 August 2007, a few weeks after Hannad was sentenced, Ray died in a car crash. When I received that call, I was in shock.

Thankfully, I was able to keep my head fully focused and soon I got my first invite to speak at a school in South London with parents, kids and teachers. I didn't have a clue what to talk about and here's the thing, I'd never been a speaker.

Everyone who meets me now assumes I was always this confident guy who would just stand in front of people and say the right things. Nope. I was really nervous. I was sweating and my mouth was so dry, I was struggling to get my words out.

One big thing that helped me through was God. I prayed to

him and said, 'I don't know how to be a speaker. You're going to have to teach me even though I'm scared.'

Similar to the boxing, once I got started, and with God behind me, my confidence grew. I talked about Kiyan, parenting, making the right choices in life, but I also wanted to enhance people's self-esteem and give them a sense of purpose.

Afterwards, I was scared everyone was going to walk off bored, but it wasn't like that. People asked question after question and then parents and kids would tell me I was an inspiration. I got an insight into where my future was.

That's where it started. More calls, more schools. For a long time, I still went in shitting my pants, but no matter how bad I felt, I always walked away feeling I'd done something useful. Something for Kiyan. I had new emotions. Something other than grief. These new emotions felt better than anger.

★★★★★★★★★★★★★★★★★★

The day after Kiyan was killed, the then Mayor of London, Ken Livingstone called for maximum sentences for all those who carry or use knives and for the age to be increased from 16 to 18 for a youth to be able to buy a knife.

Kiyan was murdered a week before the Home Office launched a national 'No-Knife' amnesty, so I genuinely thought we'd see some changes quickly, but we didn't. It's all well and good talking, but it's all about the law being enforced.

People carrying straps [guns] get a minimum of five years just for possession. That's why straps aren't as prevalent. Carry a knife and you get a maximum of four. Knives need to carry the same threat for possession, simply because the final outcome is the same; injury and death. There's guys walking around with Rambo knives, swords and some of them are walking away with a slap on the wrist. Come on, man.

That's where KPF comes into play. Giving someone a Mickey Mouse sentence for possession just tells them they can do it again. I'll give you an example. When I started doing talks at schools, I heard about this one kid who'd got arrested and kicked out of the school, when a knife dropped out from his jacket. What happened? He just got moved to another school.

He should have gone on a knife crime programme, which would have taken him through the focus on why he's carrying it. Is it out of fear? Or something else?

I ended up mentoring this kid who was expelled. He'd only been to one of my workshops when he'd been kicked out. The new school asked if I could keep mentoring him, so I did.

I asked him why he was carrying the knife and he said: "It looks nice. I like the look of the blade."

It made me think about the times I took my knife out. I wondered what the draw was, even though it was never to be used to kill someone. This kid was basically me 20-odd years ago. When I said: "I believe you," he then wanted to listen.

I told him: "I know you had no intention to use it, but because you are carrying it, the knife has got some power and there will be a situation where it will call on you and say, 'Pick me up. Use me to solve this conflict'."

Not all the kids were taking on board what I had to say, but if at least one was influenced, it was a good day.

Within a year, I was visiting around four schools a month, which soon rose to about eight. Then colleges, prisons and youth offending centres were also knocking on my door.

A lot of people thought I was this guy hanging out on the streets looking to sort people's lives out, but it wasn't like that. I didn't say, 'Let's go out on the streets and create some noise.'

There's a place for that as well, but most of my time was now spent trying to create a forum and not just shout to any Joe Bloggs out there. I knew it needed to be structured.

★★★★★★★★★★★★★★★★★

With the best will in the world, by 2008, I needed help with KPF. Demand was overtaking all the time and non-existent money I had. This wasn't some hobby volunteering I wanted to do. I needed it to be an efficient organisation, run like a business. Thankfully, my PA Ellen Bryant could see this.

Ellen was genuinely interested in seeing KPF become a success and without me knowing, she contacted the people from Noel Edmonds' show *HQ*. They sent round a television crew to my house and said they wanted to have a talk about knife crime and Kiyan, just as part of some documentary and that I'd talk about the benefits of KPF. I thought nothing of it. I talked, got a bit emotional, then they left later that day.

So I was in this studio a few weeks later, front row of this huge audience and Noel came over with the microphone and said: "Mark. Thank you for coming here to talk about knife crime."

I was getting ready to answer whatever questions were coming my way when he said: "Actually Mark, that's not true. For once Mark, I'm going to do the talking." Then he walked me up on stage to sit on this sofa, while the audience are clapping and whistling. I thought, 'What's going on here?'

Noel then started talking about Kiyan and this video came up on screen with people like my brother Junior, Gareth Ainsworth and Andy Evans from QPR, and some of the kids I'd mentored. Even Ricky Hatton wished me the best on a video link. They were all talking about KPF and the difference it had made.

I'm thinking, 'OK. I understand. They're going to give KPF a plug. Nice.'

But then Noel started talking about how I was going to need more PR, better business acumen and better communication skills. And they'd identified experts from each of these areas to help me. In fact, throughout the show people were calling in with all kinds of generous offers.

I couldn't believe it. I was genuinely touched and started getting a bit teary eyed, but then when he said they were going to give me a people carrier for a year to help cover the miles, I was sobbing like a baby. A dream come true! Or was it?

Once the cameras were off, it was a different story. Some offers were genuine, like a lovely guy called Dave who offered me facilities to do outdoor pursuits with the kids. I was very grateful and we had a great time.

Then you had the in-between offers. For example, I accepted an offer for office space from a guy up in Liverpool Street. His company was in charge of a magazine or something.

The office had furniture, phones, the works, but then his company went into liquidation after a few months. That left KPF in a situation, because we'd been spending the previous months marketing to people that this was KPF's new office address and had new stationery made up.

One guy wanted to mentor me as a businessman, which I was excited about, because I didn't have business savvy. I wanted him to help me look at the charity as a business. Maximise its potential, work within budgets, create a five-year strategy and get it functioning to its full potential.

Unfortunately, it never worked out that way. He kindly invited me to some great networking events and I met some great people, but I never got the strategy guidance I was desperate for to help the foundation.

The worst was this guy who was going to help with marketing and promotion. Firstly, he never wanted to meet us in his office, he only wanted to meet us in some juice bar down Liverpool Street. We thought he'd be coming up with PR suggestions, but it was more like us trying to add structure to the meeting.

Les Quinn came with me for the first meeting and ended up paying for the juices. That summed up how cheap this guy was. He taught us nothing and everything seemed like a rush.

So that only left me with the people carrier. When they brought out this VW for the audience to see, you'd expect that's what you were taking away. I thought I'd walk outside, they'd hand me the keys and I'd drive home. Nope.

They kept saying it would be next week but it actually took almost a year. I knew when I got the people carrier that it would only be for 12 months, but the problem is, it became a big help to the foundation and I'd been able to cover a lot of ground and deliver a number of sessions to a lot of people.

So when they took it back, a lot of the work I'd set up came to an end, because I couldn't afford to travel out. There was never once a conversation about sustainability, how I could raise funds or perhaps find another car company to help me.

I'm not being ungrateful, but the whole point of all that bullshit on the show was to assist me with the direction of the charity.

It gave the impression to the people watching the show that KPF was up and running rich in all kinds of resources, when it was the complete opposite. All they did was throw me a boomerang. I was right back where I started.

The only ones who delivered fully on their promise were QPR. On 25 November 2008, Kiyan's birthday, they dedicated their match against Charlton Athletic to KPF. I was presented with a massive canvas of Kiyan and they put on images of him on the big screen and had information about KPF.

They also put stuff on their website and newsletters, while the matchday programme had Kiyan's photo on the cover. On top of that, they allowed us to do collections after matches. Once again, QPR to the rescue.

One very positive story from that year happened while I was walking down Leyton to get my hair cut. This black kid stopped me and said: "Are you Mark Prince?"

"Yeah, that's me."

So I walked down the road with this guy and he told me that a few years back, he'd only just come over to this country and was at the London Academy school and he didn't know anyone.

He was in the playground and he was standing there on his own as the other kids played.

This guy came over to him and asked: "What you doing just standing there on your own? Come over and join us in the football game." This guy brought him over, introduced him to everyone and made him feel welcome. That was Kiyan.

He helped him to make friends, be part of a group and everyone accepted him because Kiyan brought him in. He wanted to include him. Something very dear to my heart.

When he spoke, my eyes welled up. That was such a good

feeling in my belly. Children are normally a certain way at home and a certain way outside. It was good to know how Kiyan was away from home.

★★★★★★★★★★★★★★★★★★

With or without the people carrier, I still needed to deliver the sessions. I looked at the most important issues that needed addressing regarding knife crime. It wasn't that I ignored the financial side, I just didn't focus on it. Story of my life.

I wanted to offer young people the love and life skills that I gave to my children. Those were the roots of KPF. It wasn't born out of fancy words about vision, it was born out of the fact that many kids don't have good role models or a father.

I needed to address all the factors that led to knife crime in the first place, starting with parenting.

Things have changed in terms of the amount of input parents have. Taking care of kids, bringing them up, being that authoritative figure. When I listen to how kids and parents are now, it's like the kids are taking the parents shopping. They're in control.

That's a shift in authority and it has a huge impact on how kids behave when they get older.

I realised modern society had many dangers that parents were blind to. There were obvious things like crossing the road, steering them clear of dodgy looking adults, but they were not protecting them from the telly and social media.

I realised we had to get children of any age to understand the value of what they were watching and listening to. We all like to watch a gangster movie or listen to a gangster rapper, but it's understanding that it's fantasy. Even if it's based on a true story, it's not your life. I wanted them to understand they'd been sold a dream and told a lie and I was the one telling them the truth. I kept it real. Where were all these guys that they wanted to be like? Did they come to visit them and talk to them? No.

They weren't interested in sharing experiences with them, uplifting them and helping them on their journey. They were just interested in making their money.

I wanted the children to understand that if they followed these 'idols,' they'd end up broke, dead or in prison. That would be their future.

I wanted young people to understand they were at such a special stage in their lives. How they would take care of themselves from a young age would shape how their future developed, both physically and mentally.

I wanted them to understand that their youth was a time for building blocks. The earlier you start, the earlier you can attain your success. I wanted to encourage young people to get on that journey as early as possible. It was all about changing mindsets. My job was to let the youth understand the importance of this.

I tried to make them feel proud that one day they might have a child who'd act like them. Then I made them understand how their decision-making now was going to impact on that little one. I'd ask them: "Can you imagine you telling your child you are in a gang, carry a knife and stab people? How do you think that child will turn out? That child hangs off every word you say. Is that the legacy you want to leave for your child?"

I made them understand the choice which changed me was boxing, because of the discipline it brought. Sport is a great forum for learning life skills while you're being active.

You learn communication, determination, perseverance,

sacrifice and teamwork. All these qualities are needed in life and I wanted the youth to understand that. I wasn't saying that everyone would become a sportsperson. But the discipline from sport would mould that person's mindset to enable them to dedicate themselves to becoming a qualified plumber, an electrician, an accountant, whatever.

But sport doesn't solve everything. Getting involved in 'something' is what's needed. Anything productive that can channel your energy into something positive. That's the key.

Inevitably, some of the youths got in trouble, but I tried to help them choose the right path. Revenge became a big talking topic and many used to say: "I'd have killed Kiyan's murderer."

I used to then ask them: 'Would you prefer for me to be standing in front of you or to be in prison?"

All of a sudden it would go quiet and they'd start looking at each other. I'd then say: "You have to make the right choice, regardless of the feeling. You have to think ahead. If I do a revenge attack, where's this going to put me?

"How will my kids grow up without me there for them to guide them? They might even think it's OK to go to prison because I'm there. No. That ain't the right choice."

I'm the first person to know that when you're emotional, it's hard to make the right choice. But if there's that thing in you that wants to make the right choice, then you'll do it. That's what saved me. I was hoping if these kids got into a similar position, hopefully that talk would come to mind.

One of the topics that took me a while to get to grips with was gang crime. It was an area I believed needed steering in another direction in the public eye. I still believe that.

When I was growing up, we had gangs, but it was different.

The gang was like a team, a bunch of mates. What makes a gang? Two people? Fifteen? How do you earn that label? It's bullshit. You see three or four kids together in a rough end of town and think 'gang.' If you went over and told them they were in a gang, they'd probably be more surprised than you.

Listen; I'm not trying to soften up the whole gang concept, because it does exist. There's some nasty organised outfits operating on the streets and they need to be stamped out.

However, what I wanted to do was to deglamorise it for kids.

The media love to pump up propaganda. They start making assumptions about gang boundaries, start claiming this gang did this, or that gang did that, it stirs up bad blood, but worse, it creates fear and we look at young people with labels.

Someone wears a hoodie – are they a criminal? No. But there was a stage when the press went mad on it and kids walking back in the rain with their hood up were getting stopped and searched, with some even arrested, innocently. This had an effect of making people go down the wrong path.

It seemed the second a violent crime has been committed, they always try and connect it with a group. We're not talking about the mafia here, we're talking about a few youths with a tag. More than likely that 'gang' won't exist in a year's time.

If I could make those kids understand that they were not part of anything substantial, something that didn't enhance them as a person, they'd hopefully walk away before getting involved.

★★★★★★★★★★★★★★★★

Funnily enough though, it was a newspaper sponsored award that gave me my last highlight of 2008. I was presented with the

News of The World Children's Champion award, which came in two parts. The first part was at Downing Street, which was cool.

As I walked in, I was really excited and started filming on my phone for all of five seconds, before we were politely shown where the lockers were as no filming was allowed inside.

There were a number of parents who'd all done something amazing. Whether it was a fire in the house and their kids saved people or they'd saved someone from drowning, those sort of things. My story was what happened to Kiyan and how I responded to help a number of kids.

I was presented with a big certificate, signed by then Prime Minister Gordon Brown, for championing the lives of children. Gordon was a nice bloke who seemed genuine and had the softest hands I've ever felt. I don't think those hands had done much building work.

As he extended his hand for the shake, I pulled him in for the hug, which caught him a bit off-guard. You could see that 'oh gosh!' look on his face. We had a little chat after and I'll always remember him telling me: "I could never do what you're doing. Well done."

Part two was live on Sky TV, where I was presented with a glass trophy by Ross Kemp. We were at some massive five-star hotel ballroom, surrounded by celebrities and other very worthy contenders for this prize. I was genuinely humbled and honoured, when I went up and accepted the prize and did my acceptance speech.

The next 24 months would also provide me with some memorable moments, but not all of them were so glamorous.

20

Fight For The Foundation

"Don't call this a comeback, I've been here for years." **LL Cool J**

2010 was a proper mixed bag. In April, I was asked to go on Sky's *School of Hard Knocks* programme. Will Greenwood was hosting and each week somebody would come in to take the session and chat with a bunch of guys from all walks of life and who'd done a bit of bird. Will was a lovely, humble man. I got on with him very well.

These guys didn't really know who I was. I was introduced as a former professional boxer, but they had no idea about what I'd been through and how I was in tune with the darker side of the law, before and after Kiyan. I rehearsed nothing. Everything was off the top off my head, but by the end of it, I'd earned their respect in sweat and stories.

From Sky television studios, to going back to court rooms. One of the best things about KPF during this year was helping out a number of people from going to jail and instead, giving them the chance to turn their life around. Not just kids, but adults alike. I started receiving e-mails from everyone, including prisons. The talks inside were always positive, discussing adversity, the future and goal-setting once released.

I was constantly invited back and learnt a lot by speaking with adult offenders. Things like the mindset behind re-offending and how temptations never went away irrespective of age.

Probably the most memorable of all offenders was Chris Murray, although I didn't meet him behind bars. Les Quinn had told me there was this guy looking likely to go to jail.

Through KPF and Les's Angels with Dirty Faces [AWDF] programme, we could not only save taxpayers money, but by keeping him out of jail we could also help his rehabilitation.

Chris had no previous. He'd been caught growing cannabis. Yes, he'd done wrong, but there was a different way to deal with this. We did our research and we didn't see him as a big danger to the community. He'd done it because he was skint, had a young child and wanted food on the table.

Whereas many saw an outcast, I saw a first-time offender who could be guided into turning his life around. I'd never met him, but I saw someone who, once he'd paid his dues, would be able to say to others in his shoes, 'Stay away from this.' If he went to prison, he probably would have come out with exactly the same head on him, or even worse.

I went with him to Blackfriars Crown Court and made an emotional plea for the judge to spare him jail time and come and work with me instead.

We'd written up a programme and handed it over to the judge, who said he'd go away and read it. Instead of receiving a 21-month jail sentence, Chris got 100 hours of community service and a 12-month suspended jail sentence, provided that he stuck to the outlined programme.

That was a landmark for me. When I was in court myself at the age of 17, I could have done with an older version of myself to have mentored me back then.

When we walked out the court, we planned his next move. He'd been taking from the community, now it was time to give back. Over the next year, he helped rebuild a playground which had been burned down by vandals. He really put in the work.

He also helped raise funds for AWDF and KPF. I've lost touch with Chris now, but wherever he is, I hope he's doing well.

AWDF is something Les was very passionate about, because it helped a number of people get back on the straight and narrow, in a similar way to KPF.

Les was born and bred in Islington, and used to run market stalls. Everyone knew who he was in the local area because he had a bit of a bad past, but was better known as the bad boy turned good. That's why he called himself an angel with a dirty face.

In fact, he was so passionate about AWDF, he had it tattooed on his body. He loves his ink, Les. He also had another very memorable tattoo which read, 'We never want to see one of our mates bury their baby.' He had that after Kiyan was murdered.

Me personally, I've never been into ink. Or so I thought.

Towards the end of 2010, one of my friends went to get a tattoo done and I just went along with her as company. While I was sitting down watching her, waiting for her to screw up her face, she said: "Why don't you get one done?"

I said: "No way."

For the record, she never screwed her face up when hers was

getting done. She was ridiculously calm. Then I got chatting with this tattoo guy about Kiyan and he showed me some potential designs. I then shocked myself when I said: "You know what. Yeah. Let's do it."

He then asked where I wanted it and I pointed to the right hand side of my neck. He said: "That's a very painful place to have one, especially if you've never had a tattoo before."

"That's a small price to pay," I replied. He then drew it on a piece of paper, stuck it down on my neck and asked what I thought. I told him I liked it.

Although Kiyan will never move from my heart, it's nice to see his name and for everyone else to be reminded of my incredible son. And as far as the pain went, it was even worse than I thought it would be!

I stayed still for about 90 minutes and when he brought the mirror over and showed it to me, I started crying. The tattoo tapped into an emotional reservoir.

I don't know what people are thinking when they see me, a middle-aged man with a tattoo on his neck, but it's different to when I used to have piercings on my face or gold teeth, which were just for show. This was the total opposite.

★★★★★★★★★★★★★★★★★

KPF by this time was struggling more than ever financially. While I was delivering sessions, I was struggling to pay the rent and I'll be honest when I say I was tempted so many times to give it up and just get a job to keep my head above water.

When I left my house in 2007 after splitting up with Laurel, my mate said I could sleep at his flat in Leyton. I stayed there for a couple of years, until one day, he told me there was a problem with the lady in the flat above.

"What problem?' I asked. She'd been phoning him to complain I was a nuisance and that she could hear me making love all night, non-stop "like a beast." I was never sure whether to take that as a compliment or an insult.

This lady was a slice short of a full loaf of bread. She used to leave her child in the house alone and go out all day, and he was only about six years old. He'd always leave the flat and I'd always find him walking around the street and return him.

If anyone else had found out, social services would have taken her kid away on many occasions. No thanks to me!

So I left my mate's in 2010 and went to this great swanky little pad, down Shernhall Street in Walthamstow. Kevin used to call it 'the penthouse'. I was paying £1,200 a month on rent. The problem was, I hadn't organised myself long-term.

I was working more with the mentality of, 'This place is great. Get it, pay the deposit, worry about it later.'

I loved that place and did it up really nicely. It had a big bedroom and these nice patio doors with a balcony. My kids even had their own room for when they stayed over. I was so happy. This is all I wanted. At the beginning I was finding the money to pay for it, then work went dry.

All of a sudden I was two months behind, then three. Before I knew it, I was about five grand down and I was moving out. I could have let out a room which would have covered half the rent, but I just wasn't thinking. Stupid really.

Without a roof over my head I was back to Mum's again. Although financially I wasn't in a great place, at least I knew I wasn't living out of a suitcase again. I spoke too soon. In 2012,

I was doing a talk at a community centre and got a phone call that my daughter Jodeci had been attacked by another family member. I immediately left and when I saw the blood on her lips and her teeth loose, I went mad.

Without going into detail, that caused a huge rift and that's how I became homeless again.

Back to the drawing board, living from pillar to post.

At the time, Les Quinn was in the process of selling his flat and said to me: "Why not move in with me until further notice. Until I flog the flat at least?" That became my home for the next six months.

I need to say a few words about Les. He's a true friend who's never asked for anything in return. He was someone I could trust when a lot of people I'd put my faith in had let me down. Les was and still is the real deal. Not many people like him exist and I'll never forget his kindness on so many levels.

★★★★★★★★★★★★★★★★★★

After leaving Les's, I was on the road again, travelling with a blanket and a sleeping bag. I was tired of struggling on with KPF. The flaw in the model was still my lack of business knowledge. So I thought, 'What can I do which I'm good at, to get KPF to another level? I can fight.'

At any stage in my life, I always had order when I was boxing and this time was no exception. At the age of 43, I decided to make a professional boxing comeback, but with a new focus. First time round, I was boxing to make my kids proud and stay out of prison. This time round, I was doing it to get KPF sorted.

I wasn't hunting down titles and knew boxing wasn't going to provide me with a living. It was all about networking through this brief journey and making as much noise as I possibly could.

However, having been out of the ring for 13 years, there were a few adjustments I'd need to make. Light heavyweight wasn't happening anymore, but making the cruiser limit of 14st 4lbs [200lbs] was realistic.

Next hurdle was getting my boxing licence back, which I thought would be plain sailing. I went to the British Boxing Boxing of Control [BBBofC], did all their tests and they said they had concerns and rejected my application. Not based on my age, but on my knee injury.

I had independent physical assessments in Brighton, which I passed with flying colours, just so I could demonstrate to the board I was OK. Tests like velocity, jumping, endurance, flexibility, cardiovascular, strength, you name it. I smashed them all, but the BBBofC didn't want to know.

In the end, I had a chat with a nice guy called Rio [Gianluca Di Caro], from the Malta Boxing Commission and went through the same tests again. Brain scan, the lot. Again, I passed everything. The only difference was that these guys said yes and that they'd love to have me on board.

Now I had the green light, I had to knuckle down to training. Without Dad or Carly around, I started training myself.

One person who did help was pro boxing trainer Don Charles. I had a chat with him and I explained that I wanted to train at his gym, but didn't have the money to pay him. Don never questioned my motives and he just let me crack on, for free. I even used to sleep in the boxing ring, using my bag as a pillow. I'd explained to Don that I had nowhere permanent to stay. I did this for a few days at a time and then other days would sleep on a mate's sofas. The benefit of sleeping in the gym was that I'd get up early and train, then finish late.

I remember Spencer Oliver, the former super bantamweight European champ, used to come in the morning and say in his cockney accent: "Who's that?"

"It's me, Prince."

"Prince. Did you stay here all night mate? Faaaackin 'ell."

He was shocked, especially as I was so upbeat in that gym, making jokes and first in the queue for dishing out the banter.

The only downside to sleeping in the gym was the temperature. It was freezing cold. I remember once lying in that ring about two in the morning, shivering, and looked up at the ceiling thinking about my situation.

'Remember this moment. Use this to keep pushing you forward, because when you come out the other end of this journey, you're going to look back and smile.'

★★★★★★★★★★★★★★★★★★

Between the boxing and the KPF stuff, I was also trying to earn money. But it was all a struggle. I'd asked God to help in some form, and again he didn't let me down.

Around this time, my mate, former middleweight champion Jason Matthews called me and said: "I heard you ain't got nowhere to stay. We can't have that. Let me make some calls."

He called me back and said: "Listen. I know this girl who has a house and has a room to rent. No harm in going over to see what you think and maybe we can get her price down."

The room was nice, but didn't know where I was going to get the 500 notes per month to pay for it. Then about a week later,

I received a call from some guy called Ryan Dudfield. He'd read something in the media and contacted me, saying he'd like to offer £500 sponsorship per month. We met up and when he mentioned what he wanted to do for me, I hugged him and said: "God bless you!"

My comeback was all set for 4 October 2013 at the York Hall.

With a date to aim for, I needed to knuckle down with some serious sparring. I had the option of jumping in the ring with guys who were not serious boxers, were smaller and slower than me, or to jump into the lion's den. I chose the last option.

The first big spar I had for my comeback was against Nathan Cleverly, who was undefeated WBO light heavyweight world champion at the time and had already made a couple of defences. He was two weeks away from defending his title against Shawn Hawk and needed sparring partners.

I had decided my first spar back needed to be my toughest. I said to Don: "I need to test myself. I need to find out if I'm having delusions of grandeur, or if this is for real." The only way I could find this out was if I went in against a top fighter.

There was a few people saying: "Why are you taking this? He's fighting in a fortnight and has been knocking sparring partners out. You don't need this. He's been a real handful for Dereck Chisora, a heavyweight. Why risk getting hurt?"

They knew me as this hot-headed fighter from before, but I was a different person. I entered the ring with a cool head and was working behind knowledge and experience, not emotion.

I used to be world class and I needed to see how far I was from that level. I needed to know if I could I see his punches, read what he was trying to do, return shots and get my footwork right. I soon found out.

We did five rounds of sparring and the first thing that struck me was his speed and how he could switch to the head and body with serious accuracy. Nathan's punches weren't concussive, they were more shocking. They'd stop you in your tracks.

At one point, he knew he'd hit me with a good shot, but I didn't give him any signs of wilting. However, inside I was thinking, 'Oh, oh. I felt that one,' but I was able to continue.

He also had a great guard, which was very deceiving, and also had one of the best engines in boxing at the time.

At the end of the spar he said: "You've still got it! You're still sharp. I can't see how you couldn't win the British title."

What a story that would have been, after 13 years out of the game to come back and win it. The people that shattered me attempting that dream was the British Boxing Board of Control.

Don Charles was excited and impressed with what he saw, but at the time, I thought I'd underperformed. It wasn't until I sat down and watched the video of the spar that I thought, 'That wasn't so bad. You boxed well, moved well, didn't take a beating and held your own. You're ready for this comeback.'

I also sparred with cruiserweight Wadi Camacho, who was 5-0 at the time and super middleweight Frank Buglioni, was also 5-0 and went on challenge for the world title. By now, I was 44 and I'm sure Frank and Wadi thought, 'Here we go. They're rolling out the old man here.'

But it was nothing like that. Sparring is a two-way process. Each fighter needs to develop and that's exactly what I was trying to do. I wanted to help me, but at the same time, I helped develop their talent and not just go in and bash them up.

One thing I noticed this time round was that I was trying to hone my defensive skills more. Attacking was something I knew

I could do. It was a raw instinct I was born with, but defending myself after years of inactivity is where I needed to sharpen up.

In the past, when I was under the lights in the ring, I had a tendency to try and smash people up, but now I found myself going in and for half the rounds do nothing but defending.

I enjoyed the calmness which came with being on the back foot and using my intelligence to conserve energy, look for openings and basically be the smarter fighter, instead of the aggressor.

Mind you, I knew I was getting away with things that I could never get away with Carly, like dropping my hands down and leaning my head in to bait my sparring partners.

The only big test left now was to fight for real. Did I still have enough in the tank to grind out a win?

★★★★★★★★★★★★★★★★★★

I got in touch with QPR and asked if I could use their logo and colours for my shorts and they were happy and supportive. Not only that, they did absolutely loads of publicity, trying to generate further media and funds for KPF. The most important part about the shorts was the waistband, which had Kiyan's name embroidered into it.

Going for the weigh-in was such a calm experience. My mate Zain sent his driver and it felt good to have this nice car coming to my house. It made me realise what I'd been doing for KPF was worth every bead of sweat.

When I arrived at the weigh-in, I did some television interviews, which was almost surreal.

I kept thinking about all the training I'd done. I had days

when I'd ask myself, 'What you doing? Look how much pain you're in. You're knackered from carrying all your gear to the gym and now you want to train? Give up. Just give up.'

Then the other side of me would say, 'Do this man. Don't forget where you've come from. Don't forget why you are doing this. For Kiyan. For Kiyan.'

That side would always win.

Come fight night, the reception for me was massive. Family, school friends, everyone. The last time I'd fought as a pro was 14 years before and although the buzz was incredible, it was all different this time round.

Last time I boxed I didn't want my kids in the changing room, but this time I wanted my whole family there. I was a lot more relaxed and that was nice, because I enjoyed it so much more.

Many boxers have regrets after they've retired, but I was back and had the chance to implement and appreciate some of the things I'd thought about after I stopped the first time.

I wanted to enjoy the crowd and take in their energy. I wanted to be able to see my children enjoy these moments. I never got the chance to see my dad fighting, so it was a great thing to be able to share this moment with them now.

When I put my shorts on, tears poured down my face as I looked at Kiyan's name across my waist. When it came for my time to walk to the ring, with a small crew by my side, including my brother Colin, I was calmer than I'd ever been before.

My comeback was against a guy called Jindrich Velecky and I stopped him in the fourth round. The feeling that soared through me was incredible. I was jumping up high, releasing my emotions. I then banged my shorts while pointing to Kiyan's name. That was intense.

The MC let me take the mic and I said a few words about KPF, which was the reason I was in the ring in the first place.

When I'd fought previously, I wanted to go from pro to champion in a heartbeat. I didn't appreciate the journey. In my head it was just one fight to another. My focus was 100 per cent boxing then, but now, although I was still focussed, I was enjoying it more, because the pressure was off me.

Five months later I stopped Olegs Lopajevs in the first round with a heavy counter-punch. The fight would have lasted longer, but he came steaming at me looking for the knockout, and that's the worst thing you can do with me.

Then on 2 August 2014, I was up against Jiri Svacina, in a 10-round contest. My tank was never in doubt and proved to the British Boxing Board of Control that all their reservations were rubbish. I went championship rounds and I could have gone another five.

In terms of the fight itself, I didn't enjoy it. Svacina used to spar with the Klitschkos. I soon realised he was a very awkward fighter. I needed Carly for that one. He would have given me the instructions to knock him out.

As it goes, I won a very wide points decision on all three of the judges' scorecards.

My next fight was on 23 October, against Mathew Ellis, who had a half-decent record. I was hoping to get some rounds in, but instead I smashed him inside the first.

A month later I was hosting an event for KPF and had some help from someone who should have originally been in the opposite corner to me 17 years earlier. Mr Christopher Livingstone Eubank.

I'd bumped into him a few months earlier on the train, while

I was on the way to the gym. I asked him if he could come to this event in November and he agreed straight away.

A lot of people say negative things about Chris, but I've always been cool with him. He enjoys being centre stage and took control of the microphone on the day, which I was fine with, because he'd taken his time to support KPF.

He told some stories and poetry, did his thing and had loads of photos with anyone who wanted one. I'll always appreciate his support that day to help increase awareness of KPF.

I then got a call from Carly, who was by now living in Gambia, but still training fighters in the US and Caribbean. He asked if I'd like to fight against the former WBC world cruiserweight champion Wayne 'The Truck' Braithwaite, who was from Guyana and was apparently being promoted by Don King. It was for some WBA title. Surprisingly, I declined.

The thing now, I wasn't back into boxing for boxing's sake. In the 10 months in between the last two fights, I delivered loads of talks and was able to continue with my crusade against knife crime. I wanted to put KPF on a pedestal that nobody could ignore us and after four fights, I'd made a good dent into achieving that goal.

The thought of killing myself training for some title didn't appeal to me. Time is the most important commodity on the planet and it now needed to be dedicated 100 per cent to KPF.

After a comeback trail of four fights, three stoppages and no losses, I decided it was time to hang up the pro gloves for good and concentrate on the real battle that lay outside of the ring.

21

Restorative Justice

"I was consumed with anger. I really wanted to kill this guy that killed my son. He took a piece of me. But why was I going to give him all of me? I wanted something left for Kiyan. With everything I've got left, I'm going to do something good. If I have to forgive, I'll forgive. If I have to love, I'll love. If I have to teach people by example, I'll do that. I don't want to hate, because that's what killed Kiyan."
Mark Prince, 2008

Not long before Kiyan was killed, I'd already been thinking that it wouldn't be long before me and him would have started hanging out as grown men. I'd thought that far forward that I even used to think about him starting a family and him being out with his own kids. It's hard to believe that at the time of writing this book, Kiyan would have been 27 years old. None of that can ever happen now.

And whenever I watch football on the telly, I instantly think about him. A few years ago, I was watching Manchester City, and this player Micah Richards reminded me of Kiyan in terms of his looks and build. Then I started thinking, 'Kiyan should be out there playing.'

I also wonder how he might have done if he'd have pursued boxing. We trained to keep fit, but it wasn't to make him into a boxer, he just liked the training that came with the sport.

It wasn't until a video of his emerged on YouTube after he was killed, showing him shadow boxing, that I realised he was into it that much. He was putting together some nice combinations. They were good quick punches! Seriously.

I also get harsher reminders of Kiyan's absence on the telly. Whenever I see someone get stabbed with a knife in a film, it still has an effect on me. In the early days after Kiyan was murdered, it was too real for me to be able to watch.

Even though it was just a film, it felt like I was going through what really happened to Kiyan and what he would have been thinking when that knife went into his chest.

Nowadays, it's not that bad, but I still feel uncomfortable. I don't think that feeling will ever fully disappear. The same goes for whenever 18 May comes around. Each year is different, but I've learned how to process my thoughts with better clarity.

Kiyan's friends are still furious. Apparently Hannad has been beaten up in prison for boasting about what he did to Kiyan and was put in solitary confinement for his own safety.

Years back I would have wanted anyone behind bars to go to work on him, but I've got a different head on me now. The greatest thing that could happen would be for him to come and work at KPF. You can't talk the talk about being Christ-like and full of forgiveness and love, and when you have an opportunity to demonstrate it, you turn your back. That's hypocrisy.

One of the tabloids tried to set up a meeting with me and Hannad at the prison. They asked: "Do you forgive him?" "Yeah," I replied. However, forgiveness is a decision you make, but the process you go through doesn't happen at the same time.

I had all these emotions when Kiyan was killed and knew at some point I had to move on, because, with the work of KPF, I'd be having to deal with kids like Hannad. And there's no way I could deal with these kids while still holding this anger for him in my heart, because it would transfer to them.

Hannad's release date is 2019, which is getting really close. More and more I'm starting to think, 'What about if we had a conversation. How's that gonna turn out?'

If he was sitting in front of me now, I'd ask him. 'What's changed? The guy I knew was a coward, didn't take responsibility and didn't care about other people. You're now 30 years old. What's changed?'

I'd also really like to know his take of what happened on May 18 2006. I'd ask, 'I've heard the take from the kids who were there on the day, but you never actually spoke at the trial. What's your story? What do you tell people when they ask?'

Yeah. Those would be my questions.

★★★★★★★★★★★★★★★★★

Twelve years later and knife crime continues to be a major issue in the UK. The roots of knife crime have not been tackled and the laws surrounding it are still not a big enough deterrent in my opinion. Non-negotiable sentences for possession of a deadly weapon needs to be enforced.

Also, the whole three-inch knife thing being legal needs to be scrapped. A blade of any length will open you up. It should be 'No knives.' Standard. We need zero tolerance.

We should try to support those thinking of hurting someone. With my children, I don't just want them to understand the consequences of being naughty, I want them to understand how not to continue with this behaviour, so they then don't need to continue facing consequences.

Our job should be more focussed on education and prevention, rather than punishment, which only works to an extent. And it's not only the youths we need to influence, it's those who wield power in the justice system.

A couple of years after the Chris Murray case, I was invited by the Prison Association to talk about restorative justice. This is when you get the victims of crime and the offenders, and collectively try to get everyone to play a part in repairing the harm done and look to find a way to move forward positively.

My audience was wardens and governors and I talked about the state of prisons, treatment of prisoners and dealing with them as individuals. I wanted to explain the merits of making individual programmes for rehabilitation, like I did with Chris Murray. I wanted to let them know there were other options to locking a person up, especially when they are not always a threat to the community. Then I talked about how education would be more cost-effective in the long run.

On the surface, many people think education and prevention take a lot longer and cost a lot more, but it's not like that.

It costs over 60 grand a year to put a person behind bars and when you take into account court costs and then over 40 grand for every year that person spends inside, it adds up big time.

Education and prevention are many times more effective

than just locking people away or prosecuting them, and I'm not just talking financially. If you address the consequences of the future actions, you hopefully won't need to address the weapon.

On 18 May 2016, www.tes.com had a headline of, 'Ten years after 15-year-old Kiyan Prince's murder, his father is reaching out to schools to help end knife crime.' Despite all the work I've done, I'm getting more requests than ever before from schools to come and do talks.

But in an ideal world, I'd like to be redundant.

If you're reading this and are either thinking of carrying a weapon or have one on you, please get rid of it. If you're struggling to do so, for whatever reason, contact me. The power is in our hands, let's use it correctly.

★★★★★★★★★★★★★★★★★★

I've got no problem with speaking to people at an operational level and trying to help those who need it, but now I need the strategic infrastructure around me to help the foundation grow.

Like boxing, I've always been a grass-roots performer. I never promoted or managed and the same goes with the strategic side of KPF. I want to cover wider geography, deliver more sessions, get a business plan together to drive a fresh vision, all of that.

We want to present ourselves as a larger charity with a good infrastructure. That means business. It's almost like going from amateur to professional ranks now.

Thankfully, that's all coming together nicely. The website is being reconstructed as we speak, and it carries KPF's new strapline, 'Bringing people together. Ending violence.'

With some great support from friends and advisors, I've

also just conducted a skills audit to make sure I've got a good blend of people as trustees and patrons for KPF. People who bring a skill to the table like finance, an interest in anti-knife campaigning, marketing, all that kind of stuff. People that can not only support the activities of the foundation, but will be able to help it expand realistically.

I'm also waiting to hear about some major funding applications, which will support a three-year business plan we've written. Part of that plan is to set up a gym where we can deliver sessions. We want to use sport to channel people's negative energy into a positive force.

★★★★★★★★★★★★★★★★★★

It's funny in life how things can go full circle. When I was 18, me and my mates were wild. When someone older tried to offer us guidance, we'd just laugh and walk the other way.

Living in my flat in Oatfield House, taking drugs, thieving, violence, it was all fun. In fact, for years and years later, that flat never left my head.

I dreamt many times that I was back there. I used to dream that people were knocking on the door and I'd have to hide because the police were after me.

Looking back, if my kids behaved like that, it would be my worst nightmare. That's why I try so hard to influence my kids and other youths who are at a crossroads. But it's not just me.

Since 2010, Tracy has been a family support worker for the local authority, working with gangs. She'll get a referral and it will say something like, 'Child involved in gang activity. Mother and child relationship is very fractured. Child does not go to school.' Her job is to go in there and bring the family back together, instead of letting the child to be lost to the streets.

And my mate Kevin, he works at a people referral unit, called Enfield Secondary Tuition Centre, working with 14-16 year olds. These are kids that get kicked out of school for behavioural issues and he's that last port of call when they're about to get excluded.

Me and Kevin now have conversations about the youth, which is crazy, as these kids were us 30-odd years ago.

When I went into boxing, I didn't see him as much as I used to but through our work with kids we've got back together again.

In 2015 Kevin asked me to do a black history talk alongside some other guest speakers, including some famous actors and a police officer. When I arrived, I sat down with my headphones on, singing, and loads of kids were watching me thinking, 'Who's this guy?' Then when I went into my talk, everyone was in tears, including the staff and the copper.

At the end, Kevin came over and said: "The other talks were good, but you were the cherry on top. You smashed it." The memorable thing wasn't the praise, it was me and Kevin having a conversation like this, under these circumstances. If somebody had told us we'd be like this 30 years before, we'd have laughed ourselves senseless.

Another friendship which was lost over the years was my old schoolmate, Paul Furlong. After we left school, I went on the streets and got involved in criminal activity and he played top-level professional football. When Kiyan was killed in 2006, coincidentally, Paul was playing for the QPR first team and through bad circumstances we rekindled our friendship.

Fast forward to 2016 and Paul was now the Under-18s coach

at the QPR academy. He gave me a call and asked me to speak to the players about living their lives the right way, being aware of negative influences and making the most of their opportunities when they presented themselves.

Paul told me: "You had the boys really switched on to what you were saying because you weren't somebody just standing there reading a speech. You gave real-life experiences."

It was a sincere pleasure to have been given the opportunity to help youths within QPR that were on the same path that Kiyan was on. Interestingly, Paul's son Darnell was at the talk and he now plays for the first team. A different time, a different place, Kiyan and Darnell may well have been team-mates.

Unsurprisingly, it's always QPR who get the final shout-out when it comes praise. After everything they've done as a club for Kiyan and KPF over the years, it's amazing how they continued to raise the bar with no prompting.

In addition to creating the 'Kiyan Prince Goal of The Month' competition, which is awarded at each home match, Kiyan was posthumously inducted in the Forever R's alongside some terrific players.

Here's the thing. I'm not surprised. They've always been like that. I'm not being nonchalant, it's just that they've always stuck by him and this was another example of that.

They say you don't always repay a debt the day you make it, but I don't think I could repay QPR's kindness over a number of lifetimes. Thank you to every player, fan and member of staff who have done your bit. I'll never forget you.

22

From Boxer To Doctor

"A dream doesn't become reality through magic; it takes sweat, determination and hard work." **Colin Powell**

2016 had some real gems in store for me. After three years of seeing a lady called Daz [Daszine], we finally tied the knot on 3 August 2016. Having Daz in my life, from day one, has given me a greater sense of order, priorities and vision.

Just over a month after getting married, on 11 September 2016, I decided to use my new-found organisational skills and clear the shed in the garden, which had loads of junk in it.

Exactly 19 years ago to the day, I'd fought Bruce Rumbolz and defended my WBO light heavyweight Intercontinental title. I walked away without a scratch, which is more than could be said for this particular day in 2016.

There I was going back and forth out of the rear gate, which had a brick wall either side of it. Daz's sons had just kicked a ball into the neighbours garden – again. Thankfully they are really cool. The neighbours from heaven.

While I told the kids to bugger off to the park to play football, the neighbours just laughed and said: "Leave them. It's alright."

As the boys walked through the gate, I heard screaming and I saw the expression on D'Angelo's face [Daz's son] as the wall to the left of me started to collapse. I put my hands up for what seemed like a second and thought, 'I've got this. I'm holding the wall!' A split second later I'm thinking, 'No I haven't!'

It's strange, as the next bit happened in a heartbeat, but a million things went through my head. I thought, 'If the wall's got me, I'm screwed, because I'll hit my head on the concrete floor.' So as the wall was collapsing, I turned to my side.

I turned, hit the ground, then the whole wall collapsed on me, with the top part hitting me on the side of the head. It felt like my insides were being squashed like an orange. I couldn't move.

The neighbour and Daz both called the ambulance. Daz was screaming hysterically. The next bit was a blur. I made an almighty effort and pulled myself out in one crazy move, while scraping loads of my skin off. I felt dizzy and the pain was horrible. It was more than anything I'd ever experienced in boxing. It was like six Mike Tyson body punches in one blow.

Every breath was like shallow gasping. Short breaths that took a lot of effort. I wanted to lie on my back but it made the pain even worse. I spent 45 minutes in and out of consciousness until a quick response unit arrived.

They did the usual checks and I tried to answer, but I was mumbling, struggling to get my words out. Then the ambulance finally came and they didn't know where they were going. It was like being in a cab in a foreign country. It didn't even have sat-nav. I could hear the ambulance guys up front saying: "What's the best way to get to Barnet?"

I thought, 'You've got to be shitting me.' Daz worked at the hospital and ended up giving them directions. When we got there, the doctors gave me a good dose of morphine.

The doctor then said: "Judging from the level of pain you are in, it's likely you have some form of internal injury. Possibly cracked ribs and maybe even a punctured lung."

Before she could carry on, I said, in a non-arrogant, but confident way: "You won't find anything. God's taking me through this. You won't find any internal injuries."

She looked at me a bit strange, probably thinking I was delirious from the wall falling on me. One thing I'd learnt about the characters in the Bible was the faith levels they had. Faith is the substance of things not seen. I was putting that into practice.

A couple of hours later, after they'd taken me through loads of scans, the doctor looked like she'd seen a ghost.

"I don't understand this," she said. "We're going to have to let you go as we can't find anything wrong with you internally. Obviously you are in a lot of pain, but nothing is broken or ruptured. You're free to go home, Mr Prince."

Boy, did I hobble out of that place. I looked like I was 120 years old. Thankfully my neighbours from heaven were outside to pick me up and take me home.

★★★★★★★★★★★★★★★★★

Within a few months I'd got my strength back, which was a good thing as I was about to put some of the old boxing moves to the test. On 1 June 2017, I'd had a meeting with the Borough

Commander of Kensington and Chelsea, had just got home and was absolutely knackered.

My son Kishon, who was 16 by this point, said there was a barbecue round the corner. I asked who was organising it, doing the food and all that. It was on a green, surrounded by flats, about three floors high. There were about 30 kids there.

I had a chat and then left these people to set it up. We told them we would pass back soon, just to make sure everything was OK.

We went away, did some shopping and when we came back we had a chat with some of the youths again. But by now there were about 150 young people there, three police vans and a couple of undercover police cars which you can spot a mile away.

The problem is, when people look out of their window and see 150 kids from mixed races and backgrounds, they start to get fearful and think something is about to go down. It didn't help that there had been three recent stabbings nearby.

On top of that, someone had their speakers out of their window and was playing loud music from their house, so the police had been called. I could see the police getting ready to make a beeline for the kids, so I went over and told them this was a great opportunity to talk to the young people. Meet them, gain their trust. But they weren't buying into it. Instead they tried to get me to ask them to turn off the music and disperse the youths from the park. They told me: "This can't carry on."

I said: "They ain't making no trouble, so that ain't happening. If there's a problem, I'll tackle it, but there isn't one."

They didn't reply, but just hung around. I thought, 'Let me get involved with these kids and show everyone that there's nothing to worry about.' My aim was for the community to take back their community, not be scared of it. You can't do that by calling the police. People in the community don't do that. We, the parents, the elders, come out to take care of things.

Depending how that pans out, then you might have to call the police. But it wasn't like that, it was just kids outside on a hot summer's evening having fun. I was trying to get the neighbours to come outside and join in. With the barbecue going, it was a great chance for everyone to forge some new relationships.

I said to Kishon: "Get the boxing gloves out of the car. Let's create another forum, so when the police do eventually get the music off, there will still be a focus for the young people."

We started doing some light sparring and at first there was nobody coming over. The kids were just doing their own thing.

Next minute, whoosh, loads of them came over. The police were watching like hawks, but because they could see there was no trouble and everything was controlled, they let us continue.

It was about 9pm and now everyone wanted to have a go at sparring. I said: "No problem. Everyone can join in. If you think you can bang me up, let's go."

I wasn't trying to act the big man, I just wanted people to realise that this was fun, but also understand what goes into becoming a good boxer. It's different to a drunken street fight.

Next thing, this big guy comes over: "Can I have a go? I've never done this before."

"Yeah of course. Pop on the gloves," I said as I sized him up.

This guy was at least 17 stone and was in his 20s, so I wasn't going to sit back and let him bash me up, but I also wasn't going to hit him properly. He came out swinging, but I just blocked, staying in the pocket so he'd get tired.

I let him do all his power punches and just blocked, covered up, slip-slided while he growled away and wasted loads of power. In less than five minutes he was knackered. It finished in good spirits.

Next thing, another guy in his 20s wanted a go. There was a real buzz from the kids, because when he walked over they thought this was going to be a serious fight. This guy was a hood legend among the youths.

I'd never met him before, but I'd heard he was a really good street fighter. I sized him up and I knew he could fight. I wasn't going to get hustled. He must have been thinking there was a man nearly 50 in front of him, how difficult could this be?

As soon as he put on the gloves, all the kids came running over. I'm now thinking, 'Ooooookkkaaay.' Mentally I changed my strategy. I didn't want to allow him to be able to get close like the other guy.

From his first punch I could feel he knew how to strike. He threw a one-two and the straight right hand at the end just caught me a little bit at the top of my head.

I could feel the power and knew he needed defusing. I decided to just touch him with one jab, just to calm him down, as this was sparring. That was the whole point of the exercise. Learning about having fun, but within the parameters of discipline.

He had his stance going, he was moving around nicely, still throwing the heavy one-twos. But now I was studying him as opposed to just letting him fire shots at me. The boxer's survival instinct kicked back in.

I flicked out the jab right down the middle with about 50 per cent power and it caught him on the nose. I just touched him, but I knew it had an effect, because he didn't throw another punch for about 40 seconds. He was still in the fight, but now he was on the back foot and I was stalking him. I threw a one-two of my own and he decided to stop. I was never going to hurt him, just show him who was boss, but he'd reached the level he was happy with and we gained a mutual level of respect.

I spent five minutes talking to the youths after, explaining how 'this' was how to deal with conflict. As I said on Twitter after, in terms of what I was trying to achieve, #FightWithFistNotKnives.

It comes down to that whole thing of the gang mentality. A group of people together doesn't make a gang. The way they behave turns them into that. Look at how they behave.

A group of youths laughing, having a barbecue and a bit of music was hardly gang warfare. Instead, I'd managed to change the mindsets of a few people and also get them interested in boxing. It was a great exercise in the community.

★★★★★★★★★★★★★★★★★

Although the Tinie Tempah track never generated any mass publicity back in 2007, 10 years later, an unexpected bonus happened on the music front.

I got e-mailed over the summer of 2017 by these two guys. One was British and the other American. They made films, mainly short documentaries and had just received an award from HBO. So I thought, 'They must be of a good standard.' They said they'd followed my story, knew about Kiyan and were captivated by it all. One of them was in the UK at the time Kiyan was murdered and was about his age. His death had a profound effect on him. They said they wanted to do a short film on me. They came over a couple of months later and I showed them around and had a chat with them.

They went away to discuss the film, but in the meantime, they told me some people would be in touch about a Sam Smith music video. My first thoughts were, 'That guy can sing! Cool. Let's see what it's about.'

We had a chat and I liked the sound of things. The track was called *Too Good At Goodbyes* and they wanted people who could bring genuine pain and grief to the video from their experiences of saying goodbye to a loved one.

My part of the video was filmed in Miguel's gym in Brixton and I brought along a big canvas of Kiyan, which I picked up from Mum's. It was the very same canvas that was presented to me on the Loftus Road pitch back in November 2008.

They told me the video would involve a bit of acting to get those emotions on screen, but I was like: "Mate. Ain't gonna be no acting. This is real for me. All I need to do is look at that canvas of Kiyan." And that's exactly what happened.

"Take one," the guy shouted. He told me to hit the punchbag, look back at Kiyan's picture and then back at the camera. The second I looked at Kiyan's face, I was in floods of tears. That's what they were looking for and were like "Brilliant! That was so powerful," thinking I'd put on some Oscar-winning acting performance. That was real. People probably think my face was covered in sweat, but that's not it. The tears covered my face.

Within six weeks of the video going live in September 2017, it had over 250 million views on YouTube. Hopefully it's inspired a few people to want to know why I was in that video and who was in the canvas behind me. Kiyan is still making a huge impact on people. When we meet again one day, we'll have a laugh talking about that video.

While Sam Smith's video was generating positive marketing for Kiyan, October brought a surreal opportunity my way.

Barnet council had decided to pilot a programme for their youth offenders that would show them what it would be like to go through the court system, especially in a murder case.

They wanted to show that's it's nothing like the movies and that there's nothing cool going into court as an offender.

There were 10 youths, ranging from about 13 to 19 years old. They'd go to the Old Bailey and sit in the court where they would listen to real judges, real barristers, paramedics etc. It wasn't about scaring them, but showing them the reality that lay ahead if they didn't change their ways.

I got to the Old Bailey and decided to have a walk around the courtrooms, not to be disrespectful, but because the last time I'd been there was for Kiyan's murder trial and so all the memories had come flooding back.

I started visualising the moment Hannad walked in and my anger. I could see the prosecutor, the judge and then remembered everyone's reactions when the second case broke down. I went into a bit of a haze.

We all walked to court number one and I was hanging at the back trying to do a live Facebook feed on my phone. Next thing a policeman came over and said: "You're not supposed to be filming in here. All phones are supposed to be off."

"No problem," I said. That would have been a great start to the programme, with me getting arrested at the Old Bailey!

The moment I walked into the courtroom, that feeling of the past hit me again. I started to remember how the police used to bring us round the back ahead of another hard day. Ah man.

It brought back memories of our brief, Nick Hillyard. But guess what – he was there! Nick was leading the programme. I had no idea he was going to be there. I went over and gave him a big hug. It was emotional, but awesome. What were the chances of us meeting in the same courtroom? After a little chat I asked if I could take a look around.

"You can go anywhere you want," he replied. I went to the dock. I thought, 'This is where Hannad should have been, instead of sitting there with his brief.' But I also wanted to know what it was like to see the courtroom as the offender.

I also bumped into someone else, which was way more random than Hillyard. This lady was looking at me and I looked at her back. She then walked over and said: "Do you remember me?"

I said: "You look familiar, but nothing jumps into my head."

She replied: "Remember the incident with your brother-in-law and the dustbin man? I was the first one on the scene."

It suddenly clicked. "What?! Never! That was you?"

We embraced and I thanked her for everything the police did for us back then and how they dealt with our case sensitively, not pressing charges straight away.

Here's the crazy thing. She carried on talking and then said: "You'll never guess what happened to the dustbin man..."

I was thinking he had to be behind bars when she said with a smile: "You're not going to believe this. He's a policeman now!"

How mad is that? You've got to love life haven't you. I actually helped that guy sort his life out by banging him out. I knocked some sense into him.

There was a mixture of people talking on the day. Barnet council wanted the programme to give the youth offenders the full colour of what that courtroom offered on the day of a trial.

There was a barrister, a paramedic, a trauma surgeon, a high ranking police officer, a guy from the youth offending team who had reformed himself and a guy from the Ben Kinsella Trust, who showed a very powerful and emotional video. Then there was me as a parent, who's been a victim of this crime.

The first person up was an ambulance guy. He talked about what he had to deal with when arriving at a crime scene. The blood, the stab wounds, but also the grief he's witnessed over the years from loved ones as their child dies in front of them.

I was up third. Everyone spoke from the public gallery, but I walked over to the dock. My opening line was: "Why did I decide to talk from the dock? What am I doing here?"

I had their full undivided attention. Then one of them said: "You're there because that's where the criminals go."

I replied: "What happens to people in a murder trial when things don't go their way?" I left a few seconds silence then said: "They get sentenced to life." Then I paused before saying: "That's what I got. A life sentence."

You could see them initially thinking, 'What crime did he commit to get a life sentence?' Then it hit them. It's not what I did, but what happened to me that gave me that life sentence.

I then said: "I'm standing here because people with a certain mindset carry knives and guns. That's what you do. Give people like me life sentences."

When I finished speaking I got chatting with someone, then from the corner of my eye could see a line of people wanting to talk to me. The youths and the parents.

The day went so well they've decided to repeat it every few months, which I was delighted to hear. As long as those offenders attending can get positively affected by the programme, it's worth keeping this going for a long time to come.

2017 still had one more surprise in store for me.

At 10.18pm on 9 November 2017, Tannisa had a beautiful

baby boy. Incidentally, my dad was born on the same date. Tannisa had her baby at Tracy's house with a natural pool birth.

Soon after I went to meet my first grandchild, Akai Yaw Prince-Slade, who weighed in at eight pounds 11 ounces. Compared to me at birth, he was a heavyweight. In a baby fight he would have bashed me up!

As I drove up, I started getting emotional as I thought, 'I'm driving up to see my grandson and Kiyan's not here. He'd have been uncle Kiyan.' When I got to the house, Tannisa was out of it and the baby was feeding.

It was a great moment to watch my daughter and her partner, just looking at how happy and proud they were of their child.

After about an hour I got up to leave and as I was walking out I saw this photo of Kiyan on the fridge with his cousin. The way his cousin was looking at Kiyan in the photo was a great reflection of how people saw Kiyan in general. He made everyone smile and gave out positive vibes all the time.

I took the photo and said to Tracy: "Look at this…"

Then we both started to get all emotional. We cried and hugged for about five minutes.

I find it difficult to cast my mind back to when he was young and those happy times. Taking him on the swings, those sort of memories. I get angry and upset. It was sad that a moment of joy had stirred up pain and sorrow, but that's something me and Tracy will have to live with every waking day.

★★★★★★★★★★★★★★★★★★

In 2004, I had a dream and in that dream it said, 'Write a book and call it 'From Boxer To Doctor.' Although, at the time, the title made no sense, I started writing my life story, but for whatever reasons, I could never fully get into it.

Early 2016, I received an e-mail from Excel university in Luton saying they wanted to award me some degree for my youth work and dedication to my Christian faith over the last 10 years. I thought, 'This has got to be junk mail or a virus.'

I sent it to Les Quinn to look at and it turned out it wasn't a scam. 18 November 2016, I was awarded an honorary doctorate in Ministry. It was an awesome ceremony and something I will never forget.

I was now Dr Mark Anthony Prince.

It took a while to understand what the dream meant when it said 'boxer to doctor' but then it became clearer. As a boxer, my mission was to duck under the ropes, step into the prize ring and muster all my strength to smash the person in front of me.

Now I try and pick up those people who have been knocked down by life. Doctors can either heal people physically or mentally and that's what I want to do now. Heal the minds of young people and teach them how to be healthy and prosperous. That's where the real power comes from.

With Kiyan as my inspiration and God leading me, the journey that began back in 2006 will have no ending. As long as I've got air in my lungs to spread the word, I'm walking that journey. Then one day it will be the turn of someone else to step in and carry that torch.

But that day won't be for a long time.

My work is far from done.

Man On A Mission

May 2006. I was an ITV correspondent and news had reached us that a 15-year-old boy, Kiyan Prince, had been stabbed to death at his school gates. It was a big story, because the fatal stabbings of young people had been rare for a few years.

I ended up reporting on the story all day and said something live on air that had been playing on my mind: "While this stabbing and loss of a young promising life is shocking, it has also destroyed other lives. There's two parents out there, whose son went to school today and didn't come back..."

That obviously struck a chord with Mark Prince and he got in touch. "I've been watching news reports all day and you were the one I felt appreciated my pain and I want to thank you for that," he said. And that's how our conversations began.

Two weeks later another teenager had been stabbed and it became apparent there was a big problem. I wanted to make a film to highlight this. I got the green light from ITN and the *Put The Knives And Guns Down* documentary was born.

The first time I ever met Mark face to face and with a camera was at the grave of Kiyan, shortly after the funeral. I filmed him sobbing. We had a little chat off camera and I said, "Are you really sure you want to do this? If you are comfortable, let's perhaps keep filming and see what happens?" He agreed.

Five months later the trial of Hannad Hasan started. I was with Mark the first day he saw this lad in court. He said to me, "I can't stop looking at him. I just want to ask him 'Why?'"

One thing that struck me at this time was how drained Mark was of his personality and soul. I was speaking to a broken man.

I gave Mark a camera to create video diaries. The ones he sent during that first trial were pretty angry. Then he worried about what he'd said, and whether it should go in the film. I tried to reassure him that people would understand his anger.

The first trial collapsed and although I still wasn't sure where this film was going, I kept meeting and filming Mark whenever possible. The second trial started a couple of months later.

Then Mark phoned me. "I've messed up. I just can't keep going in that court and hearing the defence saying, 'He [Hannad] is just a child. He's not a murderer. He's got a troubled background'. Who's the victim here, Chris? I was at the train station when I saw one of the jurors and had a word. The case has collapsed again." "Oh, Mark. What have you done?"

We met in the park, where I interviewed him. That went on air on ITV that night. Mark wanted people to realise that although he'd done something really stupid, he was a broken, angry man, who just wanted justice for his son.

When the second trial had ended, I met Kiyan's mum, Tracy Cumberbatch. She told me not to give up on Mark. I promised Tracy I'd keep going with it, but it wasn't easy. The filming continued for 16 months.

Mark started to get stronger. He knew he had a choice – he either got bitter or he got better. He wanted to do something for Kiyan. He wanted to tackle the very culture that killed his son. He decided he wanted to set up the Kiyan Prince Foundation.

That summer, there was a horrific spate of teenagers being killed. Mark suggested we got all of the bereaved parents together to discuss how they could make a difference together.

It was incredible to see one bereaved parent after another talking about their pain, their anger, their sorrow and their need to find some positivity, some way of making sure their kid's death wasn't in vain.

Mark wanted to give these kids other options other than joining a gang. I told him we needed more publicity, so he came up with the idea of doing a charity record. I used to be a radio DJ, so I still had a few contacts. I called a woman called Anne Barrett, who had her own record label. She said: "We've got two new artists, one is called Maresa Macbeth, who's an opera singer. The other artist is called Tinie Tempah. He's from Peckham, understands the culture Mark is tackling. I'd like to use them." Tinie was only 18 and pretty much unknown.

Maresa, Anne, Mike Stobbie, Tinie and myself were at the Power House [Metropolis] Studios in Chiswick waiting for Mark to turn up. Anne was paying for studio time at God knows how many hundred pounds an hour and…no sign of Mark. I was thinking, 'I've done this for you, so the least you can do is turn up on bloody time!' The trouble with Mark is, no matter how angry you are with him, there's always something that makes you forgive him, because he's such an endearing character.

Tinie said: "What I think we should do is a rap, with Maresa doing the melody. But I need some inspiration for the rap."

Mark pulled out a folder and said: "I knew you'd say that Tinie. Since Kiyan's died, I've been writing poems about him." The room fell silent as Mark and Tinie read out touching words about Kiyan's magnetic character, his life and his goals. Tinie starts trying to rap the poems and a tear emerged from the corner of his eye. Tinie and Maresa said: "Can you leave us for an hour?" We walked out and left them to practise.

Exactly one hour later we went in the studio and Maresa and Tinie had brought these poems alive. The song *Put the Knives and Guns Down* was born. It was so incredibly powerful, we were all sat around the mixing desk in tears.

We took the single to all the commercial stations around the country, and nobody would play it. They said it was too contentious. They didn't want to play a record because it was about a dead teenager. They were happy to play rap music that was about killing people, drugs and weapons.

One organisation who didn't hesitate to help was QPR. They invited Mark and his family. We were standing on the pitch where Kiyan played as a junior. Mark and Tracy held hands as over 12,000 people fell silent as they announced the song was going to be played to raise money for the Kiyan Prince Foundation. Then the crowd started singing and clapping along.

When the song finished, everyone applauded and that moment was just incredible. Mark and Tracy were sobbing and I'll be lying if I said I didn't get emotional.

It was almost as if Kiyan's spirit was there. It added purpose and structure to Mark. It helped him devise a plan. Knife crime is a problem we're never going to totally get rid of, but I'm convinced that Mark has saved an awful lot of kids from imprisonment, or from being murdered, by following his heart and ensuring Kiyan Prince did not die in vain.

I'm positive of that.

Chris Rogers,
Investigative journalist
and broadcaster

Guiding young people together

On 18 May 2006, I remember being in the stadium and hearing there had been an awful incident. There was the media focus on Kiyan which was inescapable. That image of Kiyan in the Hoops shirt across all the newspapers and every TV screen.

We knew our priority was the immediate support of the Prince family, but how do you deal with it? That's when you're reminded about this really positive side of QPR.

Everyone says we're a family club and quite soon after the shock, Mark and Tracy got that outpouring of support and love from everyone who had any affiliation with QPR. My relationship with Mark became very strong. He wanted to do something positive in Kiyan's memory and started talking about the Kiyan Prince Foundation. We wanted to lend our complete support. Fast forward about two years and QPR in the Community Trust and KPF were working in partnership.

We have a youth and communities department, which works with the most vulnerable young people in London. Whenever we need to educate them on the perils of gang and weapon crime, we ask Mark to come out and share his story. Whichever direction Mark wants to take the Foundation, he knows that QPR and the Community Trust will be there as a partner.

Andy Evans, 2017
CEO – QPR in the Community Trust

I never got to meet Kiyan in person, but what I did know of him from everyone I spoke with at the club, was that he was an extremely talented young lad. He had a lifetime ahead of him, of hopes, dreams and aspirations. He had it all to look forward to. Tragically, that was all taken away from him.

The Forever R's Club was set up to recognise players from QPR who had made a substantial contribution on the pitch. Kiyan was the only player to be inducted who had not played for the first team, but his merits as a player stood out and if he hadn't of been murdered, he would have no doubt been playing in our current squad today.

It was an honour to have Mark Prince with us at the QPR v Huddersfield match, to receive the award on behalf of Kiyan. When Mark walked out onto the pitch the fans were on their feet clapping, which was a touching moment. QPR as a football club had made a pledge that we would continue to support Kiyan's name, his legacy, his family and his dad's foundation. Inducting Kiyan into the Forever R's was a fitting way of making sure his memory lived on at Loftus Road.

Kiyan's name has a firm place in QPR culture, by way of the Kiyan Prince Goal of the Month. Similar to the Forever R's it's another way for Kiyan's memory to live on. It's a fitting tribute to make sure his memory continues to be there and we, as a club, intend to carry this initiative forward into the future.

Unfortunately, knife crime is still very active and every time someone like Kiyan is lost, it's one too many. Kiyan Prince – gone, but never ever forgotten. The QPR family salutes you.

Andy Sinton, 2017
Former QPR player and current ambassador

THE
PRINCE
OF PEACE

Kiyan Prince
1990-2006